Allen G. Noble

WOOD, BRICK, AND STONE

The North American Settlement Landscape   Volume 1: Houses

Drawings by M. Margaret Geib

The University of Massachusetts Press

Amherst, 1984

Publication of this book was assisted by the
American Council of Learned Societies
under a grant from the
Andrew W. Mellon Foundation.

Designed by Mary Mendell

Library of Congress Cataloging in
Publication Data
Noble, Allen George, 1930–
Wood, brick, and stone.
Includes bibliographical references and index.
Contents: v. 1. Houses.
1. Vernacular architecture—North America.
I. Geib, M. Margaret. II. Title.
NA703.N6 1984 728′.097 83–24110
ISBN 0–87023–410–2 (v. 1)

Contents

Acknowledgments

Throughout the long process of assembling materials and preparing the text for this book, I have encountered helpful assistance from so many individuals and organizations that I take a great risk in singling out particular contributions. However, the help of some has been so valuable that I must thank them publicly.

The drawings and sketches that contribute so much to this volume are the work of M. Margaret Geib. Reproductions of these sketches and drawings, as well as the numerous photographs, have been made in the University of Akron Laboratory for Cartographic and Spatial Analysis under the direction of Debbie Phillips. The enormous task of typing and proofreading the manuscript and copying research materials has been performed efficiently by Teri Blount and a number of outstanding typists which at various times included Lisa Amato, Andrea Centola, Lisa Manville, Linda Rogers, and Bridget Hoffert, all supervised with wit and wisdom by Hilda Kendron. Research assistance was provided by Mark Stuller, Michael Coe, Mark Catlin, Mohammed Khan, and Brian Coffey. Because of the widely scattered nature of the studies in material culture, the diligence, efficiency, and unfailing good humor of Valerie Johnson, Sara Lorenz, and Jean Danis of the interlibrary loan office, Bierce Library at the University of Akron have been invaluable. Others who have been particularly helpful include Andrew Modelski, Library of Congress Map Division; Martin Perkins, Old World Wisconsin Outdoor Museum; Charles Calkins, Carroll College; William Noble, University of Missouri; William Laatsch, University of Wisconsin–Green Bay; and John Lehr, University of Winnipeg. Several scholars have read all or part of the final manuscript or earlier drafts and have offered valuable critical comments and suggestions. These have included Peter Wacker, Rutgers University; William Tishler, University of Wisconsin–Madison; Edward Mueller, University of Pittsburgh; Albert Korsok, University of Akron; and Stephen Jett, University of California–Davis.

A special word of appreciation needs to be expressed for the patience and forbearance with which my wife, Jane, and our children, Lisa, Matthew, and Douglas, have endured my preoccupation with crumbling barns, abandoned houses, and other mysterious rural features.

To all of those mentioned above, and to many more who inadvertently remain nameless, go my special thanks and gratitude. Most have helped more than they know.

Preface

This book is intended to be an introduction to the major features of the American settlement landscape, as it has evolved from the colonial period to the present time. Emphasis is placed on the differentiation of the houses in which Americans have lived, and on the farm barns and secondary farm structures in which most of them worked. The wide range of other buildings, which also gave character to the landscape, has not been covered for two reasons. First, such an attempt would produce a work of unreasonable size. (I entertain some hope that this book will be used in college-level courses.) Furthermore, inclusion of all structures would introduce a mass of detail and obscure major points by requiring readers to follow several lines of development. Throughout the book an attempt is made to trace the process of cultural diffusion that accompanied settlement. I have not hesitated to cross the political borders of the United States when it seemed desirable in order to follow settlement or to explain the rationale for structures.

Certain advanced readers will wish that I had included more detail, particularly in the opening chapters. This book, despite its length, is not exhaustive, and I request readers to keep in mind the strategy on which the two volumes are based. The first chapter is a simple statement of the significance of building forms as representative of ethnic groups, together with a brief introduction of some ideas of cultural diffusion, stressing cultural hearths.

The chapters of Part Two examine house types in five locations, introducing additional levels of complexity with each succeeding set of houses. Thus, Chapter 2 discusses only external appearance, the simplest characteristic and, hence, the easiest for beginning readers to grasp. In Chapter 3 the identification of the structural parts of a timber frame house and the importance that the arrangement of rooms or the plan has in the study of house type evolution are added to external appearance. The treatment of Dutch hearth houses in Chapter 4 adds a discussion of various important building materials, including types of brick bonding. At the close of this chapter Dutch house types are used to show that plan and exterior appearance do not always have a constant relationship.

Chapter 5 introduces further complexities. The early houses of the Delaware valley are products of a mixed ethnic heritage. The evolutionary sequence involves a series of shifting combinations of plans, exterior form, structural members, and building materials. The discussion of Chesapeake Bay houses in Chapter 6 focuses upon the possible lines of evolutionary development that suggest not only interconnections of house types, but increasing diversity over time. My hope is that, with Chapter 6, readers will recognize that earlier chapters simplified material in order to demonstrate principles or relationships.

Part Three relates early dwellings to the various environmental conditions existing in different sections of the continent. Chapter 7 examines the approaches of the English and the Spanish, both of whom brought Caribbean influences into southeastern United States. The scope of Chapter 8 is exceptionally broad, dealing with three quite disparate western environments and the shelter adjustments that were made to them over very long periods of time, by groups having different economies and levels of technology. The final chapter of this section examines in greater detail the French reaction to the physical environment of the Mississippi valley and delta. Included is the west African and Haitian origin of the shotgun house.

The evolution of houses in the late eighteenth and entire nineteenth centuries is covered in Part Four. Chapter 10 analyzes the changes that occurred both as New England houses spread into the Midwest, and as the log houses of the Upland South culture area diffused throughout the Southeast. Also reviewed is the introduction in the Midwest and Great Plains of domestic structures derived directly from European sources and brought by newly emigrating groups. Chapter 11 is a summary of the stylistic changes occurring in domestic architecture in the nineteenth century, as popular and academic houses largely replaced those of folk origins.

In volume 2, Part One discusses the farm barns, which, together with houses, have dominated the rural cultural landscape. Three chapters trace the origins of farm barn design, whereas Chapter 4 discusses the geographical pattern of distribution of barns.

The complete range of farm outbuildings and secondary structures is the subject of Part Two of the second volume. Chapter 5 is devoted to a review of the design evolution and the geographical diffusion of various types of silos. The following chapter is exceptionally long, containing discussions of a very wide variety of secondary farm structures, ranging from spring houses and windmills to corncribs, granaries, and hay derricks. In most instances the form of these structures is related to their function, and often to environmental conditions. In a few cases, statements can be made about evolutionary development or geographical distribution and appropriate maps are included. Chapter 7 discusses the various types of fences, hedges, and walls that have been employed in rural North America.

The final section contains two chapters. The first reviews the literature of material culture studies and attempts to classify the research approaches that have been made by various workers. It also provides examples of cultural landscapes viewed in their entirety by examining those of seven ethnic groups not extensively studied previously, each of which demonstrates research possibilities not addressed in this volume. The last chapter suggests lines of inquiry for further research in this fascinating field of material-settlement landscape study.

PART ONE Introduction

1 Settlement Landscapes and Cultural Hearths

Nothing reveals so much about an area and its civilization as the buildings that people construct for shelter, economic support, defense, and worship. Not only is a region's range of resources, its environmental conditions, and the level of society's development within it revealed, but also much about the history, ethnic origin and composition, and even ways of thinking of the inhabitants of the region.

Certain structures clearly are associated with different ethnic groups and thus provide a means for identification and study of those people. The form of Ukrainian houses in Manitoba, for example, helps establish the European provincial origin of these settlers, despite the lack of precise documentary evidence.[1] The three-room arrangement of so-called Quaker-plan houses in the piedmont of North Carolina implies a connection with similar houses constructed by German settlers in southeastern Pennsylvania. That identical plans occur in the two widely separated areas, as well as along the Great Valley between, testifies to the direction and ethnic composition of settlement patterns. Colonial houses in eastern Massachusetts, eastern Long Island, and eastern New Jersey show remarkable similarity, which reveals a common settlement connection. Migrants from the early colonial settlements around Massachusetts Bay made their way in the middle of the seventeenth-century, first to Long Island and somewhat later to New Jersey. The Cape Cod cottages of New England are little altered on Long Island, and are still basically similar in New Jersey.[2] Many more examples exist, some to be identified later, of the association of particular buildings and ethnic groups.

The relationship is so definite that many structures are identified by means of ethnic designations. "Dutch," "English," and "German Bank" barns are each clearly distinguishable types, for example. As Thomas Wertenbaker observed, "There is no possibility of confusing the Dutch barn with the German barn or the English barn. As one motors westward from New Brunswick, when he sees an old barn with the wagon entrance on the long side, he may be fairly certain that it is of English or New England antecedents; if the entrance is in the gable-end it is Dutch; and when, after crossing the Delaware, he finds barns with the stalls on the ground level and the threshing floor above he knows it is a Pennsylvania Swiss or German barn."[3]

That buildings are a reflection both of the level of development of society and of the range of resources available seems to be so axiomatic that to state the relationship appears to some readers as almost superfluous. However, others may wish to have some confirmation of these pronouncements, which in any case is rather easy to provide. Wertenbaker was the first to state the now well known observation that a line on a map between Princeton, New Jersey, and Wilmington, Delaware, would mark a general division between stone buildings to the north and west and brick buildings to the south and east.[4] Such a differentiation reflects the geological resources of the two areas. To cite just two examples, in Lancaster County, Pennsylvania, the blue-gray limestone houses and barns produce a cultural landscape that is quite distinct from the patterned red-brick houses of Salem County, New Jersey. Less than fifty miles separate the two areas.

Building materials may indicate more than just the occurrence of geological resources, however. Alan Gowans notes that in areas of Dutch settlement, stone was used for dwellings occupied by people with lower incomes, whereas brick structures housed upper-income groups.[5] Certain materials either possess or gain status. Another well-known instance is that of log houses. A dwelling built of logs on the frontier, although admirably suited to the existing primitive settlement conditions, was often considered a mark of inferior status. Thus, when replaced, it was succeeded by a timber frame structure, or, when enlarged, the addition was frame and the original log house was covered to hide the log construction.

That fashion and status seeking has a lot to do with the popularity of particular house styles is not difficult to ascertain. Almost every small town has at least a few nineteenth-century houses with elaborate "gingerbread work," one of the hallmarks of a style called *Gothic Revival*, which became so popular that it was added to all sorts of house types.

One of the most distinctive features of any structure, and one likely to be affected by stylistic changes, is the roof.

At the same time, the perceptive observer may detect the inertia that is incorporated into building by observing some roofs and the persistence of a form long after the rationale for it has disappeared. This is nowhere clearer than with very early houses, some of which have roofs with slopes of up to sixty degrees. Such a high pitch was required to shed rain when roofs were constructed of thatch. Good thatching materials, however, were not widely available in North America and excellent substitutes such as wooden shakes, shingles, and planks were, and the result was that these other materials rapidly were adopted. The roof pitch remained steep for some time even though the new materials did not require it.

The bell-cast roof of Quebec cottages is another example of a design that persisted despite the removal of the conditions that had given rise originally to the feature. On cottages in France the bell-cast of the eaves was strictly functional —a device to throw water from the roof away from the base of the clay or earthen walls in order to slow down the process of deterioration. In Quebec, however, the walls were constructed of durable timber or of stone and the need for the bell-cast disappeared. But not only did the bell-cast persist long after its function had ceased, it actually increased (fig. 1–1). From an average of about eight inches around 1720, the eave overhang grew to between thirty-six and forty inches by roughly 1850.[6] Such an increase appears to have been a response entirely to the dictates of fashion, with a functional need totally absent.

After the colonial and pioneer periods passed, and especially in the nineteenth

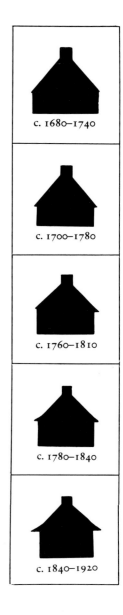

1–1 Silhouettes of French-Canadian houses, showing the increase in the bell-cast eaves with the passage of time (modified from Michel Lessard and Gilles Vilandre, *La Maison Traditionnelle au Québec*)

century when economic conditions had stabilized somewhat, fashion and changing tastes were sufficiently important to produce great changes in roof styling, often in existing structures (fig. 1–2). The magnitude of such changes makes house classification in some instances a perilous exercise.

As the North American economy shifted from an agricultural base to that of urban-oriented industry, building motifs also altered. Even more significant was the ever-widening spread of wealth derived both directly and indirectly from industrialization. Such wealth supported a shift from folk building in a traditional manner, which had evolved slowly over centuries on both sides of the Atlantic, to popular building styles derived from academic origins, which changed rapidly and often in radically different directions. Such modifications, although widely supported, were artificially created and thus each "style" was fated to last only a few decades, to be succeeded by some new fashion.

Before alteration

After alteration

1–2 Fashion dictates a roof change (from William M. Woollett, *Old Homes Made New*, 1878)

Settlement landscape and material culture

In the twentieth century, American geographers have been increasingly concerned with the study of cultural landscapes, although their investigations generally have lagged far behind those of their European colleagues. The dominant American figure promoting cultural geographic study in the first half of the century was Carl O. Sauer of the University of California-Berkeley. Although not primarily interested in the geographic study of architectural features, Sauer did direct several generations of graduate students in studies of diffusion and cultural phenomena in general. Among his outstanding students was Fred B. Kniffen who, more than any other geographer, has influenced the study of the settlement landscape in North America.

Despite a few earlier important but isolated studies, the beginning of systematic attention to the subject of the spatial variations in building types may be said to date from the presidential address that Kniffen delivered in 1965 before the Association of American Geographers.[7] Since that address a growing number of cultural and historical geographers have been devoting increasing effort to identifying, classifying, arranging, and studying the rationale of buildings and other major features incident to human occupation of an area. Such work focuses upon the *settlement landscape*, which includes not only structures of all types but also a large number of folk and popular items such

3

as furniture, modes of transportation, and handicrafts. These often have strong ethnic associations and they may be valuable in delineating cultural regions. Furthermore, the pattern of settlement itself, including methods of land subdivision, shape and size of fields, arrangement of houses and other buildings, road and other transportation patterns, and land use also may be considered part of the settlement landscape. Other terms, such as *cultural landscape* or *material settlement landscape* are sometimes used in place of settlement landscape.

A number of folklorists have also made important contributions. Among folklorists, this field of study is usually given the designation *material culture*, a term that has a large overlap with the geographer's term *settlement landscape*, although the direction and objectives of study of the two disciplines normally are quite distinct. The dominant material-culture folklorist is Henry Glassie, whose writings have had both a broad and a specific focus, and who produced the earliest general statement integrating the vernacular architecture of the eastern United States with other cultural elements.[8] In contrast to cultural geography—where a single center of settlement landscape research, the Department of Geography and Anthropology at Louisiana State University—has dominated the field, material-culture study among folklorists is diffused in a number of important academic locations. Among the most significant of these are the Department of Folklore at

Indiana University, The Cooperstown Graduate Program in Folklore in New York, and the departments of Folklore and American Studies at the University of Pennsylvania.

Among historians, interest in the study of vernacular architecture seems to have peaked initially in the period prior to World War II, although the most significant work of these scholars appears as late as 1952 in the great study of Hugh Morrison entitled *Early American Architecture*.[9] Most of the best-known historians specializing in vernacular architecture have dealt primarily with the precolonial, colonial, or immediately postcolonial periods as expressed along the eastern seaboard of the United States. Foremost among these early historians were Thomas Jefferson Wertenbaker, Talbot Hamlin, Harold Eberlein, and Fiske Kimball. Special mention must be made of Thomas T. Waterman, who is notable for his wide range of research interests, including early work on American Indian dwellings and on vernacular structures in North Carolina, as well as on colonial architecture.

Closely associated with the historians around, or just after, the turn of the century were a number of professional architects who produced the first comprehensive studies of colonial architecture based upon measured drawings. Henry Chandlee Forman pursued three careers —art historian, archaeologist, and architect/restoration specialist. Also particularly influential were Norman Isham and Frederick Kelly. In recent years, a number of landscape architects and architectural historians trained in schools of architecture have begun to exert a growing influence on the study of vernacular architecture. The more

important centers of such study presently include the University of Virginia, the University of Wisconsin-Madison, and North Carolina State University.

A rather different sort of orientation which, nevertheless, provides a significant opportunity for study of architectural forms is offered by the larger outdoor museum restorations, such as Old Sturbridge Village in Massachusetts and Colonial Williamsburg in Virginia. The research facilities provided at these establishments have enabled scholars, such as Abbott Lowell Cummings and Marcus Whiffen, to produce extended works dealing with the periods and areas represented in these museums. The Old World Wisconsin outdoor ethnic museum may, in future, offer the same sort of opportunity for scholars concerned with ethnic vernacular architecture.

With so many disciplines of such diverse viewpoints concerned with the structures of the landscapes, it is not surprising that no one yet has attempted to integrate the enormous number of existing and widely scattered studies, to say nothing about reconciling the various philosophical approaches. The aims of the present volume are largely limited to providing a synthesis from existing studies, which can function both as an introduction and review of the field for students and as a point of departure for additional research. This subject is dealt with more fully in the second volume.

The scope of the present volume is limited to a discussion of certain aspects of the settlement landscape of North America. Because houses are the most basic structures that people build, these will be treated in considerable detail. An insight into the operation of the components that have functioned in the settlement process may be gained by noting the alterations that have occurred in housing and relating such modifications to changing social and economic conditions. Such study also will provide a framework for understanding much of the present-day cultural landscape of North America and especially its variations from region to region.

Barns and silos, structures of major importance in farming, will be studied in the second volume. The reasons for their inclusion are simple. Until recently, agriculture has been the major support of the population, hence barns and secondary farm structures were the most common buildings after houses. Furthermore, these structures are still commonplace in most regions of North America and thus they serve to give a distinctive identification to those regions.

The North American settlement landscape

North America has many advantages and a few disadvantages for the study of the material-cultural landscape. First, *settlement* is a recent phenomenon. At the beginning of the seventeenth century, the eastern half of North America contained less than 1 million American Indian inhabitants. By the close of the eighteenth century, a European population, combined in the South with an African slave population, largely had replaced the American Indian population, but numbers for the entire area were still low, just slightly over 4 million. Overall population densities of not much more than two persons per square mile prevailed, although much clustering was evident. The effective occupation of eastern North America is, in truth, a phenomenon of the last century and a half. Thus, in all sections of the continent, many of the original pioneering structures still stand.

Not all early original structures are museums or protected buildings, although many are. Students often are surprised to learn how many simple, private residences can be identified as representatives of early types by the careful researcher. More houses than barns or other economic structures survive because the basic function of the house has remained unchanged.

Another condition favoring settlement study is that different ethnic groups, drawn from various distinct areas of Europe, tended to settle in separate regions in North America. Thus, more or less clearly defined regional *settlement ensembles*, consisting of houses, barns, churches, mills, and smaller structures can be perceived. Such distinctive ethnic settlements became the *cultural hearths*, of which more will be said.

Even in areas where settlement by various ethnic groups was not geographically separate, one group tended to succeed another so that periods of dominance of a particular group may usually be defined. In any case, the number of such "layers" of settlement is small, thus reducing the complexity of material-settlement study. In certain areas the groups that arrived first occupied the land and succeeding groups went to villages and towns, effecting an almost immediate separation of cultures.

With occupation so recent and cross currents of migration so few, the serious student has little difficulty in dissecting the material-cultural landscape and identifying the origins of its components. Because population was sparse and the land not completely occupied, it is relatively easy to trace the migration and assess the impact of ethnic groups by noting the distribution of structures or architectural features typically associated with each group. The examples of the Quaker-plan house and the Cape Cod cottage have been mentioned above. Another somewhat different instance, first noted by Kniffen, is that of the evolutionary sequence of New England–derived houses, which can be traced right across central New York into northern Ohio and southern Michigan.[10]

Finally, as Wilbur Zelinsky has commented, another important advantage is the abundance of data available for scholarly study.[11] Not only are many early structures preserved (largely because of the tranquil conditions in most portions of the area), but also a great mass of documentation has been preserved. Accounts of travelers and scientific observers are supplemented by volumes of drawings, measurements, maps, and even photographs. Despite this abundance of source materials, no comprehensive bibliography on the settlement landscape has been compiled for North America, the United States, Canada, or any large region thereof.[12]

Two important factors operate to inhibit the study of the material-cultural landscape in eastern North America, however. First, the rapid population growth during the past one hundred and fifty years has encouraged the destruction of small early structures and their replacement with "modern," larger buildings. In many instances, population growth has encouraged physical redevelopment with reconstruction or "renewal" of areas containing outmoded structures. The replacement buildings are usually more efficient, but often less important architecturally, than the ones demolished. Unfortunately, it is just those areas of towns in which the most architecturally important buildings are found that are the oldest and, thus, most susceptible to modernization. In other instances, earlier rural buildings are being replaced by later urban or suburban structures.

Another great disadvantage for the serious student of material-cultural landscape is the North American unconcern for the past. One of the psychological characteristics most often noticed by foreign observers of the North American personality is the tendency to ignore whatever is not current or modern or progressive. In the process, many of the significant buildings that would help explain architectural evolution in the New World have been ignored and ultimately destroyed. In other instances, early buildings have been modernized, with little or no thought of preserving a record of the original plan, facade, interior decoration, or other architectural elements. Even seemingly competent authority sometimes errs in its enthusiasm for reconstruction. Several decades ago when I first visited Fort Necessity National Battlefield, the reconstructed fort was a rectangular log structure. Fortunately, in more recent times the fort has been altered to a more faithful circular structure of vertical poles. Not every organization engaged in historic preservation or reconstruction possesses the resources and integrity to correct its own, or others', earlier mistakes.

A casual examination of eastern North America reveals a confusing array of material-cultural landscape features. Older structures are scattered amid newer ones and often appear to be unrelated to their present surroundings. Organizing concepts are required to create some order and to reveal both the systematic relationships that exist between the features and the connection of the cultural landscape to the environment, or physical landscape, in which the features occur. The process whereby cultural traits have been diffused has not been studied adequately, although some beginnings have been made. Despite the current lack of sufficient materials, diffusion studies show promise of eventually becoming an effective analytical tool.

One of the most limiting difficulties has been the lack of a widely accepted terminology that would serve to establish a common base from which diffusion studies might proceed. This book, which is the first attempt to correlate geographical and other writings on houses and agricultural buildings for all North America, may provide the common nomenclature from which further studies may advance.

Another useful basic concept is that of the *cultural hearth*, which may be defined as an original source area with distinctive settlement forms, as well as other cultural attributes, from which certain clearly identifiable elements were carried to other parts of the continent.

American cultural hearths

The concept of *cultural hearths* was proposed in different terminology by Donald Meinig in his study of the Mormon culture area of western United States.[13] In Meinig's analysis the concept was originally identified as the *cultural core*. Meinig defined this as a centralized zone in which a culture displayed most strongly its essential features. The hearth coincided with the core because Mormon culture developed in relative isolation and expanded outward with no competition from other cultures.

In eastern North America, as noted by Richard Pillsbury,[14] the advent of European colonists produced a rather different cultural evolution, largely because the environmental and geographical conditions were different. Several independent cultural hearths developed, mostly along the littoral and in the major river valleys near the coast. Expansion of each of the different regional cultures was highly directional, partly because of the restriction imposed by initial littoral location and partly because of competition from other expanding cultures. Free land remained mostly on the western frontier so expansion occurred largely in that general direction. In Pillsbury's view the advancing westward streams of culture eventually coalesced to produce a national cultural hearth in the eastern Midwest (fig. 1–3).

At about the time Meinig was formulating his ideas concerning culture areas, Kniffen was identifying *source areas* along the Atlantic Coast from which distinctive house and barn types spread across the remainder of eastern

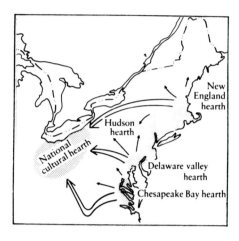

1–3 The process of settlement landscape development in eastern United States (after Pillsbury)

United States. The source areas of Kniffen fit the definition of cultural cores or hearths as proposed by Meinig and Pillsbury. Kniffen identified only three cultural source areas: New England; the Middle Atlantic, centering on southeastern Pennsylvania; and the lower Chesapeake, centering on tidewater Virginia.[15]

The source areas of Kniffen were subsequently refined and delimited by Henry Glassie, who added a fourth source area, the coast from southern North Carolina through Georgia. In contrast to Pillsbury's view, Glassie suggests that the interior portions of the eastern United States contain at least

two distinct national cultural areas[16] which he terms the *Upland South* and the *Midwest* (fig. 1–4). Definitive study is still needed to determine the validity of these two alternative approaches.

Subsequent studies of the cultural hearths of Kniffen and Glassie suggest that they can be refined and extended to cover the entire continent. For example, in eastern North America, both Kniffen and Glassie dealt only with the United States, ignoring Canada and the important original source of French settlement.

1–4 Material folk-culture regions in eastern United States (after Glassie)

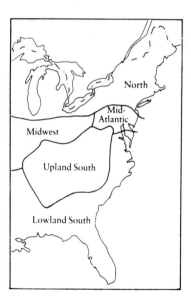

7

At least ten cultural hearths can be delineated (fig. 1–5), from which settlement proceeded, although the entire distributional process has not been studied in complete detail. Most of the original hearth areas are situated in eastern North America, which reflects the significance of European colonization. The hearths are that of French settlement along the lower St. Lawrence River; southern New England, the northern hearth of early English culture; the Hudson valley, the center of early Dutch settlement; the Delaware River–Lancaster plain hearth from which spread a cultural mixture containing Swedish, German, English, and Scotch-Irish elements; Chesapeake Bay, extending northward into southern Maryland and southward into northern North Carolina, in which an English culture somewhat different from that of New England developed; the southern tidewater, the coastal region between Charleston, South Carolina, and Savannah, Georgia, where an English culture modified by Huguenot and West Indian influences evolved; a small area in northern Florida from which the Spanish attempted to extend their influence, but with limited success; the delta of the Mississippi River in Louisiana, with a mixture of French, Spanish, and Haitian Negro cultural elements; a Native American hearth centered on the Colorado plateau in northeastern Arizona; and the Mormon cultural hearth of the Utah oasis.

On the periphery, but outside North America, lie two other cultural source areas whose influence has spread over different portions of the United States and/or Canada. Mexican settlement, an amalgam of Spanish and mestizo components, has indelibly stamped roughly the entire southwestern quadrant of the United States. The hearth of Mexican culture lies far to the south in the intermontane basins of the southern extremities of the Meseta Central. Russian settlement affected a much smaller area in the Pacific Northwest, and to a more limited degree than Mexican settlement. Hence, Russian cultural features are less evident, less clearly defined, and fewer in number.

1–5 North American cultural hearths

The process of cultural diffusion

One of the principal tasks facing the cultural geographer is more detailed study of the cultural diffusion process. Meinig has suggested that two concepts in addition to that of the core or hearth can be utilized. Beyond the hearth is a larger area termed the *domain* into which the features of the core have been transported. "The *domain* refers to those areas in which the particular culture under study is *dominant*, but with markedly less intensity and complexity of development than in the core, where the bonds of connection are fewer and more tenuous and where regional peculiarities are clearly evident."[17] The domain of the Mormon culture region as delineated by Meinig is shown in figure 1–6. If expansion of settlement continues, ultimately the influence of a cul-

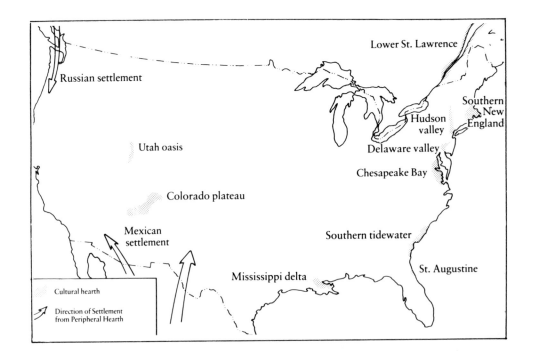

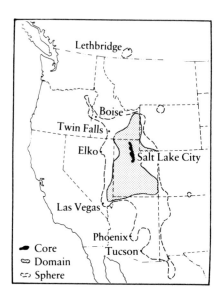

1–6 The Mormon culture region: hearth, domain, and sphere (after Meinig)

tural hearth will extend beyond the area in which it is dominant. If the culture is growing rapidly and vigorously this outer zone at some future stage may be incorporated within the domain. If, however, cultural expansion is weak the outer territories may continue to be marginally affected. Such an outer zone of influence of a culture has been termed its *sphere*. Within the area of the sphere, the "culture is represented only by certain of its elements or . . . its peoples reside as minorities among those of a different culture."[18]

The process by which the culture of a people is transmitted beyond the core or hearth is complex and as yet only partially and imperfectly known. Part of the difficulty lies in the fact that *culture*

covers so many varied features, not all of which have a physical expression.

Two basic types of cultural diffusion have been suggested. One is *relocation diffusion*, which is the transfer of culture from one area to a noncontiguous second area. This is a process that has produced the cultural hearths in North America. European immigrant groups transported the culture of their home areas across the Atlantic Ocean to the New World. The second type of cultural diffusion is termed *expansion diffusion* and is the process by which North American cultural hearths have expanded into their surrounding domains and spheres. It is this process that Meinig is discussing when he talks about Mormon expansion across the intermontane West of the United States.

The precise extent of cultural areas is difficult to measure. This is partly because *culture* is such a vast phenomenon and its material forms represent only one aspect. The number of people who speak a particular language and the number of adherents of different religions are two criteria that have been most widely utilized in the past to measure the extent of cultural areas. In the future, a study of the settlement landscape may provide similar utility as the cultural geographer attempts to understand the cultural diffusion processes that have produced today's world.

The major routes of settlement diffusion are reasonably clear, as are certain distinctive building types associated with each hearth and its domain and sphere. Using an analogy from geology, such distinctive building types, easily recognized from the hundreds of structures that exist in the landscape, may be considered to be somewhat similar to

index fossils that identify particular geological strata. "Index" buildings always identify a particular cultural origin or influence, regardless of where they are found. However, the problems of classification are more difficult than those faced by the natural scientist, whether geologist, biologist, or other. As Kniffen noted, "The biologist never finds the tail of a lion grafted to the body of a cow; the classifier of cultural forms has no such assurance. He must judiciously generalize, and he can never be completely objective. Without the necessary historical and comparative data he cannot safely accept apparent genetic relationships. In his morphologic data he must look for central themes, and must temporarily obscure minor variations in the individual forms."[19]

Unfortunately, no census exists of structures and much painstaking fieldwork will be required before definitive statements can be made about the settlement landscape of North America. Though the task is large, its magnitude ought not to deter the investigator. The balance of this book is a review of the studies that presently exist and a synthesis of their results.

9

PART TWO
Evolution of Colonial Houses
in Northeastern Hearths

---

2   French Colonial Houses in the St. Lawrence Valley Hearth

Beginning early in the seventeenth century, European colonists established beachheads of occupation in eastern North America, which were eventually to become the cultural hearths from which subsequent settlement proceeded. These cultural source areas, enumerated in the previous chapter, each produced a set of distinctive buildings that evolved in response to the local environmental conditions, reflecting the particular economic structure of the area and that were patterned after buildings in regions the settlers had left behind. In effect, building types were a large part of the colonists' cultural baggage that was to be discarded or modified only very gradually, usually by a process of slow modification until the original building type was no longer easily recognizable.

In some instances, the environmental conditions were so different on this side of the Atlantic Ocean that certain buildings were no longer especially well suited to the new locations and these structures, or certain features thereof, immediately began to change. The process of modification often took a very long time, however. The substitution of sliding barn doors that could be opened easily after the heavy snowfalls of northeastern North America, in place of the original swinging or hinged doors typical of western Europe where snowfall is light, is only one example of such modification. In other instances, new features were added to better accommodate a structure to its environment. Such alterations are abundant in the southern United States, for example, where verandahs to provide shade, single-file arrangement of rooms to provide cross ventilation, and elevated basements to raise houses above the damp ground of the subtropical environment occur widely on many types of houses.

This chapter examines the house types that first appeared in the colonial period in the St. Lawrence valley cultural hearth. Only those houses that are associated with the French settlers are included and only the exterior form of the houses is discussed.

The reason for such restriction is twofold. First, by limiting consideration to the outside of the building, emphasis is placed on a single element of the structure. Thus, the task confronting the student of material culture is greatly simplified. A second cogent reason for such simplification is that the exterior form is the most immediately and clearly recognizable feature of a building. It is generally what the observer notices first. It is, thus, the place to begin analysis.

2–1 Aerial view of the rang land system of the St. Lawrence valley. Photo taken near Montreal, May 1976.

French occupation and division of the land

Although Quebec was founded by traders as early as 1608, it was not until after 1632 that much colonization was contemplated, and not until after 1663 that actual settlement by farmers took place on any important scale.[1] It was well into the eighteenth century before the initial phase of land occupation was completed.

The system of land subdivision in the St. Lawrence valley divided properties into "long lots" which were normally perpendicular to the rivers, the earliest and for a long time the principal means of transport and communication (fig. 2–1). The "long lots," typically about ten times longer than they were wide, produced a settlement pattern of tiers or ranges (*rangs*) parallel with the river courses (fig. 2–2). The oldest settlements normally are those along the river in the first range, with each subsequent range or tier possessing later settlement and younger structures. The system of land division utilized in the St. Lawrence valley is similar to that employed in several parts of France, as well as in other parts of Europe. Its use in the St. Lawrence valley apparently arose from settler preference and familiarity, rather than as an officially imposed system.[2] In any event, it had the advantage of dividing adjacent farms into properties possessing balanced amounts of high quality land along the floodplain, land of lesser fertility on the river terraces, and remote lands of poor quality, serving mainly as wood lots, along the far valley slopes.

The main roads along the valleys usually followed the edge of the first terrace, to be above normal flood level and to permit maximum cultivation of the best quality farmlands along the floodplain. Houses were situated on individual farm properties with little nucleation of settlement, so that an elongated pattern of occupance called a *cote* was created. "Even today, lines of closely spaced farmhouses have a gregarious feel—as if, in rejecting village for cote, the inhabitants had struck a balance between their wishes to associate with their fellows and to be isolated from authority."[3]

2–2 A model of the rang land-division system used by the French

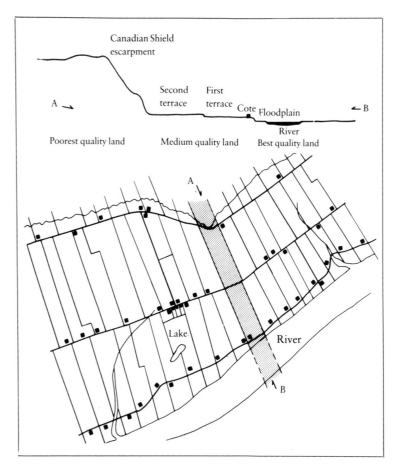

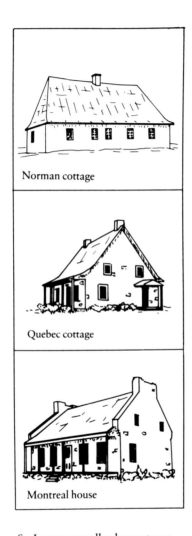

Norman cottage

Quebec cottage

Montreal house

2–3 St. Lawrence valley house types

French colonial house types

Three distinctive house types are associated with the French settlement of the St. Lawrence cultural hearth (fig. 2–3). Two, which were brought by early settlers and craftsmen, represent transplants from France. The third, in the view of Ramsey Traquair, is a Canadian-evolved type,[4] although produced from French antecedents. Gerald Morisset, however, considers this latter house to be a type brought without modification from western France.[5]

These three house types form the basis for most later housing throughout French Canada. With the passage of time, although political control passed to the British and their descendants, French culture persisted and houses derived from these early structures continue to create the distinct cultural landscape of French Canada.

Within the lower St. Lawrence cultural hearth, the study and classification of houses largely has centered on the analysis of the external form and features of the structure.[6] Plan or internal room arrangement has not always been a primary consideration.

The Norman cottage

The Norman cottage (fig. 2–4),[7] as its name suggests, has strong French associations and there are identical structures located in northwestern France. Norman cottages are decidedly oblong and much longer than deep. External walls of local fieldstone that was bedded in lime mortar and whitewashed frequently were boarded over to guard against frost damage and ultimate wall disintegration in the severe winters of Quebec. Walls were two or more feet thick to achieve stability. "Such walls give good protection. They are cool in summer and in winter, once warmed, they retain heat for a long time."[8] The distinguishing characteristic of Norman cottages, which are most likely to be encountered in the St. Lawrence valley below Quebec City, is the immense roof, steeply pitched, bell-cast at the eaves, and hipped at the ends (fig. 2–5). It is this feature that makes the Norman cottage unmistakable.

2–4 The Norman cottage

2–5 A Norman cottage on the Isle d'Orleans, near Quebec City, 1976

The steepness of the roof was largely a relict feature which had been needed in France where the roof was typically comprised of thatching. A steep pitch was required on thatch roofs in order for the roof to shed water effectively. If the pitch was too low, water would drip through the thatch. A steep pitch, however, permitted water to run along the individual reeds or straw lengths until ultimately it was shed at the eaves. In New France, roofs were made of wood rather than thatch, but they still retained their earlier design, providing a good example of cultural inertia. However, it is also true that snow would accumulate on roofs that were too low in pitch, and its alternate thawing and freezing would allow ice to form at the eaves and cause water to back up and leak through.[9]

The Quebec cottage

The second imported French house type has such a wide distribution across the entire St. Lawrence valley that it reasonably may be called the Quebec cottage (fig. 2–6). Furthermore, these dwellings are especially characteristic of the Isle d'Orleans and the region immediately around Quebec City, where they have exerted an influence on house architecture that has continued into the twentieth century.

Georges Gauthier-Larouche calls attention to four aspects of the Quebec cottage that are significant and that can be utilized to trace the evolutionary development of Quebec cottages.[10] These are the pitch of the roof, the general size and shape of the house, the exaggeration of the eave overhang, and the elevation of the gallery or porch.

Generally speaking, as time passed, the pitch of the roof decreased from sixty degrees, common in the seventeenth century, to forty-five degrees, which typifies the middle of the nineteenth century. At the same time, the shape and size of the structure also were changing.

2–6 The Quebec cottage

Although Quebec cottages steadily increased in floor area, they became shorter and more massive. The bell-cast of the roof became more pronounced with time, even though the original rationale for the feature had disappeared (see chap. 1). An eave overhang of eight to eighteen inches was typical of the first half of the eighteenth century, whereas by the middle of the nineteenth century the projection had grown to between thirty-six and forty inches. Finally, the porch or gallery, which may be an addition derived from the French colonial connection to the West Indies, shows a steady process of elevation from ground level in the seventeenth century to a position averaging eight feet above ground level by the mid-nineteenth century. Some scholars have suggested that this elevation of a design feature not conducive to the cold climate of Quebec may have been in response to the accumulations of snow, a common feature of the Canadian winter.

Both size and arrangement of plan tended to vary (the former somewhat more than the latter). Dimensions of between forty and fifty feet in length and twenty to thirty-five feet in width appear to have been more or less normal. The plan of the Quebec cottage usually consists of two rooms of unequal size, the larger, termed the *winter room*, originally was occupied and utilized primarily in winter months. In many instances the outside end of the room is subdivided into two tiny unheated bedrooms.

13

The smaller *summer room*, which was dominated by its immense fireplace hearth, was used in early days primarily as a kitchen. Into this room open the outside doors and from this room leads the narrow stairway to the loft above. The walls of these cottages may be built of stone rubble covered with white-washed mortar, of sawn lumber weatherboarding over a timber frame, or of hewn logs in the *pièce-sur-pièce* mode of construction (see chap. 10).

In earlier houses the chimney is centrally but asymmetrically positioned. Often a single hearth provided heat to the kitchen and the winter room received only what heat was radiated from the back of the chimney stones. In some other houses, back-to-back hearths were constructed, and in still others, distinctive large brick stoves were utilized as heat sources.[11]

In all early houses the appearance is largely medieval: doors are set off on the side, window openings are narrow with small multiple panes set in frames which are fixed or which open outward, roof pitch is steep, and the chimney is positioned near the center of the structure. In later houses, two chimneys located inside but near the gable walls are usual (fig. 2–7), facades are balanced, and roof pitch is lower (but still at least forty-five degrees). In the latter half of the nineteenth century some of these houses received fashionable mansard roofs (fig. 2–8).[12]

The Quebec cottage had a remarkable persistence in the St. Lawrence valley.

With only slight modifications it has lasted for over three hundred years. Many houses built in the twentieth century are clearly derivatives of this earlier type.

2–7 A Quebec cottage with dormer additions, front galerie, and "gingerbread" scrollwork typical of the Victorian period. The balanced facade and the gable window placement suggest a center hallway, four-room plan. (Isle d'Orleans, 1975)

2–8 Two views of a Quebec cottage with bell-cast mansard roof (Isle d'Orleans, 1976)

The Montreal house

The third of the early French-Canadian house types can be termed the Montreal house (fig. 2–9) from its concentration in the upper portions of the St. Lawrence lowland. In form the Montreal house, generally deeper than the other types, produces a more massive building.[13] Particularly noteworthy are the large, heavy stone gables often incorporating double-flue chimneys.[14] Such great gables normally are carried above the roof line creating prominent parapets. This feature evolved as a safeguard against windblown roof fires spreading from adjacent houses.[15] Obviously the design was worked out in towns, where houses were situated close together. The fact that it was incorporated in rural houses is a confirmation of the leadership provided by town dwellers. In plan these houses have two rows of rooms, front and rear. The size of rooms and the interior arrangement of the doors is quite variable and often irregular. Stone is the most typical building material of these houses (fig. 2–10).

2–10 A Montreal house in St. Lambert, Quebec. The parapet is missing and the house is raised somewhat over a cellar. (May 1976)

The French colonial houses evolve

As already noted, other and often rather picturesque features were added to the basic early Canadian houses. Extended or overhanging eaves, mansard roofs evolving into curved cove or bell-cast roofs, narrow dormer windows, extensive verandahs, and snow galleries three to four feet high along both the front and the back of the house were emphasized in the eighteenth and nineteenth centuries.[16] The conquest of French Canada by the English in 1763 and the influx of English Loyalists to Upper Canada from the United States after the American Revolution effectively limited the expansion of French settlement and thus of the early French-Canadian houses. In New England no such restrictions to expansion occurred.

2–9 The Montreal house

3 English Colonial Houses in the New England Hearth

The houses erected in the New England cultural hearth by English colonists differed significantly from those built by the French in the St. Lawrence valley. Not only are the houses of the two cultural hearths quite different, so also are the methods by which the land was divided and occupied, and the result is that the overall appearance of each area is quite distinctive.

This chapter examines the difference in exterior appearance of the colonial English houses. It also introduces the idea of an evolutionary relationship of house types that can be deduced only by an examination of floor plans. Thus, five colonial houses that do not resemble one another externally can be seen to be closely related when their floor plans are compared. Examining the floor plan represents a better method of analysis than simply looking at the external form, the procedure followed in the preceding chapter. Of course, ultimately, both external form and internal plan contribute to an understanding of the house.

Land division and settlement in the southern New England hearth

Settlement in southern New England commenced only a dozen years after that in the St. Lawrence valley, but the pace or rate of settlement was far more intensive in New England.[1] Probably much of the explanation for this can be traced to the fact that English settlers came in quest of free land, whereas French settlers came as tenants. (It is true that the French managed to escape the grasp of landlords almost from the inception of settlement.)

Unlike the orderly *rang* pattern that obtained in the St. Lawrence valley, English settlement appears almost haphazard or random, although the appearance is really deceiving, mostly because the land was divided originally utilizing the metes-and-bounds system, which produces irregular properties of uneven size (fig. 3–1). This system of land subdivision was based upon units of human measure (i.e., feet, paces, spans) and natural landmarks. Direction as well as distance often was rather imprecisely stated, especially in earlier days. Thus this system had serious drawbacks that originated primarily in the variability of its measurement components. As settlement progressed and formerly isolated holdings were connected by newly created properties, the potential for disputed boundaries and subsequent lawsuits was fully realized.

The landscape produced under the metes-and-bounds land division system in New England consisted of irregularly shaped lots organized into townships (simply called *towns* in New England). Within the area of the New England hearth, each town consisted of a village

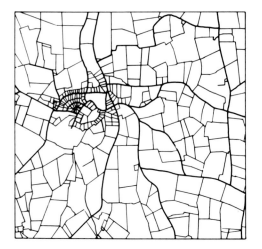

3–1 The metes-and-bounds land system used in New England. Compass orientation is lacking and properties are irregular. Smaller town lots surround the village common.

—which was the single major focus of settlement—and its surrounding agricultural fields. In the early agricultural market villages, the meetinghouse or town hall and the adjacent local tavern provided the focal point for the settlements. Later on, the now-familiar New England village form of public buildings and business establishments fronting on a central green or commons evolved.[2]

In the beginning, the three-field system of European agriculture was introduced, although it was soon abandoned in favor of more individual agricultural efforts.[3] As population increased, subsidiary hamlets were established.[4] A pattern of nucleated settlements separated by agricultural land persists throughout the domain of New England culture, even though isolated individual farmsteads also have become a common feature.

Timber frame construction

The earliest domestic structures in the New England hearth were simple, single-room huts constructed of wattle and daub, covered with crude thatched roofs.[5] The reconstructed huts standing today at the popular historical tourist attraction of Plimouth Plantations in Plymouth, Massachusetts, are reproductions of some of these early dwellings. A variety of dug-out caves were also employed in the earliest period.[6] The temporary shelters were quickly supplanted by more substantial houses. The building techniques existing then in England were utilized, but with some modification.

It must be emphasized that log construction was not employed in New England because the early settlers came largely from southeastern England, where timber frame structures were almost universal.[7] Nonetheless, it is difficult to dislodge the popular idea that all early settlers were somehow associated with log cabins, despite the fact that extensive scholarly study has failed to establish any such connection. The problem has been well stated by Harold Shurtleff.

To deny that log cabins or log dwelling houses existed in the early English settlements, or to maintain the fact that framed houses were built by the English without passing through a log cabin stage, is to take issue with an American belief that is both deep-seated and tenacious.

The reasons for this emotional basis for the Log Cabin Myth are not far to seek. In the nineteenth century Americans began to marvel at their own progress, and to make a virtue of their early struggles with the wilderness. The log cabin as a symbol of democracy was dramatized in two famous presidential campaigns, those of 1840 and 1860. In literature the popular "Log-Cabin to the White House" series firmly fixed the log cabin as the proper scenario for the birth of a great American; as early as 1840 Daniel Webster was apologizing for not having been born in one, and as late as 1935, we are told, a "considerable legend" had already grown up around the "log-cabin origins" of Roy Harris, the Oklahoman composer. Thus, the log cabin came to be identified with "Old

3–2 Typical timber frame for a house

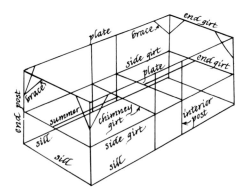

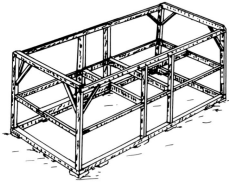

17

Hickory," "Tippecanoe," and Abraham Lincoln, with democracy and the frontier spirit, with the common man and his dream of the good life, and those persons, types, and forces of which Americans are justly proud. The log cabin, along with the Indian, the long rifle, and the hunting shirt is associated with one of the greatest of all conquests, the winning of the West. It gives us that sense of the dramatic which we seek in our history. Add to this that the log cabin has been the typical dwelling in timber frontiers, and in the backwoods of the older states, for at least two centuries, and we need not be surprised that careless historians projected it back into the earliest colonial settlements, or that many Americans today feel a sense of outrage when told that neither Captain John Smith nor Governor Bradford nor any of the founding fathers dwelt in a log cabin, or ever saw one.[8]

The permanent timber frame structures that the migrants erected in New England (fig. 3–2) were sided with overlapping clapboards or flush weatherboards, and roofed with lighter planks, wooden shingles, or thatch. Tile was not used much for roofing, probably for the same reason that bricks were not used for walls: good clay deposits were small and scattered but timber was plentiful and cheap. Thatch disappeared early on houses, although it persisted on barns well into the nineteenth century.

The reasons for the decline of thatch are several. First, the supply of suitable reeds in North America was decidedly limited. Winters were also colder than those in England, making a tighter roof covering more necessary. Most important, the "irregular New England climate could not be relied upon to wet down the thatching every few days" and hence the roof became a serious fire hazard.[9]

Whereas the thatch roof rapidly disappeared in the New World, the tradition of oak framing did not. Oak was abundant in New England and was used extensively in early houses, not only for framing but for siding and floors as well.[10] Despite its hardness and the difficulty that it presented in working it, oak was valued for its durability and strength. Cedar was often used for shingles and shakes in place of oak because it split more easily.

The tools used to hew timber were quite simple, principally the broadax and the adze, the latter for finishing work. The first step in hewing is to score the log with the broadax, i.e., to make a series of short cuts perpendicular to the grain, at frequent and regular intervals. The broadax is then employed to "hew to the line" of chalk marks placed lengthwise along the log in such a manner as to provide a guide for squaring up

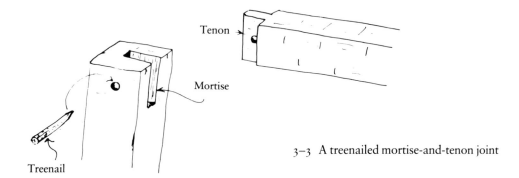

3–3   A treenailed mortise-and-tenon joint

the timber. The finishing is done with the adze,

a hoelike cutting instrument with a curved blade and long handle. Grasping the handle of the foot adze with his right hand about one-third of the way up from the blade, the carpenter rests the bottom of his right forearm on his right thigh. His left hand holds the handle near the butt end. Straddling the log, he makes short chopping strokes parallel to the surface of the log, chipping off the rounded bark surface in small chunks between each score. The craftsman moves backwards as his work progresses.[11]

The heavy vertical and horizontal timbers were joined together by sturdy mortise-and-tenon joints reinforced by wooden pegs (fig. 3–3). Holes for the octagonal treenails (trunnels) were bored through both mortise and tenon with a large auger or a hand-powered drilling machine. Driven home, the treenail usually became more or less permanently emplaced. Such rigid and strongly reinforced joints made these timber frame houses virtually hurricane proof. Diagonal braces (see fig. 3–2) also helped tie the horizontal and vertical timbers together.

The vertical members are referred to as *posts*. One is positioned at every corner of the house, on either side of doorways, and every sixteen feet or less along side walls. Between the posts there often are smaller lighter uprights, which do not bear any weight and which are called *studs*. To the posts and studs is attached the horizontal wall boarding. Many early houses, however, employed vertical wall planks instead of studs.[12] Examples may be found throughout colonial New England, although they are rare in the Boston area.[13] These planks, which are often two inches thick, may be attached by treenails to the outside of the horizontal beams of the house or, if designed to be load bearing, the planks may be mortised into both the plate and sill of the house.

Between the outside wall covering and the plaster-covered lath of the inside wall, a variety of insulating materials were often used to fill the wall. These could include wattle and daub, clay and straw rolls called *cats*, and soft brick nogging. Some speculation has centered around the use of half-timber construction with exposed brick, plaster, or clay filling in between the timbers, a type of

construction known to have been common in England. However, Hugh Morrison concludes that "the New England climate, with its driving rains and extremes of temperature, would have disintegrated exposed clay daubing in a short while. Since clapboards were exported to England from Plymouth within the first year, it is reasonable to suppose they would have been used for local building." Furthermore, the New England colonists came from southeastern England, which was the only part of that country where weatherboarding of houses was common practice.[14]

The horizontal timbers are spoken of generally as *beams*, but many are given special names (see fig. 3–2). Thus, beams along the foundation, upon which the posts and studs rest, are called *sills*, whereas those on top of the posts and studs, just under the eaves of the house, are termed *plates*. A basic house would have four sills and two plates, the latter connected by end girts. Beams between posts in the outer wall

of a building (with one exception) carry the designation of *girts*. They are specifically identified by their location, e.g., front girt, end girt. The one exception, the chimney girt, does not lie in the outside wall, but always athwart the house, adjacent to the chimney structure. Normally at right angles to the chimney girt is the major beam, called the *summer*, which carries the weight of the upper floors. Perpendicular to and resting on the summer, are the *joists*, smaller timbers upon which the floor boards are fixed.

The frame of the house had to be rigid and securely pegged to carry the weight of the roof structure and to withstand its thrust which was outward as well as downward.[15] The simplest and most common roof was the gable, i.e., a roof with two slopes, one forward and one to the rear (fig. 3–4). The slope was determined by sloping pairs of timbers called *rafters*, which were attached to the plates. Each pair of rafters was kept together by a horizontal member called a *collar* or a *tie beam*. Adjacent pairs of rafters were attached to one another by horizontal *purlins*. Ridge poles were considered to be too heavy and were generally absent on early timber frame houses.[16]

The English colonists erected these timber frame houses according to ideas and traditions that had been handed down from one generation to another "of carpenters slow to change their ways, so that seventeenth century architecture in America is marked by medieval methods and medieval forms."[17]

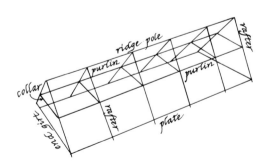

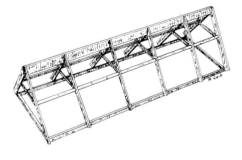

3–4 Typical framing for a gable roof

New England colonial house types

At least five distinct house types evolved in the New England cultural hearth (fig. 3–5). It is tempting to hypothesize a progressive development from simple one-room structures, to two-room houses, and, finally, to larger dwellings, and basically this must have been the original sequence of appearance of the types. But the investigator should recognize that earlier house types continued to be built long after later types first appeared. Both the one-room plan and the basic two-room plan discussed below were known in England and clearly were transported intact across the Atlantic.[18] Thus they were contemporaneous in New England, although they may have had an evolutionary connection in England at an earlier period. A clear chronology of house types is difficult to establish and defend for New England, especially since so many of the earliest structures have disappeared. Anthony Garvan estimates that only 1 percent of the seventeenth-century houses built in Connecticut have survived into the middle of the twentieth century.[19] Surely whatever statements are made concerning chronology of types must be tentative at best.

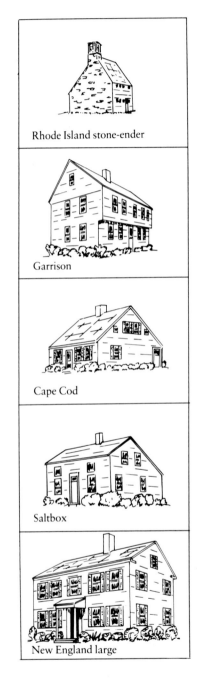

Rhode Island stone-ender

Garrison

Cape Cod

Saltbox

New England large

3–5 Early New England house types

The floor plan as a diagnostic element

Examination of floor plans generally reveals much more about relationships between house types than does the exterior appearance of those houses. Frequently, the exterior is significantly modified as fashions and styles change (see fig. 1–2). One recent and well-known example from the 1950s is the placement of picture windows in older houses designed for narrow windows.

The exterior of the house is subject to stylistic alteration because it is visible. The less often seen interior tends not to change as drastically. Furniture is replaced, decoration may follow the current mode, and light-weight partitions are shifted, but the position of the load-bearing walls usually does not vary. If more space is needed or desired, usually a room is added. Thus, the floor plan is apt to grow as time passes since, in the normal course of events, simple structures become more and more complex.[20] This additive principle permits one house to be related to another and allows classification and study of domestic structures to follow a rational method. Colonial New England offers an excellent opportunity to demonstrate how floor plans can reveal the close relationship between houses, even though the exteriors of these houses show no apparent similarity.[21]

The Rhode Island stone-ender house

The simplest permanent house type in colonial New England consisted of a single room. Its most distinctive version is called the Rhode Island stone-ender (fig. 3–6). In its most basic form, the Rhode Island stone-ender had one chamber affixed to a massive stone gable containing a fireplace and chimney (fig. 3–7). Very few of these early structures have survived, and those that have are mostly later modifications of the basic form.

What happened to the plans of the Rhode Island stone-enders illustrates the most commonly encountered changes in design of all houses, together with some quite unusual modifications. First, additions in the form of rear sheds provided more room. Second, extensions to the gable added further space and other rooms. Third, the position of

3–6 The Rhode Island stone-ender house (from Isham and Brown, *Early Rhode Island Houses*)

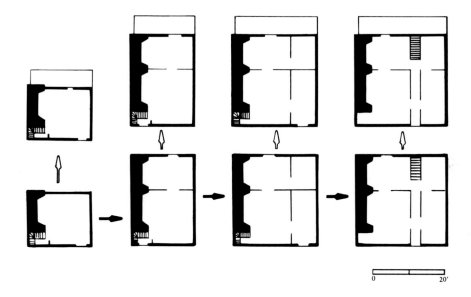

the door shifted. Initially, the door was off-center, located away from the chimney gable. In the first modification, the door location shifted to an entry vestibule adjacent to the chimney. Subsequently, the door moved toward its original position, away from the chimney gable. A final alteration was the addition of a second story.

Enlarging the chimney to accommodate side-by-side hearths, which was done in the Rhode Island stone-ender, was unusual. Much more common was the opening of additional hearths on the other sides of the chimney, a development that served to shift the chimney to a central position within the house. This line of evolutionary development became the major one for other New England colonial houses.

Single-room houses were built in parts of the New England hearth other than Rhode Island but, because of the scarcity of lime for mortar in other areas,

3–7 Conjectural evolution of Rhode Island stone-ender floor plans. Additions were made to both the gable and the side of the house.

the chimney was enclosed within the gable wall, and thus was a much less prominent feature of the house. The main part of the Paul Revere House in Boston (see fig. 3–10) is one well-known example.

21

The garrison house

A second house type in New England has been widely termed the *garrison house* (fig. 3–8), but this designation is misleading. Although not at all connected with military affairs or defense, the garrison house was given its name by early investigators who assumed the second-story overhang was a defensive feature similar to that found in forts and blockhouses. More careful examination reveals that there were no openings, which would have been necessary for defensive action, and that the overhang usually appears on only one or, at most, two sides of the structure.[22] In reality, the second-story overhang is a relict feature stemming from house design in medieval Europe. Its origin is probably twofold, one environmental and the other economic. In England a projecting second story afforded protection against wind-driven rain for the lower-story walls of half-timber houses. Protection was only needed on the exposed front of the house facing the street. The sides were sheltered by the eaves of the roof, and neighboring structures broke the force of the wind from those directions.

On expensive European town lots, the second-story overhang projecting out over streets and roadways maximized the floor area on each small space. Anthony Garvan suggests that the overhang was transferred from town to countryside in England as a status symbol, indicating the owner's contact with trend-setting London.[23] From the En-

3–8   The garrison house

glish countryside this building technique migrated across the Atlantic with early colonists and was incorporated in their new houses, although its original rationale was no longer present in spacious New England where buildings were weather boarded instead of half-timbered and land was cheap. Its persistence is another example of the inertia of house design, where features continue long after their rationales have disappeared.

The floor plan of a garrison house consists of two rooms of roughly equal size separated by a central chimney and a very small entry hallway (fig. 3–9). It is about twice the size of a Rhode Island stone-ender or of other early, single-room New England houses. Between the chimney and the entry is a narrow, turned stairway giving access to the unheated second floor, which is normally divided into two "chambers" or bed-

rooms. Each lower room was heated originally from a large hearth, incorporated into the central chimney stack. One room served as both kitchen and general activity area for the family. The other slightly smaller room doubled as the master bedroom and formal entertaining room. Not only did garrison houses offer more space, the rooms of the upper floor typically were drier and warmer than those of the ground floor.[24] Hence, two-floor dwellings steadily became more popular and numerous in New England.

Garrison houses were apparently quite common in the New England hearth, and there was an especially high concentration in the Connecticut River valley. One well-known structure, which is not a garrison house but which shows the external features of one, is the Paul Revere House in Boston (fig. 3–10).

3–9   Floor plan of a garrison house

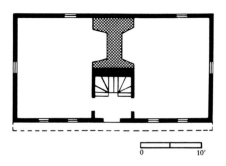

0   10'

3–10 The Paul Revere House, Boston, rear view. The kitchen ell is to the left, the main house to the right. (A. G. Noble, 1969)

The Cape Cod cottage

Among the early and most rudimentary of New England houses was the cottage that has come to be associated especially with the Cape Cod peninsula.[25] A derivation of common English rural dwellings, the Cape Cod cottage is simplicity itself (fig. 3–11). The plain gable roof, with minimum gable and eave overhang, rises at about a forty-five degree angle from a roughly square plan, creating a boxlike structure often divided internally into three rooms (fig. 3–12). The great massive central chimney accommodates three hearths; the slightly smaller side-facing hearths were designed for heating only, whereas the larger rear-facing hearth provides heat and a cooking place as well. The kitchen at the rear of the house is long and rather narrow. In other aspects the plan resembles that of the garrison house, as can be seen by comparing figure 3–9 with figure 3–12.

The Cape Cod cottage sits low in the landscape, which makes sense in an environment characterized by raw, windswept winters. The intimate connection of the cottage with its surroundings is emphasized by the low eaves, which are often only six or seven feet above ground level. In consequence, the steeply pitched gable roof, when viewed from the side (fig. 3–13), appears to be outsized.

In many respects the Cape Cod cottage resembles the garrison house. Each possesses a gable roof initially covered by wooden shingles, a central chimney

3–11 The Cape Cod cottage

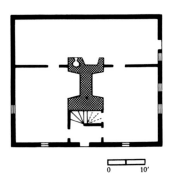

3–12 Floor plan of a Cape Cod cottage

large enough to accommodate multiple flues, a steep roof pitch with narrow eave and gable overhang, an asymmetrical facade, a timber frame pinned together by oak pegs in mortise-and-tenon joints, narrow clapboards overlaid on the frame, casement windows, and, most distinctively, a general lack of embellishment and decoration.

However, certain clear differences exist between the two types of houses. Most important are variations in floor plan and in elevation. The two or two-and-a-half-story garrison house is more rectangular than square, and this shape combined with its height gives it a tall narrow appearance. The Cape Cod cottage possesses a lower silhouette and is much more compact.

The saltbox house

Another house evolving in colonial New England was called the saltbox (fig. 3–14), a type derived in part from

3–13 The roof of a Cape Cod cottage is a prominent feature of the structure, Orleans, Massachusetts, 1935 (HABS)

the Cape Cod and in part from the garrison. Its designation results from the resemblance of the house to early small chests used for storing salt. During the eighteenth century as the frontier of settlement passed beyond New England, as Indian danger declined, and as the colonial New England economy expanded, many craftsmen and entrepreneurs prospered. A market was created for larger buildings to house their expanding families and, sometimes, their workplaces as well. The same process in the South produced a proliferation of outbuildings and "dependencies."

In the colder climate of New England the problem was solved by expanding the house's basic structure. A compromise between the full two-story garrison and the one-and-a-half-story Cape Cod resulted in a roof line more than one-and-a-half, but less than two full stories. This, plus a rear addition, gave these structures an asymmetrical gable roof, the most distinctive feature of this house.

In the earliest saltboxes, the rear shed lean-to was an afterthought, added subsequent to the construction of the main structure. These sheds can be detected easily by noticing a change in the slope of the longer side of the roof (fig. 3–15). Later, changes in the house framing allowed the shed to be incorporated as part of the house when originally built. Such changes removed the breaks in the roof slope, providing a roof of constant pitch.

The ground floor plan of the saltbox house closely resembles that of the Cape Cod cottage, with the further division of the shed addition creating two small unheated rooms on either side of the rear kitchen (fig. 3–16). Of these two new

24

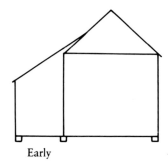
Early

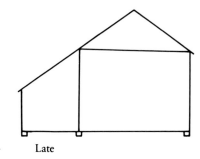
Late

3–15 Variations in the roof line of early and later saltbox houses

3–14 The saltbox house

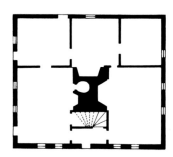

3–16 Floor plan of a saltbox house

rooms, one functioned as a pantry or storage room, while the one generally on the leeward, and hence warmer, side of the house served as a bedroom.

The second story is not truly a full story. Headroom is rather limited and because of the long rear-roof slope, often only two rooms are present in the upper level. These are similar in position and size to those of the ground floor. Second-story rooms were normally unheated, except by whatever warm air rose up the stairwell or through small heat openings in the floor. In many saltbox houses the second-story windows, because of the low headroom on that floor, are of considerably smaller size than those of the main floor.

Evolving in the middle of the eighteenth century, saltboxes have a generally wider distribution than either the garrison or Cape Cod type.[26] During the eighteenth century, saltbox houses gradually acquired balanced facades as Georgian ideas of classical symmetry began to gain acceptance. However, these stylistic changes were adopted only slowly, and not all saltboxes display such symmetrical facades.

The New England large house

The final house to emerge in the New England hearth during the colonial period was one called the New England large house (fig. 3–17). This house has also been called the central-chimney colonial house.[27]

In the view of Richard Pillsbury and Andrew Kardos, this house was "the initial New England response to Classical Revivalism," since all external elements are in apparent balance.[28] The enormous chimney remains centrally placed—in the exact middle, never slightly off center as was true of many earlier New England houses. The main door is always in the middle of the facade, and the window openings, all of

25

3–17 The New England large house

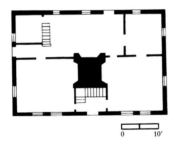

3–18 Floor plan of a New England large house

equal size, are evenly placed. The greater width and height of the house gives it a blocky, squarish form, yet it is still quite stately and majestic. Unlike the saltbox house, the roof form is symmetrical and the plan of the upper floor roughly duplicates that of the ground floor.

The floor plan of the New England large house illustrates quite clearly the antecedents of the house and its close connection to all the earlier New England house types (fig. 3–18). Compare figures 3–9, 3–12, 3–16, and 3–18. The greater size of the New England large house (ten rooms) allowed inclusion of a side entry hall and an additional stairway to the second floor. The larger size of the house and the greater number of rooms also favored some variations in the basic room arrangements, so that New England large houses have a greater range of plans

3–19 A New England large house in southern central New York state. Located in the village of Randolph. The porch and the eave treatment are of later style. (1976)

than do earlier colonial New England houses.

Colonial New England houses diffuse

Although the Cape Cod cottage has been revived in different sections of North America at various times, the New England colonial house types generally did not spread much beyond their area of origin. The major exception is the New England large house, which occurs throughout New England and along the settlement migration route across New York state (fig. 3–19). The type remained popular in several variations well into the nineteenth century as a house accommodating large families of middle and upper income. Eventually, the central-chimney New England houses were succeeded by Georgian structures containing paired chimneys, central hallways, and balanced facades. The evolution in the nineteenth century of those house types derived from New England origins and associated with New England migration is discussed in chapter 10.

26

The third of the colonial hearths is that which Dutch settlers established along the Hudson valley and in adjacent areas of Long Island and northern and central New Jersey (fig. 4–1).[1]

Utilizing the metes-and-bounds system of land division, the Dutch and other ethnic groups created a landscape more like that of New England than of the St. Lawrence valley, despite the attempt by the Dutch to create patroonships, which resembled the seigneuries of French Canada. Neither attempt was successful and both left only a minimal impress on the land.

Compared to the other cultural hearths of eastern North America, very little scholarly investigation has been done of the early settlement features of this area.[2] In this chapter, in addition to a discussion of the early colonial house types, attention will be paid to brick and stone as building materials, because of their importance in the Hudson valley hearth. The discussion of these materials is also relevant to structures beyond this particular area. Thus, for example, descriptions of brick bonding can be applied to all brick structures, not just to Dutch buildings.

The settlement process in the Hudson valley hearth

Settlement by the Dutch in the Hudson valley area began about the same time as that by the English in Massachusetts. Although a fort was built as early as 1614, the first permanent settlements in New Netherlands, as the Dutch colony was called, date only from 1623.[3] Not until after 1638 did settlers in any considerable numbers begin to arrive.

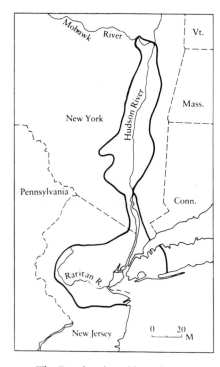

4–1 The Dutch colonial hearth

Although New Netherlands was officially a Dutch colony until 1664, the actual settlers were a mixture of Europeans, attracted by the Dutch reputation for protection of religious minorities. Because Protestants felt especially secure here, New Netherlands became a haven for Flemings, French Huguenots, Britons, Germans, and others. Even after the British seized control of the colony in 1664, the Dutch and others continued to migrate here from Europe. As a consequence, the early houses of the so-called Dutch areas are a complementary mixture of folk architectural contributions drawn from several ethnic sources.

4   Dutch Colonial Houses in the Hudson Valley Hearth

Throughout the period of Dutch rule, the number of settlers remained small, fewer than ten thousand, whereas the New England colonial population in the same period was at least five times greater.[4] Such slow growth in New Netherlands resulted primarily from the restrictions placed upon individual settlers to engage in commercial activities, and the government's attempt to direct agricultural settlement into a framework of feudal patroonships. Although most settlers upon arrival in the colony promptly ignored the governmental restrictions, those policies did discourage many potential immigrants from embarking. With too few colonists to effectively counter the British challenge, the Dutch colony succumbed and Dutch settlement officially ceased, with the result that "Dutch style" houses rarely occur beyond the original hearth area. Even within the area, the pressure of population has become so great that the colonial houses are all but lost in the sea of later dwellings. Every decade sees a few less of these structures that represent the original colonial landscape.

Early colonial Dutch houses

Out of necessity, the earliest colonists in New Netherlands (and in early Dutch settlements along the Delaware River), constructed partly excavated, crude shelters of light poles covered with mud daub, thatch, and bark.[5] Such structures, which could be constructed quickly, were intended only as tempo-

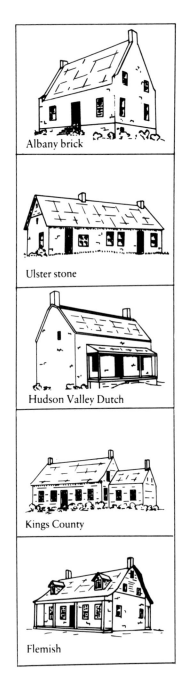

Albany brick

Ulster stone

Hudson Valley Dutch

Kings County

Flemish

4-2 Hudson valley hearth house types

rary residences and were abandoned in favor of timber frame houses, or those of brick and stone, as soon as it was convenient. Simple one-room cottages probably were the earliest fully elaborated houses, but virtually none of these has survived as such. The best extant example of such a dwelling is the seventeenth-century Pieter Bronck House in Greene County, New York. Early one-room houses often were incorporated in later structures in such a way as to lose their original identity.

The one-room cottage soon gave way to more clearly differentiated and more elaborate structures. Except on Long Island, timber frame houses apparently were not as common as those of brick or stone, which gradually became the standard dwellings of the region.[6] Study of existing Dutch houses and of those recorded before they disappeared suggests that five distinct Dutch house types evolved during the later colonial period (fig. 4-2).

The Dutch houses of New York and New Jersey were unique in that they did not have closely associated structures in the metropolitan country, as did houses in all the other colonial hearths. Thomas Wertenbaker has suggested that this may be a result of the physical separation of house and barn that occurred when settlement was transferred across the Atlantic.[7] In the Netherlands, houses tended to be engulfed by large animal barns, incorporated to a greater degree than elsewhere in western Europe.

In the colony of New Netherlands, land pressures were not so great and the disadvantages of a combined structure outweighed the pressures for retaining it. Among the most important reasons

28

for separating barn and house were the reduction of fire loss and the improvement of the quality of life, especially if the barn had to be upwind. Standards of cleanliness and sanitation were dramatically improved at a single stroke.

As the Dutch groped for a housing type, not unnaturally some settlers constructed structures resembling the detached urban houses of the Netherlands. These houses were especially suitable for the towns and appeared early in New Amsterdam and the smaller urban centers. The gable faced the street to conserve street frontage, with the main entrance on the gable, leading directly into one of the two ground-floor rooms (fig. 4–3).[8]

In the countryside, however, the front entrance normally was on the side of the house. In the earliest period, the structure consisted of just two rooms (fig. 4–4), but quite soon a center hallway evolved. Much later, other smaller rooms were added to the two main rooms. A steep enclosed stairway in the hallway gave access to the unpartitioned second floor, which served as a

4–3 The Abraham Yates House, an urban version of the Albany brick cottage. Located in the Stockade district, Schenectady, New York. (April 1979)

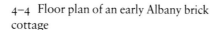

4–4 Floor plan of an early Albany brick cottage

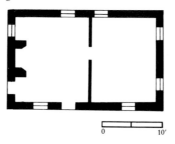

4–5 The Albany brick cottage

grain storage area.[9] The second floor was later partitioned with walls that did not reach entirely to the ceiling to enclose two, three, or four bedrooms. The average outside dimensions of the earlier houses were about eighteen by twelve feet.

Having come from the delta of the Rhine River, where clay deposits were widespread, the Dutch settlers were experienced in techniques of brick making and brick construction. In fact, the only really abundant building materials in Holland were bricks.[10] Thus, brick is the commonest building material of these cottages. Because this type of house (fig. 4–5) appears to have been concentrated in the Albany region of the Hudson valley, it may be termed the *Albany brick cottage*.

Brick as a building material

Brick kilns were operating in New Amsterdam as early as 1628, and near Albany by 1630.[11] Brick had certain advantages over timber as a building material in the colonial period. Bricks were not significantly more expensive than hewn-timber framing and much cheaper than sawn timber. Although considerable skill was necessary to construct buildings in brick, the material was easier for a single craftsman to handle than were heavy timbers. Brick houses were fire resistant and, when well built, a brick house would outlast a wooden one. A certain stigma also may have been attached to wooden dwellings among the Dutch settlers, who often replaced earlier light timber structures with more substantial buildings of brick or stone.

The most common problem facing the craftsman erecting a brick structure is to arrange the individual bricks so that they interlock to add strength to the structure. This is called *bonding* and there are several distinct, but related, methods of brick bonding (fig. 4–6). The different patterns are created by laying the bricks in mortar in distinct layers called *courses* and by exposing the sides of the bricks, in which case they are called *stretchers*, or the ends, in which case they are called *headers*.

The simplest bonding pattern is called *American* or *common bond*. In its most elemental form it consists of courses of stretchers with the bricks of each succeeding course centered over the joints

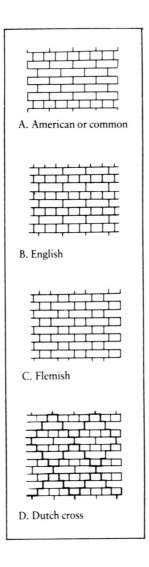

A. American or common

B. English

C. Flemish

D. Dutch cross

4–6 Examples of brick bonding

of the next lower course. Normally, every sixth course consists of headers (fig. 4–6a). Common bond was never as popular in colonial buildings as certain other types, but it did gain acceptance in the eighteenth and nineteenth centuries. Common bond is the strongest of all bonds and is the cheapest and quickest to lay.[12]

English bond consists of alternating courses of headers and stretchers (fig. 4–6b), centered over each other. Walls built in English bond present a distinctive horizontally bonded effect, because of the much larger number of joints in the header courses and also because the end of a brick is frequently slightly different in color from the side. Despite its name, English bond was widely used in Holland. It produces a very strong wall, but the brick must be of such proportions that two headers and their joint is equal to the length of one stretcher. If not, bricks must be cut, which is time-consuming and costly.

A third major type of brick bonding is that referred to as *Flemish bond*, which consists of headers and stretchers alternating in each course. The headers are centered over the stretchers of previous courses (fig. 4–6c). Because Flemish bond has no decided diagonal lines when viewed from a distance as is true with other bonds, not much attention needs to be paid to vertical alignment of bricks. Furthermore, leveling is easier because headers and stretchers alternate. Hence, it is cheaper and easier to lay Flemish than English bond.

The most attractive and sophisticated of the various bonds is one that may be called *Dutch cross bond*. A variant of the English bond, it was perfected in the Low Countries and brought at an early

30

date to New Netherlands. It is basically similar to English bond, with alternating courses of headers and stretchers, except that successive stretcher courses are centered over the joints of earlier stretcher courses. By slightly widening certain joints, or by careful selection of brick colors, the natural diagonal lines of the wall are emphasized, producing attractive diamond patterns (fig. 4–6d). Dutch cross bond is, of course, the most difficult to lay and the most expensive of all the brick bonds.

All these brick bonds were used throughout the colonial areas of eastern United States, wherever suitable clay deposits were found. Particularly effective is the elaborate brick bonding used in houses built in Salem County, New Jersey.[13] The brick work of these structures is much more decorative than that of the Albany brick cottages, whose walls are most frequently laid in English bond.

4–7 An Albany brick cottage built in stone. Note the steep roof pitch, the lack of eave overhang, and the continental-type dormer. (Hurley, New York, March 1979)

The Albany brick cottage

The most distinctive feature of the Albany brick cottage is the gable roof with its very steep pitch and limited eave overhang (fig. 4–7). Some have low parapets with distinctive "knees" at the eave line (cf. fig. 4–5). The pitch of the roof is so steep that although these cottages are technically one-and-a-half stories in height, the upper story is only slightly restricted in area, and a garret or loft is common above the second floor (see fig. 4–3). In order to add light, ventilation, and some additional headroom, dormers frequently were added. The style of dormer most typically employed in the Dutch settlement area is called *continental*, and is characterized by a single slope roof with a pitch in the same direction but lower than the main roof (figs. 4–7 and 4–8). Because of this characteristic roof, the dormer is also known as a *shed-roof dormer*.

Among other distinguishing characteristics of the Albany brick cottage are casement windows, often set in low rounded arches, port-hole ventilators under the ridge, and decorative iron beam anchors in the shape of trefoils or fleur-de-lis. Not all Albany brick cottages were built of brick (figs. 4–7 and 4–8), although that material was most commonly used.

4–8 An Albany brick cottage built in wood. The later porch unfortunately masks a fine structure. This house is now used as the public library in Scotia, New York. (March 1979)

Stone as a building material

A rather different house type is the Ulster stone house (fig. 4–9), so called because of its concentration along the Esopus Creek and other tributaries of the Hudson in Ulster County, although it occurs in lesser concentrations throughout the area of Dutch settlement. In form, this house bears a strong resemblance to many farmhouses found in Belgium and northern France.[14]

Stone is the normal building material for these structures, although typically the triangular portions of the gable end are of timber frame covered by rows of wooden shingles or horizontal clapboards. The abundant Devonian limestones of Ulster County yielded not only an attractive and easily workable building stone, but a source of lime mortar as well. Furthermore, a locally available, dark-colored sandstone called *bluestone* was also employed in building.[15]

Stone has certain advantages and some disadvantages as a building material. Among its advantages are its durability and resistance to weathering and decay; its strength and resistance to wind and snow; its insulating qualities which make stone structures cool in summer and, when heated, heat retentive in winter; and, finally, its significant resistance to fire, the greatest danger faced by wooden structures.

The chief disadvantages of stone are the considerable skills needed to quarry and cut building stones and, especially, to properly lay and cement the cut stone in courses; the great weight that makes handling all but very small building stones difficult; and the great cost involved in transporting building stone any great distance from their point of origin. As a result of this latter condition, domestic stone structures normally are a good index to local geology. Another reason building stone is not transported very far is that the longer that quarried stone is exposed to the atmosphere, the harder it becomes and the more difficult it is to work.[16]

Several terms are used to describe building stones. *Cut* or *finished stone* (fig. 4–10a) consists of blocks that are accurately and uniformly sized and surface tooled. These stones are usually laid in mortar in regular courses in an interlocking fashion, much as bricks are laid. Ashlar (fig. 4–10b) refers to small, rectangular blocks of varying sizes, which have sawed, planed, or rock-split surfaces. The different-sized blocks are intermixed in building a wall. *Field stone* or *rough stone* (fig. 4–10c) is the term applied to irregularly shaped and sized natural boulders, which are laid up with mortar in an irregular fashion to form a wall. Normally, the corners of such walls are formed of cut stone

4–9 The Ulster stone house

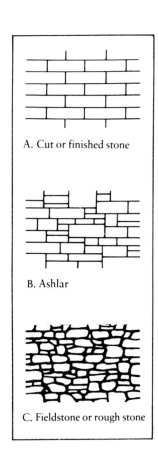

4–10 Examples of various building stone techniques

A. Cut or finished stone

B. Ashlar

C. Fieldstone or rough stone

blocks, called *quoins*, placed in an interlocking fashion to give maximum strength to the wall corners where stress is greatest (fig. 4–11). Cobblestone is a naturally formed, rounded stone, large enough for use in rough paving and walls. Most cobblestones are of glacial origin, which defines more or less the areas of their use. Rubble or rip-rap are small, irregular rock fragments thrown into a binding mortar, without order, to form a foundation.

Several types of rock are widely used for building. Perhaps the most common are sandstone and limestone, with granite, marble, and gneiss used mostly in public or monumental building. Trap rock, which consists of basalt, diabase, gabbro, or diorite, also is used in local areas.

4–11 Example of a quoined corner. The wall is laid in rough stone courses and the quoins are cut blocks of limestone. Muller House, Milbach, Pennsylvania (erected 1752). Photo taken 1976.

Slate, which has unusual properties, came to be widely used for roofing in the late eighteenth, nineteenth, and early twentieth centuries. A pronounced cleavage, together with a "grain" at more or less right angles, permits slate to be broken into blocks and then split into thin smooth sheets ideal for use as roofing material because of its fire resistance and durability. Normally, roofing slates are between four and six inches wide and ten to twenty-four inches long, with thicknesses varying between 3/16 and 1/4 inch. The standard measure used for roofing slates is the *square*, i.e., enough slate to cover one hundred square feet of sloping roof surface with a three-inch head lap.[17]

Certain factors combined in the twentieth century to reduce substantially the use of slate for roofs. First, the quarrying of slate became increasingly more expensive. The deposits that were the easiest and, therefore, the cheapest to mine, were exhausted. The slate with the best cleavage characteristics was used up and the remaining slate was more difficult to split evenly. Second, the slate roof, although quite effective, had to be constructed very carefully, especially to ensure that the slates were not cracked by too tight nailing. Third, the slate roof was heavy and required a strong frame for support. The average weight of a square of roofing slate is about 650 pounds. As the fashions in roof styles dictated lower and lower pitches in the nineteenth century, slate roofs required ever stronger frames, es-

pecially in northern areas where snow accumulation in winter was a factor to be considered. Fourth, the cost of shipment of slate remained high. As a consequence, few buildings west of the Mississippi or in the southeastern United States, locations far from the slate deposits that stretch from Virginia to Maine, were covered with slate roofs.[18] Finally, alternative roofing materials, especially composition shingles, which were cheaper and almost as suitable, came into widespread use.

Because of the abundance and cheapness of wood and its ease of handling, it was used more widely than stone, both as a roofing material and for building construction. Nevertheless, early stone structures are scattered over the entire area of eastern North America. Nowhere is their concentration greater than in Ulster County, New York, where a surprising uniformity of early stone domestic architecture prevails,[19] producing the typical Ulster stone house.

The Ulster stone house

Roof pitch of these one-and-a-half-story houses is moderate and may be broken, especially in later examples, by continental dormers to provide better light and more headroom in loft bedrooms. The ground floor plan, frequently measuring ten to twelve feet by thirty to thirty-six feet, consists of three rooms (fig. 4–12). In many instances the elongated form results from the original construction of a small single-room dwelling and the subsequent addition of two more rooms in line, either at one time or in two stages. As a consequence of this evolutionary pattern, there may be two or even three doors on the same side of the building (fig. 4–13). Furthermore, there will be two (one at or near the gable and one interior) or three (two at or near the gable and one interior) chimneys. This chimney arrangement is one of the more distinctive features of this house type.

The Ulster stone houses may have appeared somewhat later than the Albany brick cottages, but both styles reached their peaks early in the eighteenth century. Establishing an evolutionary sequence for folk house types is particularly difficult for several reasons. First, not all, and perhaps not even a majority of, the houses fit the types that are designated. Many are eclectic, and some follow no established pattern at all. Second, not all the houses of a particular type are built at the same time. This would be less of a problem if houses dis-appeared at an even rate. Unfortunately, house destruction follows no rules and one cannot be certain that surviving houses accurately reflect the original balance of types. Finally, even though communication was restricted in the colonial period, diffusion of architectural ideas did take place and hence a common though early feature of one location might be introduced at a much later date elsewhere. Thus it is probably wise not to put too much faith in the certainty of architectural evolution. Still, it remains a useful organizing concept of research.

With this caveat in mind, we can examine what appear to be the later Dutch house types. Beginning at the end of the eighteenth, and continuing well into the nineteenth century, the Hudson Valley Dutch house appeared (fig. 4–14).

4–12 Floor plan of an Ulster stone house

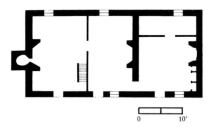

0   10'

4–13 A fine Ulster stone house in Hurley, New York, a town noted for such structures (March 1979)

The Hudson Valley Dutch house

The gambrel roof, hallmark of the Hudson Valley Dutch house, became popular in the New World about the middle of the eighteenth century. It was introduced in New England and the Middle Atlantic colonies by English settlers. The Dutch and other groups in New York and New Jersey also adopted the gambrel roof, but its basic form differed in both shape and slope. In the Hudson Valley Dutch house, more often than not, the shorter upper slope lies at an angle of thirty-five degrees and the longer lower slope inclines almost seventy-five degrees from the horizontal. Acceptance of the gambrel roof permitted erection of much wider dwellings. Breaking the slope of the roof also permitted the use of shorter rafters. Whereas the earliest Hudson Valley Dutch houses perpetuated the initial plan of a center hallway with one room on either side, later dwellings typically have two large but unequally sized rooms on each side of the hallway (fig. 4–15).

The gambrel roof also allows for much greater headroom on the second floor, or on the third floor if the house extends to two-and-a-half stories. Prior to the third quarter of the eighteenth century, virtually no houses higher than one-and-a-half stories had been built.[20] Although some houses have only a single chimney, the presence of two is much more likely. Chimneys built into the great brick or stone gable walls, together with the greater depth of the house and the gambrel roof, help give these structures a massive overall appearance, which nonetheless is still a pleasing one (fig. 4–16).

Often associated with these and other Dutch-derived houses is the stoop, a raised, uncovered entrance platform with two benches extending outward on either side of the door (fig. 4–17).

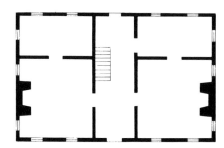

4–14 The Hudson Valley Dutch house

4–15 Floor plan of a Hudson Valley Dutch house

4–16 A rather large Hudson Valley Dutch house, now unoccupied and boarded up. The porch is a later addition. (Delmar, New York, March 1979)

4–17 A restored stoop with its characteristic wooden benches, Batsto Village, New Jersey (April 1979)

**The Kings County cottage
and the Flemish cottage**

The two final house types commonly encountered in the Dutch areas of New York and New Jersey appear to be closely related. Both are usually derived from an early single- or double-room cottage of small size, which ultimately became a kitchen wing for a much larger house. Despite the fact that one has a gable roof and the other a gambrel, both houses possess prominent bell-cast eave overhangs, although the roofs rarely extend sideward beyond the gable. Both houses are usually one-and-a-half stories high, often with a garret above the partial second story. The interior plan of the houses varies but is, more often than not, one that consists of two large front rooms and two smaller rear rooms, each set divided by a central hallway containing the stairway to the second floor (fig. 4–18). Some houses, which appear to be the earlier ones, do not possess the center hallway, but have two doors, each entering a main room. Doors are the so-called Dutch doors, i.e., divided across the center so that the upper and lower halves can open independently. Finally, late in the eighteenth century or early in the nineteenth century, a second small wing was sometimes added on the opposite side of the house to provide a symmetrical balance to the original kitchen wing.

Despite these common characteristics, certain features of the two house types were quite distinctive. The gable-roofed house appears to have been built at an earlier time, perhaps even as early as the very late seventeenth century. Because it was the predominant Dutch house in eastern Long Island, it may be termed the *Kings County cottage* (fig. 4–19). Usually, the structure is timber framed and sided with wide, white pine clapboards or, less often, with shingles. A number of these houses are elevated above full basements. The overall appearance of the main portion of the Kings County cottage reminds us of the Quebec cottage found in the St. Lawrence valley. Such resemblance may not be surprising when one considers the large proportion of French Huguenots who settled in the New Netherlands colony.

4–18 The evolution of floor plans of later Dutch colonial houses

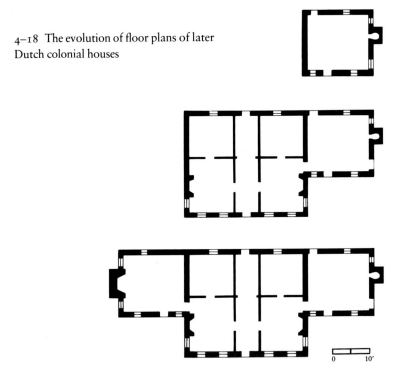

4–19 The Kings County cottage

4–20 The Flemish cottage

The gambrel-roofed house has been given the name of the *Flemish cottage*,[21] although its derivation from Flanders has been challenged.[22] The Flemish cottage (fig. 4–20) is concentrated throughout northern New Jersey[23] and in the Dutchess County portion of the Hudson valley.[24] Its distinguishing characteristic is its graceful gambrel roof, whose unusual configuration serves to unite an otherwise tall structure with the surrounding landscape. The form of the gambrel roof is quite different from that of the Hudson Valley Dutch house roof. The upper-roof slope is quite short and somewhat less steeply pitched, while the lower slope is much longer and inclined at about a forty-five degree angle. The exaggerated bell-cast of the eaves accentuates the sweep of the roof, producing a silhouette quite unlike that of any other North American house.

Some Flemish cottages are built of timber frame with shingle or clapboard covering, but most extant examples utilize a reddish Triassic sandstone, which splits easily and yet hardens upon exposure to the air.[25] Typically, this building

stone is used for the first-floor elevation and the upper gables are faced by shingles or clapboards.

The interior of the Flemish cottage shows a variety of plans, although many are identical to those used in Kings County houses. The exterior form and the diversity of plan strongly suggest that the Flemish cottage is the latest of the colonial Dutch house types, made popular during the late eighteenth century.

Variations in plans of Dutch house types

Up to this point, for the purposes of simplicity and clarity, the assumption underlying the discussion of house types has been that each type possesses just one basic floor plan. Such an assumption is not strictly correct, although each house type normally has a particular plan that predominates.

The process of house typing involves a certain amount of intuitive guesswork. In order to confirm the validity of the types, an investigation of the individual architectural components of the houses must be performed. One of the most significant diagnostic characteristics to be considered in the process is the floor plan.[26]

Information on floor plans is available for only 114 colonial Dutch houses that fall within the five types discussed in this chapter.[27] Fifteen percent of the houses consisted of just two rooms, an arrangement that may be taken as the earliest of the floor plans (fig. 4–21). The two-room plan occurs in Albany brick cottages, Kings County houses, and Ulster stone houses. Although only four of these houses were Albany brick cottages, this figure represents 40 percent of the houses of that type, suggesting it to be the oldest of the five Dutch house types.

One line of development from the original two-room plan produced houses with rooms in a row, but with no hallways. The absence of a hallway suggests these houses also to be early in design evolution. All such houses fall within the Ulster stone house type. Another Ulster variant has a floor plan of three rooms in a row, with a hallway separating two of the rooms. Houses with a laterally expanded floor plan comprise over half of all the Ulster stone houses, but less than a fifth of all Dutch houses surveyed.

Still another fairly early modification of the original two-room plan was the evolution of a four-room plan, accomplished by making the house deeper and thus adding two small rooms behind the original rooms. Although this plan occurs in only 8 percent of the houses surveyed, it shows up persistently in houses built in the Hudson valley at much later dates. It is perhaps the most distinctive arrangement found in colonial Dutch houses.

One final series of floor-plan modifications is the result of the introduction of central hallways. All house types pos-

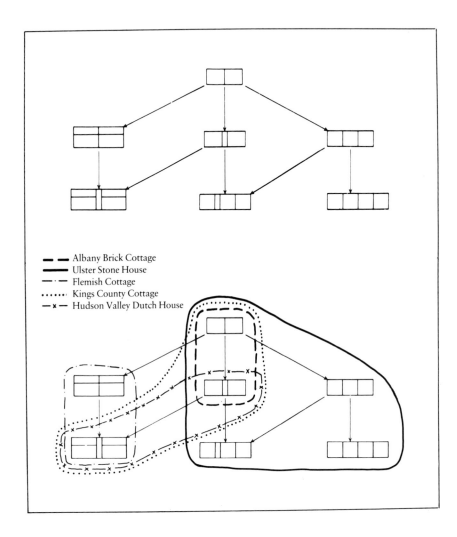

4–21 Upper diagram shows conjectural evolution of colonial Dutch floor plans. Lower diagram indicates relationship of house types to the various floor plans.

sess some houses with these room arrangements. Indeed, virtually all the Hudson Valley Dutch houses, i.e., 90 percent, have central hallways. The percentage of houses with central hallways reflected in the totals of Flemish cottages and Kings County houses is very similar, 61.1 percent and 60 percent respectively. A few Ulster stone houses also fall within this categorization. Adding three-room, interior-hallway houses brings the total up to a third of all Ulster stone houses.

If houses without central or interior hallways are considered to come early in the evolutionary sequence of colonial Dutch houses, then the Albany brick cottage and the Ulster stone house appear to be early house types. The elongation of the floor plan further identifies the Ulster stone house.

The predominance of central hallways is the distinguishing mark of both the Hudson Valley Dutch houses and the Flemish cottage. Floor plan is less a distinguishing characteristic for the Flemish cottage than for some other house types, however.

The Kings County house demonstrates the complete range of floor plans, from simple two-room arrangements to later, more complicated ones. Some of these houses have wings, which represent the earliest unit of the house to be built. These early structures normally contain just two rooms. Later Kings County houses were built in the same style, but on a larger scale. It is possible that research on Dutch floor plans may have combined some early houses to which later wings were not added, with later houses from which wings were excluded. Obviously some further study is warranted.

Dutch houses in summary

Considered together, the five Dutch house types are an interesting and harmonious architectural ensemble. They show an evolution from simple to complex and the adaptation local builders made to the availability of different building materials. The blending of diverse architectural traditions has been accomplished with little difficulty. Perhaps it is a small wonder, as Alan Gowans notes, that the "Dutch colonial revival" became the most popular of the early twentieth-century house styles.[28]

39

The various colonial settlement landscapes discussed to this point have been essentially the product of a single early immigrant group. To be sure, several groups participated in structuring the colonial Dutch landscape of New York and New Jersey, but the principal elements were clearly from the Low Countries, as is shown by the fact that these features are not duplicated elsewhere in North America, in areas largely settled by English, German, or Scotch-Irish peoples. The Delaware valley cultural hearth was settled later than the three hearths previously discussed. Furthermore, the settlement patterns and the domestic architecture associated with those patterns were the product of a combination of ethnic groups.

5 Colonial Houses in the Delaware Valley Hearth

Multiethnic settlement in the Delaware valley hearth

Early in the seventeenth century, both the Swedes and the Dutch attempted to establish settlement colonies on the Delaware. Neither was successful, although Swedish influences persisted, exerting some effect upon later settlement forms. The Swedish and Dutch settlers contributed certain elements to the domestic colonial architecture, although their numbers were so small and their impact so ephemeral that most of the elements were decorative rather than definitive.

Not until 1682, when English Quaker settlers began to arrive in numbers, did this cultural hearth assume its ultimate character. Most English settlement was directly related to the colonizing efforts of William Penn. Most settlers were Quakers and they introduced an em-

phasis on trade and commerce that continues in this area to the present day.

The English settlers tended to gravitate toward the cities and port areas along the rivers, re-creating in the process small red-brick replicas of the Georgian cities of the England they had left. Because effective settlement was late, the domestic architecture of Philadelphia and other Quaker towns of the Delaware valley reflected the building style of London, which was largely rebuilt after the Great Fire of 1666. The Quaker leaders and many of the settlers were accustomed to the new building styles of Christopher Wren and other London architects.[1]

A contribution to domestic architecture certainly as significant as that of the English Quakers was made by the large numbers of Germans who were drawn to Pennsylvania by the promise of religious freedom in Penn's colony. German settlers began to arrive in the Delaware valley almost as early as Quakers, but in much smaller numbers. Mass German migration did not begin until early in the second quarter of the seventeenth century, but it then continued up to the Revolution and resumed after the conflict.[2] The German settlers headed for the countryside, and in so doing left their cultural stamp indelibly on the landscape. The Lancaster limestone plain, sixty miles west of Philadelphia, became an important nucleus of German settlement. In contrast to that of the Quakers, early German architecture was essentially medieval in style. Furthermore, Germans moved beyond the Quaker areas to settlements where their own cultural heritage was carefully preserved.

The Scotch-Irish followed virtually on

the heels of the Germans. The last major ethnic group to enter the cultural hearth of the Delaware valley during the colonial period, the Scotch-Irish arrived in large numbers throughout the middle half of the eighteenth century.[3] Used to hardship, ready for struggle, and relegated to the poorer agricultural lands and the dangerous frontier because the Germans had already occupied the most fertile soils, the Scotch-Irish became the pioneers and frontiersmen and women of American history. It fell to them to spread European civilization ever westward across the North American continent. In the process they carried not only their own cultural elements, but also those acquired by contact with other ethnic groups.

Together these diverse groups produced a mix of distinctive house types in the Delaware valley cultural hearth (fig. 5–1), incorporating cultural elements from each ethnic source. Some of these house types subsequently diffused throughout much of eastern United States. It was here that the log cabin, which stands prominently in American folklore as a symbol of pioneer life, evolved.

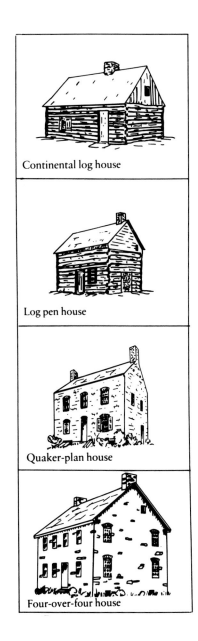

Continental log house

Log pen house

Quaker-plan house

Four-over-four house

5–1 Delaware valley house types

The continental log house

The technique of building in log materials was introduced into North America by the Swedes, but no authentic and unaltered Swedish log structures have survived, and Swedish techniques were not adopted by subsequent groups. It remained for the Germans, who also had a tradition of log building, to establish log construction firmly in the New World.

The log house that German settlers introduced was, in reality, a copy of the stone and half-timber cottages of the Rhineland and elsewhere in Germany, but here they were built of different materials. In Pennsylvania and the rest of the New World the medium of construction reflected the local resources, stone in areas underlain by limestone, sandstone, or other similar rocks (fig. 5–2), brick in regions of clay and shale (fig. 5–3), and logs virtually everywhere (indicative of the low cost and availability of rough forest materials). Because of this, log construction was often employed in the earliest period, even in those areas where other building materials were present. Hence, log construction in Pennsylvania and elsewhere in North America represents an initial construction period.[4]

German log houses, or *continental log houses* (fig. 5–4) as they are often termed, have several distinguishing traits. The central chimney is one of the most significant, although the location of this feature rarely is in the exact center of the structure.[5] It is more likely to be off center, marking the dividing wall between the kitchen (*kuche*), and the other two rooms, the "great room" (*stube*), which functioned as a combination living, entertaining, and family room, and the smaller downstairs bedroom (*kammer*) (fig. 5–5).[6] The kitchen extends entirely across one end of the house, which is almost square in plan, almost as deep as it is wide. Typically, there are two doors, front and back, both opening into the kitchen, thereby providing desirable cross ventilation. In this arrangement, the kitchen also functions as a hall passageway, giving rise to the German name of the house, *Flür-kuchenhaus* (corridor-kitchen house).[7] In some continental houses, the kitchen is partitioned to create a small fourth room, which normally functions as a pantry. Such houses have been termed *Kreuzhauser* (cross houses), but they should not be confused with English-derived cross houses (see chap. 6). The four-room continental house, which can be traced from southeastern Pennsylvania to the Shenandoah valley, seems to have a more nearly square floor plan than the three-room version.[8]

A number of continental log houses were two or two-and-a-half stories. The second floors of many early houses were hardly more than lofts reached by ladders or a steep ladderlike stairway.[9] In many instances these lofts were used for grain storage, although this practice began to die out just prior to the Revolutionary War, as larger barns with built-in granary bins or separately standing

5–2 The Hans Herr House, Lancaster County, Pennsylvania. This structure, built in 1719, is a stone version of the continental log house. Note the steep roof pitch, massive interior chimney, off-center door, rough quoined corners. (October 1976)

5–3 A brick half-timber version of the continental log house. Several similar houses have been restored in the Old Salem section of Winston-Salem, North Carolina. (August 1978)

granaries came into widespread use.[10]

The steeply sloping roof has a slight bell-cast or "kick" to assist in shedding water, but this feature was never as pronounced as in the St. Lawrence valley houses (see chap. 2). The thickening of the roof at the eave line is well shown in figure 5–6. Roof covering was originally of overlapping wooden shingles, each about twenty-four to forty inches long and four to eight inches wide. Usually made of red oak because of its uniform grain and resistance to rot, the shingles are tapered or beveled in two directions. "The thin tapered shingle produces a continuous air channel running vertically under each row across the entire roof, thus giving excellent air and water drainage and long shingle life."[11]

The floor joists of the continental log house often rested directly upon a stone foundation rather than on sills. A cellar for food storage was typical[12] and access to it was normally from outside the building.

5–4 The continental log house

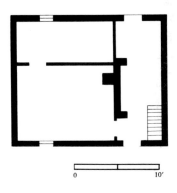

5–5 Floor plan of a continental log house

5–6 Detail of a wooden gutter and downspout. The building is a restored half-timbered, stucco-covered brick house in Old Salem, North Carolina. (August 1978)

Swiss bank houses

Robert Bucher has identified a group of gable-entry dwellings in Pennsylvania, which he calls *Swiss bank houses*, having floor plans similar or identical to those of continental log houses.[13] Edward Chappell notes similar structures in the Shenandoah valley of Virginia.[14] In Swiss bank houses the ridge line is reoriented by ninety degrees, so that the main door is on the gable. All these houses are built into hill slopes to provide direct access to a lower floor into which the kitchen and other work areas are shifted.

Rather similar to these houses is a second type of banked dwelling which Bucher believes is derived from the Swiss Weinbauern houses. The form and the plan are quite different from continental log houses. The structures are rectangular and have four rooms on the upper floor and gable chimneys. Entrance to the lower floor is by way of a large rounded-arch doorway placed at the lower edge of the bank (fig. 5–7).

A large cooking fireplace is located in the cellar at that end of the house which is outside the bank. In the rear is the large arched wine cellar for the cooling and storage of wine and dairy products. A spring located above the house provides cooling water as the water flows through one side of the cellar in a channel built wide and deep enough to hold cans of milk and other food containers. There is no interior stairway from the lower to the upper level. A stone stairway was built outside the house which led to the door which gives ingress to the upper level. Just inside

5–7 The Swiss bank house

the upper level door is another, but smaller, gable fireplace located opposite the kitchen fireplace in the lower level cellar.[15]

Complicating matters further is the existence of still a third variant of the Swiss bank house.[16] Basically it has a rectangular plan, gable chimneys, a three-and-a-half-story elevation, and a prominent elevated porch at the second-story level occupying one entire side of the building. Furthermore, it does not possess either a cellar fireplace for cooking or an arched storage cellar. Clearly the Swiss bank houses need additional study, if only to more carefully differentiate the types.

The log pen house

British and especially Scotch-Irish settlers, forced to erect a weather-tight permanent dwelling in a single season, turned away from the stone, earth, and timber frame materials of their native areas to the log construction that the Germans had utilized so successfully.[17] Although these groups abandoned traditional building materials and construction techniques, they did not turn away from established form. Thus, the log pen house retained the relative dimensions and the chimney position of cottages from the British Isles (fig. 5–8). Although actual size varied considerably, a ratio of 1:1½ or 1:2 for the relationship between gable walls and side walls usually was maintained in the log houses built by the Scotch-Irish (fig. 5–9). Thus the log pen house was considerably narrower than the continental log house of German settlers. The gable chimney also contributed to the appearance of narrowness. The other major difference between the two log houses is in their internal plans; the log pen house

5–8 The log pen house

5–9 A Canadian log pen house. This structure is in the Black Creek Pioneer Village restoration in Toronto. Windows are of later style. (August 1976)

5–10 Floor plan of a log pen house

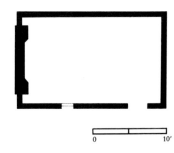

consists of one or two square or rectangular rooms with a loft of the same floor area above (fig. 5–10).

Because the Scotch-Irish were numerically superior on the westward-moving frontier, this type of log structure became the most common one and hence has become popularly associated with American pioneering settlement.[18] No other early house type is so widely distributed in eastern North America, although the number of surviving houses is fairly small (figs. 5–9 and 5–11). In many instances, original log construction has been masked by later clapboard siding, new rooms have been added, and roof lines have been altered, making these structures sometimes difficult to recognize. Later modification and evolution of the log pen house are discussed in chapter 10.

5–11 A log pen house in Mifflin, Ohio. The gable has been covered by clapboards and the roof by sheet metal. A porch has been added. (April 1977)

The Quaker-plan house

As the log pen house came to predominate on the westward and southward advancing frontier, a different house type evolved in the Delaware hearth. Variously called a Quaker-plan house,[19] a two-thirds Georgian house,[20] or a continental deep house,[21] the origins of this structure are diverse yet strongly related to the influence of Germans from the Rhine valley.[22] These settlers built not only continental log houses, they also constructed quite similar three-room stone cottages. Thus, despite its Quaker designation by Thomas Waterman, the arrangement of the Quaker-plan house (fig. 5–12) appears to be a derivation of the three-room layout of earlier German dwellings. However, Henry Glassie has suggested that the three-room plan of the Quaker-plan house is not German in origin, but is a one-third reduction of a Georgian double-pile house drawn from English sources.[23] Finally, Patricia Cooper has raised the question of the origins of the Quaker-plan house again.[24] She suggests that one structure in Georgia gives evidence for an actual Quaker origin that is much stronger than has been thought heretofore. The questions that Glassie and Cooper raise will only be resolved by additional careful research on other Quaker-plan houses.

The most important modification that distinguishes the Quaker-plan house from possible German antecedents is the position of its chimneys. The chimney heating the large room is on the gable, with the hearth parallel to the gable and the long dimension of the wall. The two smaller rooms often are heated by

5–12 The Quaker-plan house

5–13 Floor plan of a Quaker-plan house

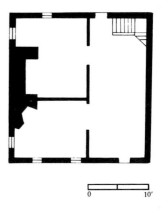

0   10'

45

fireplaces catted into a common corner in the middle of one gable. Such corner chimneys are derivative of Swedish origins (fig. 5–13).[25] In some houses the early Swedish triangular corner hearths evolved into complex rectangular fireplaces against the interior wall.

Several other standard features are associated with the Quaker-plan house. Generally, they are built of brick and are two or two-and-a-half stories in height. In earlier houses the facades may be unbalanced (fig. 5–14), whereas later versions almost always have the door centered, separating equally spaced windows. In both instances, there are two windows and a door on the lower floor and three windows on the upper floor. Both door and window openings are usually capped by low fan-shaped brick arches, a feature that may be of Dutch origin, for it is reported as early as 1699 in New Jersey.[26] The final distinguishing feature that many Quaker-plan houses possess is a pent roof, a self-supporting, projecting roof at the second-story floor level. At first the pent roof was designed to protect the chinking or wall infilling of the lower-story walls. Originally from the Germanic areas of Europe, it was also widely employed in the British Isles before being introduced into North America.

5–14 A Quaker-plan house in Elizabethtown, Pennsylvania, is built in the local fashion with no front yard. (October 1976)

The four-over-four house

The final house type to evolve in the Delaware valley cultural hearth is termed the four-over-four house,[27] in reference to its basic room arrangement. The house has an appearance of solidity derived largely from its dimensions (fig. 5–15). The ratio of width to depth is roughly three to four, and height to the eaves approximates the depth of the house.

About the middle of the eighteenth century, Georgian style concepts began to appear in southeastern Pennsylvania. The design of two-room-deep Georgian houses harmonized easily with that of two-room-deep continental houses already in common use. The result was the four-over-four house.

As Georgian styling became popular, Germanic and Georgian ideas meshed. One concept that found increased favor was the use of a balanced facade with four openings per floor. In order to pro-

5–15 The four-over-four house

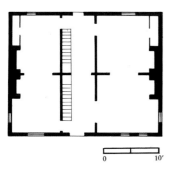

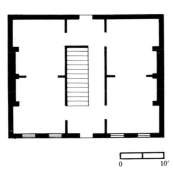

5–16 Floor plans of a four-over-four house. In the upper plan, four openings produce a markedly asymmetrical facade. The lower, five-opening house has a balanced facade.

5–17 A five-opening, four-over-four house built of limestone, Lebanon County, Pennsylvania (October 1976)

vide the maximum balance, two centrally positioned doors separated two windows. Later on, the stairway located in a corner of the large room in Quaker-plan houses was shifted toward the center of the house, and the internal arrangement of doors was modified considerably (fig. 5–16).

Continued expansion of the type produced a standardized version built after 1800, which had a balanced, five-opening facade with a central hallway (fig. 5–17). The large room of the original Quaker-plan house was now divided into two rooms of equal size, although rooms on one side of the hallway were not necessarily the same size as those on the other side. The second-floor room arrangement and sizes duplicated those of the first floor. The chimneys were generally set into the gable. Sometimes massive double chimneys added to the blocky or heavy appearance. Also, by this time the catted Swedish fireplaces had been replaced by hearths parallel to the gable wall.

Some of the house types developed in the Delaware valley hearth (e.g., the log pen house) spread widely throughout eastern United States. Some other house types never migrated much beyond the domain of the Delaware valley cultural hearth, where, however, they are a familiar component of the cultural landscape.

Initial European settlement in the Chesapeake Bay area occurred as early as 1607, when English colonists arrived in the James River estuary in tidewater Virginia. Formal colonization in Maryland dates from 1634, although isolated settlements by Virginians are known to have preceded that.

The method of land division employed in the Chesapeake Bay hearth was that of the metes-and-bounds system, also utilized in several other American cultural hearths (see chap. 3) and later throughout the eastern parts of the continent. Hence, the arrangement of the landscape is irregular and not greatly unlike elsewhere in eastern North America. However, because farms generally were larger in the southern colonies, the land was not as fragmented here as in New England.

6 English Colonial Houses in the Chesapeake Bay Hearth

Evolution of early housing in the Chesapeake Bay hearth

No other cultural hearth, with the possible exception of southern New England, has exerted such influence over the domestic architecture of eastern North America as has the Chesapeake Bay hearth. The colonial housing evolved in this area has its origins in England, especially western England, although most sections of the metropolitan country were represented by migrants to the Chesapeake Bay hearth.

The earliest housing of the English colonists was similar to that of early New England—one-room huts of wattle-and-daub walls with rough, thatched roofs. Perhaps because this was a frontier area foundations were not used but the houses were based instead on poles set directly into the ground, using a system of construction that the English had abandoned centuries before.[1] Exterior gable chimneys were generally of stick-and-clay construction. Jamestown Festival Park in Virginia contains reconstructions of these early structures, together with replicas of Indian bark houses, which, although the original common dwelling throughout eastern North America, ultimately disappeared without influencing subsequent domestic building.

Succeeding the early primitive huts were timber frame buildings built with the same simple configuration and the same size and construction techniques. Wood, which was widely available in forest-covered eastern North America, rapidly came to be the principal building material, not only in the Chesapeake Bay area, but elsewhere as well. The main structural members of the building were hewn from timbers, whereas the siding and lighter structural supports were hand sawn. A flexible framing system was adopted to minimize the stresses resulting from building deformation.[2]

In addition to the more numerous timber frame structures, a considerable number of brick dwellings were erected, a fortunate circumstance for the modern student, since virtually none of the wooden buildings has survived. Building in brick commenced almost as soon as the earliest Chesapeake Bay area colony was founded in 1607. Roofs continued to be made of thatch in most instances because of its light weight, although wood shingles gradually supplanted that material. Wooden shingles, while heavier than thatch, were less susceptible to fire, more durable, and more readily available. Chimneys built of brick, easily made from the clays of the coastal plain, replaced the earlier rougher ones. None of these simple, one-room houses, termed *single-bay* or *one-bay* structures,[3] has survived, but this model served as the basis for a series of subsequent, more elaborate dwellings that have come to characterize the area.[4]

The hall-and-parlor house and its derivatives

The first elaboration produced the hall-and-parlor house (fig. 6–1), named for its two ground-floor rooms. The parlor, used variously as a bedroom, guest chamber, and formal reception room, was the smaller of the two rooms (fig. 6–2). The somewhat larger hall combined the functions of kitchen, dining room, work area, and informal living space. Both an exterior door and a corner stairway to the garret or loft were normal features of the hall (fig.

6–2 Foundations of an eighteenth-century hall-and-parlor house at Fort Frederica National Monument, Georgia (August 1978)

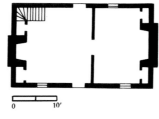

6–3 Floor plan of a hall-and-parlor house

6–3). Sleeping quarters were provided in the loft, which was either partitioned or undivided.

Each gable of the hall-and-parlor house contained a chimney, so each room had a heat source. But, because long, hot, humid summers were more significant than the short cool winters in the Chesapeake region, the chimneys usually were exterior to the house, continuing the tradition of western England.[5] In rare cases, they even had outside hearths for summer cooking. Exterior chimneys detached from the gable wall are distinctive traits associated with many early Chesapeake Bay hearth house types. Detached or free-standing chimneys not only reduced house heat in summer, they also allowed the flues to be kept away from the flammable thatched roof.[6]

The exterior dimension of the hall-and-parlor houses varies considerably,

6–4 A hall-and-parlor house in Yorktown, Virginia. Note the general lack of embellishment typical of the eighteenth century, the slight flare of the eaves, and the device over the doorway to divert rainwater runoff. (August 1978)

6–1 The hall-and-parlor house

but it rarely exceeds forty feet by twenty feet. In some instances, the house facade is balanced, with the door in the center and one window on either side; more often, however, the door is slightly off center or the windows are unevenly spaced. The irregular facade betrays the medieval origins of these houses, which are copies of the homes the immigrants knew from earlier times in England. Other medieval characteristics are the steep roof pitch (forty-five to sixty degrees) and the fixed or outward swinging narrow casement windows.

Quite rapidly, the small hall-and-parlor houses became the standard dwelling of the Chesapeake Bay colonies (fig. 6–4).[7] Subsequently, this type of house spread across the entire southeastern United States. As time passed, certain modifications were made in the basic structure, producing a series of interrelated early house types.

The evolutionary sequence, which is shown in figure 6–5, must not be taken too literally, however. Houses of the early types often were being built at the same time or even after those of later types. As Henry Forman has noted, "it cannot be laid down as a rule that all the plain, simple structures were built first, and all the complicated ones later."[8] In some instances, both in the Chesapeake Bay hearth and elsewhere, an opposite

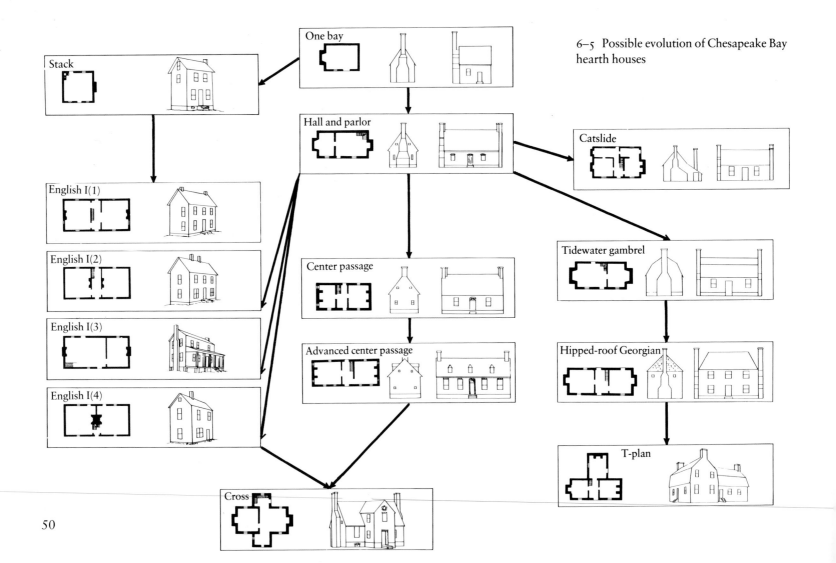

6–5 Possible evolution of Chesapeake Bay hearth houses

process operated by which less-elaborate, simpler houses were produced.[9] Folk houses, that is to say those dwellings that arise from building traditions informally perpetuated within a society, are often built in virtually an unchanged aspect for up to a century. Styles of academic architecture, i.e., structures designed by professional architects. rarely last longer than a generation. To those reared in an atmosphere of regularly and rapidly changing architectural fashions, the tenacity and persistence of folk-housing types is often surprising. Furthermore, as with style changes, modifications of folk houses never entirely replaced the earlier versions, but simply coexisted with them.

The modifications of the hall-and-parlor house were essentially of two kinds

6–6 A center-passage, hall-and-parlor house in Yorktown, Virginia. Note exterior chimneys, balanced facade, dormers, and boxed-eave overhang. (August 1978)

—alterations or additions to the plan of the house and changes in the elevation and facade. The simplest and probably the earliest modification was the expansion of the hall-and-parlor house so that it included a center passageway between the parlor and the hall (see fig. 6–5). The passageway accommodated outside doors and thus gave greater privacy to the hall room.[10] The stairway to the loft was shifted from its earlier location in a corner of the hall to the back of the center passageway. The facade of center-passageway houses is more apt to be symmetrical than that of the earlier hall-and-parlor houses, but otherwise the two houses may be quite similar (fig. 6–6).

As in New England, family size increased and the colony slowly gained economic prosperity. Larger houses were needed, but there was no need to break the long continuity of folk-building traditions. The advanced center-passageway houses not only have larger

6–7 An advanced center-passage, hall-and-parlor house in Yorktown, Virginia. An unbalanced facade and off-set chimneys are quite unusual. (August 1978)

6–8 An advanced center-passage, hall-and-parlor house in Yorktown, Virginia. This house with its five dormers and balanced facade is of a later design than the house shown in fig. 6–7. (August 1978)

dimensions (especially width [fig. 6–7]), but several other modifications as well.[11] The wider facade permitted four windows of larger size and of sliding-sash design instead of the fixed leaded casement windows typical of earlier houses (fig. 6–8).[12] Dormers were added to give greater headroom and better light to the loft, which was now often divided into separate bedrooms. The new gable dormers were different in form from the earlier continental or shed dormers. Although they were more complicated to build than the earlier types, they provided greater headroom. Part of the need for additional height in the upper floor resulted from the lower roof pitch adopted in these houses.

51

The stack house

The hall-and-parlor house and its derivatives, the central-passage house and the advanced central-passage house, are all one-and-a-half stories high. A different kind of modification, the evolution of a full second story, produced a quite different group of houses.

Stacking another room on top of the single-room, one-bay house produced an ungainly dwelling referred to variously as a *one-over-one half house*,[13] an *up-and-down cottage*,[14] or a *stack house*.[15] Virtually nothing has been written about these structures, although they are reported for tidewater Maryland and Virginia[16] and southern New Jersey.[17] Howard Marshall's description of stack houses in central Missouri refers to them as having a tall profile and as being at least two stories high and often having a loft above that. Other typical features include doors roughly centered on the side, a single gable-positioned chimney, a boxed-in or open stairway located in the corner of the room, and one-story rear frame additions containing the kitchen. Front porches are rarely encountered, but a small pent roof often provides modest weather protection for the front door.

The stack house may be related to the much more important and widely distributed structure, the English I house, which was first identified and studied by Fred Kniffen.[18] Subsequently, the designation of the structure has been shortened to just *I house* by most students of vernacular architecture.

The I house

The I house (fig. 6–9) spread far and wide throughout southeastern United States, north to Pennsylvania, and westward across the entire Middle West, at least as far as central Nebraska. In the process, the house lost some of its medieval character; the roof especially changed, as its pitch was steadily lowering, and often a front gable was added (fig. 6–10).

The I house has been a remarkably persistent type, perhaps because its origins were deeply embedded within the English culture introduced into North America in colonial times. It had the widest distribution of any folk house in America, except possibly the log pen house, and it was constructed without a lapse up to the beginning of the twentieth century, long after house building began to be affected by architectural styling. Thus, an impressive Greek Revival house (fig. 6–11) turns out on close inspection to be an I house with a formal gable and portico attached to the side. Similarly, Italianate and Gothic Revival decorative embellishments often adorn other I houses. What identifies all I houses regardless of their facade decoration are certain basic plan and form characteristics: side-facing gables, one-room depth, at least two-room width, and two full stories in elevation.[19] Furthermore, although individual measurements vary somewhat, the dimensions of the I house conform to a particular standard. The average size may be taken as sixteen to twenty-four feet deep by twenty-eight to forty-eight feet wide by twenty to twenty-four feet tall.[20]

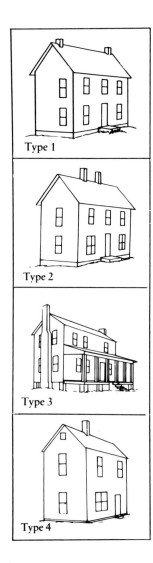

Type 1

Type 2

Type 3

Type 4

6–9 I houses

Some I houses are built in brick, and even a few are of stone or log, but the overwhelming number are constructed of timber frame, surfaced with horizontal clapboards. The overall effect produced by the I house is that of plainness and simplicity, together with a certain air of ungainliness produced by its tall, narrow form (see fig. 6–9).

At least four variants or subtypes of I houses can be discerned (see figs. 6–5 and 6–9). The first type possesses a floor plan of two rooms separated by a central hallway, quite similar to that of the advanced center-passage hall-and-parlor house, suggesting its possible derivation therefrom. The two rooms, which are usually of equal size, are heated by gable-positioned hearths, enclosed within the house walls (fig. 6–12). The facade usually contains three openings in a balanced composition, although windows in the gable are typically off center. This subtype is encountered at least from tidewater Virginia to central Indiana.

6–11 An I house to which a Greek Revival portico has been added (Harrodsburg, Kentucky, November 1978)

6–12 An I house, type 1 (Hanover, Indiana, October 1979)

6–10 An I house in the Italianate style (Lexington, Kentucky, November 1978)

A second type of I house also has a central hallway, two rooms of equal size, and three facade openings per floor across the front side. It differs primarily in the placement of chimneys and hearths, which are located on either side of the central stair hall (fig. 6–13). Windows on the ground floor are sometimes paired, the gable windows are usually centered, and a small side gable often breaks the roof line (fig. 6–14).

The adding of this third gable occurs not only with the second type of house, but in other subtypes as well. Although it does provide extra headroom in the attic of the house, the gable apparently was not added for that reason. It "appears to have arisen out of pattern books and standardized plans displaying romantic Gothic cottages and Tuscan villas. The one feature that could be taken from these plans without disturbing the requirements of the accepted house form was the decorative gable set at dead center on the facade. Tradition was maintained while a certain concession was made to fashion, and a balance was achieved between the two."[21]

Most of these center gables either were added to earlier I houses sometime in the last three decades of the nineteenth century or were incorporated as features of houses built during this time.

Type two houses are the I houses most widely distributed across Appalachia. Of all the I houses, this one is the most interesting. The hearth and chimney placement does not appear very logical and raises questions of origin which

6–13 An I house, type 2 (Tazewell County, Virginia, October 1975)

6–14 An I house, type 2, with front gable and corbeled chimney (Carroll County, Missouri, 1974)

have not been answered thus far. This chimney placement does not occur in any other house type, except for a similar appearing one-story house found in central Kentucky (fig. 6–15).

The type three house does not possess a central hallway, the two rooms are of unequal size, the gable chimneys are outside the walls, and three to five openings are typical. The facade is not always symmetrically arranged (fig. 6–16), but ideas of classical symmetry lent themselves easily to the facade of this subtype, even though the interior might not contain such balance (fig. 6–17). A long, one-story verandah covered with a hipped or shed roof often masks the facade (see fig. 6–16).[22] These houses, sometimes locally referred to as *Shenandoah* houses, are most often encountered in the piedmont or tidewater areas of southeastern United States.

The type four houses, in contrast to the

6–15 A one-story house with paired interior chimneys near Harrodsburg, Kentucky (November 1978)

6–16 The I house, type 3

other three types, have only a single chimney, roughly in the middle of the structure, serving back-to-back hearths (fig. 6–18). Such an arrangement is reminiscent of and may be associated with the saddlebag house, a structure formed of two adjacent rooms using a common central chimney stack (see chap. 10). The facade of type four houses is usually unbalanced, with two or three openings per floor. The door, set in a severely plain frame, opens into a small hallway in front of the chimney. A narrow stairway to the second floor occupies about half the small hallway area. Type four houses are found from Virginia to Missouri and seem to be most common in the Midwest.

I houses are among the most significant folk dwellings of eastern United States. In the nineteenth century the basic form was further modified by additions of large ells and wings that changed the floor plan.[23] The exterior was often distinguished by Italianate style brackets, Eastlake-style porches (see below, chap. 11), and a variety of other decorative touches. Despite the changes that occurred through the years, this house type was constructed with a basic form and integrity from the seventeenth to the twentieth century. It, thus, has a continuity among the longest of any American house type. Not only have the I houses persisted for a long time, they also are spread over a surprisingly large area. They are scattered, with fair abundance, from Pennsylvania to Georgia, from the Chesapeake Bay hearth to the heart of the Middle West, and perhaps beyond.

6–18 An I house, type 4

The cross house

The cruciform or cross house probably represents the combination of two evolutionary lines (see fig. 6–5), each derived from the basic hall-and-parlor house. The cross house is a full two or two-and-a-half stories high (fig. 6–19) and the floor plan is an elaboration of the earlier two-room arrangements. Many original features, such as the enclosed porch, the stair tower, and the steep roof pitch, were eventually modified. Both the porch and the stair tower became regular rooms, open exterior porches were added, and the roof pitch was lowered. Cross houses built in the nineteenth century with these modifications are almost as widely distributed as the English I house (fig. 6–20).

6–20 A nineteenth-century cross house (Akron, Ohio, January 1979)

6–19 Bacon's Castle, an example of a colonial cross house (Bacon's Castle, Virginia, January 1981)

Other early Chesapeake Bay houses

A third line of dwelling modifications originating from the basic hall-and-parlor house leads to three house types that are only occasionally encountered outside southeastern coastal areas (see fig. 6–5). The floor plans of all three are basically similar, not only to each other but to other derivatives of hall-and-parlor houses as well.

The first of these may be called the *tidewater gambrel house* (fig. 6–21) and is recognizable by its particular roof style (fig. 6–22). Gambrel roofs are typical of several house types. They occurred on houses in New England from the middle of the seventeenth century, and perhaps even earlier. In the Dutch areas of New York and New Jersey, gambrel roofs also became quite common during the seventeenth century and later. The essential difference between the Dutch and English gambrel roofs is the length of the upper slope and the pitch of each component (fig. 6–23). The short upper portion of the Dutch roof has a pitch of about twenty-two degrees, whereas the longer, lower part inclines at an angle of about sixty degrees. By contrast, a typical English gambrel roof possesses upper and lower slopes of generally equal length. The upper pitch is usually about twenty-five degrees and the lower, about forty-five degrees. Consequently, the visual effect of the two roofs is quite different.

Modifying the roof line of the hall-and-parlor house in a different fashion produced a house that could be called the *hipped-roof Georgian* (fig. 6–24). The hipped roof slopes in four directions from a short ridge line. Its introduction into English colonies in North America coincides with the appearance of so-called Georgian or Renaissance design. The Georgian house's central hall encouraged employment of a balanced facade. Both features are among the most characteristic architectural traits of the Georgian period. The best examples of the hipped-roof Georgian house are those built of the reddish bricks from clay deposits all along the coastal plain.

The third house type of this series, the *T-plan house*, is distinguished more by its room arrangement than by its exterior design (fig. 6–25). A third room (or more) is added to the basic two-room house so that the ground plan resembles a T. Adding rooms to the rear of the house is a widely employed way of expanding houses. This method is not limited to variants of the hall-and-parlor house, nor to the area immediately under the influence of the Chesapeake Bay cultural hearth. None of these houses, the tidewater gambrel, the hipped-roof Georgian, or the T-plan house, is an especially important type. They were not widely built, did not have any important effects upon subsequent house types, and are not found much outside southeastern United States. They do,

6–21 The tidewater gambrel house
6–22 A tidewater gambrel house in Savannah, Georgia. Note how differently the verandah roof is framed from that in fig. 6–21. (August 1978)

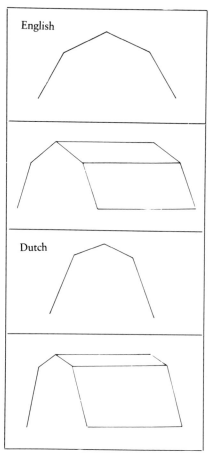

6–23 Comparison of Dutch and English gambrel roofs

57

6–24 A hipped-roof Georgian house in Savannah, Georgia. The house is raised in the fashion typical of the tidewater South. (August 1978)

however, illustrate the possible variations that can be derived from a single basic house, in this instance, the hall-and-parlor.

One final line of modification resulted in the evolution of a dwelling called the *catslide cottage* (see fig. 6–5). To the basic hall-and-parlor house have been added a full-width front porch or verandah, and a rear shed incorporating one, two, or even three rooms. The gable roof is extended from the main ridge to include both a front porch and rear shed. The slope of the roof is often broken, especially in earlier houses, and it is this feature that is referred to as the *catslide*. In later versions of the house, both front porch and rear addition are frequently incorporated within a unified roof structure. Often, the stairway to the second floor is placed in the center of the rear addition and another part is left open to function as a rear porch and work area (fig. 6–26). A further elaboration is the cottage's elevation upon a stone or brick foundation, which cre-

ates a cellar or substory, or upon stone or brick piers, which raises the cottage above ground. Such a condition facilitated the circulation of air beneath the house, thus cooling it during the long southern summers. It also reduced the possibility of wood rot and termite damage. Because of these advantages, a great many other kinds of houses in southern United States also are raised on piers.

Many of the house types originating in the Chesapeake Bay cultural hearth merged with others brought southward from the Delaware valley hearth to characterize the entire Appalachian interior of southeastern United States, where this assemblage of house types and other cultural features has been called the *Upland South culture*.[24] By contrast, the house types originating in the southern tidewater hearth, to be considered in the next chapter, had a markedly limited effect, except along the coast and in the Mississippi River valley.

6–25 The T-plan house

6–26 The catslide cottage

The southeastern coastal lands of the United States lie well within the humid subtropical climate, one in which summers are long, hot, and rainy and in which winters are brief, warm, and only somewhat less rainy. Winter is less uncomfortable than summer and hence housing is usually designed to combat the heat and humidity of summer. Both the English and the Spanish, of necessity, had to adjust to the climate. Neither group introduced houses that seem to have had profound influence upon the later house types, but each group utilized distinctive floor plans, providing room arrangements most suitable for the climate. Each group also made use of locally available construction materials and employed certain forms and building techniques that permitted better adjustment to the local climate.

The English in the tidewater South hearth

The coastal region between Charleston, South Carolina, and Savannah, Georgia, was not settled by Europeans until the end of the seventeenth century. Nevertheless, it became a focus from which certain cultural elements were introduced into American society and from which evolved a distinctive, albeit limited, series of house types (fig. 7–1). A large part of the explanation for late settlement lies in the unfavorable environmental conditions of this area. The coast is low-lying and marshy, so that diking or artificial drainage was required before extensive cultivation could take place. Because of the swampy conditions, malaria was endemic, further delaying and discourag-

PART THREE   Environment and House Evolution

7   Houses of the English and Spanish in the Humid Subtropics

Huguenot plan (early)

Charleston single

Huguenot plan (late)

7–1 Southern tidewater hearth houses

ing rapid or early settlement. Thomas
Waterman cites these environmental
conditions as a contributing reason for
the rather modest nature of South Carolina country houses, which were not
large because "the dread malaria mos-
quito forced the plantation families to
migrate to Charleston for the summer."[1] Thus, it was in and around
Charleston that the most distinctive
house of this cultural hearth developed.

7–2 Charleston single house floor plan

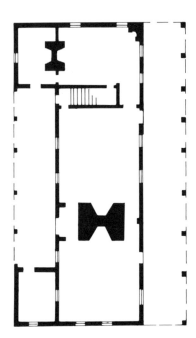

The Charleston single house

The Charleston single house is especially well designed for the climate of the
area. All the rooms are in single file to
secure cross ventilation in every room.
The earliest Charleston single houses
were mostly one story and built of
wood, but because of the toll of fire, few
of these survive; those that do are mostly brick or stucco-covered brick. Chimneys are centrally positioned so that
each serves back-to-back hearths in adjoining rooms, or they are located in
each room against the side wall, opposite the verandah that runs the full
length of the house.

  The plan is usually that of three (parlor, hall, dining room) or four rooms in
a row (fig. 7–2). At the extremities of the
house, but offset from the line of the
main house, are small rooms that functioned variously as kitchen, slaves quarters, guest bedrooms, or storage areas.
In line with these rooms and flanking
the file of main rooms is a long, shady

verandah, locally called a *piazza* (fig.
7–3). The piazza, as well as the room
arrangement, was probably introduced
by English immigrants from Barbados,
who formed one of the three main settlement groups in South Carolina.[2]

  In the countryside, piazzas flank both
sides of the house. In Charleston, where
land costs were higher, the end of the
house faces the street and the house is
generally shifted to the north or east
side of the lot, with a single piazza opening into a garden (fig. 7–4). Thus, the
main entrance of the house, which is off
the piazza, is removed from the street
(fig. 7–5). In order to eliminate casual
traffic across the piazza to the main
door, a wall was built across the street
end of the piazza (fig. 7–6). In time, as
the house itself became larger, this wall
with its main doorway became quite
elaborate and the piazza gained a second story (fig. 7–7). Because of the piazza's end wall, the facade of the house
facing the street was highly asymmetri-

7–3 The Charleston single house: side
view of a rural variant

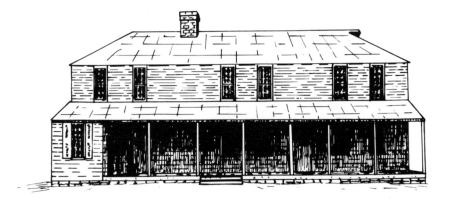

7–4 The Charleston single house: gable view of urban variant

7–5 A Charleston single house in Savannah, Georgia. Here houses tend to be wider and lower and have verandahs on two sides. (August 1978)

7–6 A Charleston single house in the Ansonburgh section of Charleston. Note the movement of the house door to the street end of the verandah. (August 1978)

7–7 Examples of piazzas and doorways, in Charleston, South Carolina (August 1978)

61

7–8 A Charleston single house showing the long verandah perpendicular to the street (August 1978)

cal, with two windows on each floor of the two- or three-story house and an offset door, above which was the open end of the second story of the piazza (fig. 7–8).

A variety of roof types crowns the Charleston single house (fig. 7–9). Some have gable roofs, others gambrel, but most have hipped roofs (a roof that slopes in four directions) or jerkin-head roofs (a gable roof that is truncated by a steeply sloping end section).[3] Tiles, as roofing material, were more common here than in most other areas of eastern

North America, although no satisfactory reason for why they were has so far been advanced.

The influence of the single-file Charleston house can be traced throughout the entire southern portion of the United States. The addition of Greek columns, other classical features, and further modifications eventually made it the archetypal antebellum "southern mansion."

7–9 Although most Charleston single houses have low, hipped roofs, some have gables. This one is particularly steeply pitched with a slight bell-cast. (August 1978)

The Huguenot-plan house

Another important house type, which originated in the southern tidewater hearth and was diffused across the South, and which also passed through significant architectural changes, is the Huguenot-plan house (figs. 7–10 and 7–11). In Charleston these houses often are referred to as "double" houses because they possess two files of rooms.[4]

It is really the plan that distinguishes this house (fig. 7–12). The dwelling is squarish in shape with two large front rooms and three smaller rear rooms, the center one of which contains the stairway to the upper floor. Chimneys are always interior and two in number. Each chimney has two back-to-back hearths.

In early versions of the Huguenot-plan house, the house is small and its exterior resembles the catslide cottage because of the wood construction, the gable roof, front porch, and rear rooms often

7–10 The Huguenot-plan house (early phase)

under a shed roof. At the same time, several differences are present. The early Huguenot-plan house usually has two front doors, one entering into each of the large front rooms. The plan is squarer than the catslide cottage and the rear stairway is enclosed in a dormer, necessary because of the relationship between the stair location and the roof line.

In later versions of the Huguenot-plan house, the size increased, wood gave way to brick as the basic building material, hipped roof replaced gable, and the

7–12 Floor plans of Huguenot-plan houses

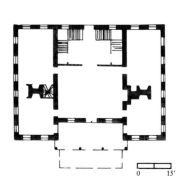
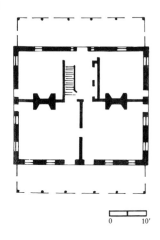

7–11 The Huguenot-plan house (late phase)

7–13 A Huguenot-plan house which has a classical roof line, but which retains the long side verandah (Charleston, S.C., August 1978)

63

7–14 A Huguenot-plan house, also called a double house, with a low, hipped roof (Charleston, S.C., August 1978)

porch became shortened but increased in height, eventually assuming a classical form under a triangular pediment (figs. 7–13 and 7–14). To the casual observer, the late Huguenot-plan house looks totally unlike the early Huguenot-plan house, but the room arrangement is essentially the same. It is not their exterior form that reveals the connection of these houses, but rather the constancy of their floor plans.

The arrangement of rooms was also distinctive in houses built by the Spanish further south. They, too, were searching for building designs that would provide a harmony with the climatic demands of southeastern North America.

As early as 1565, the Spanish were establishing a military and trading outpost at St. Augustine, Florida. Throughout its existence, the Spanish colonists were under constant pressure from Indians, the English and Americans, and French pirates, so that little expansion into the countryside was possible. Furthermore, political control fluctuated among the Spanish, English, and French. A cosmopolitan population was attracted and, consequently, not much clearly definable ethnic architecture has survived. Fire also took its toll of early buildings. What did develop in St. Augustine was a series of buildings demonstrating different methods and materials of construction, but adhering to a distinctive plan that has been termed the *St. Augustine plan*.

The settlement of St. Augustine burned down in 1702 and no houses from earlier than the eighteenth century have survived (in fact, there are only a handful at this relatively late age). The evidence provided from historical and archaeological sources indicates that the most common floor plans in St. Augustine were those encountered widely among early houses in other parts of the Atlantic seaboard. In 1788 somewhat more than a third of the houses had two-room plans and just over a quarter consisted of a single room.[5]

Only slightly less typical was the St. Augustine plan (fig. 7–15). The distinctive feature of this plan is either a sheltered porch or a loggia (a room open on at least one side, but built within the body of the building) that opens onto the backyard of the dwelling. Rarely were doors placed so as to open directly

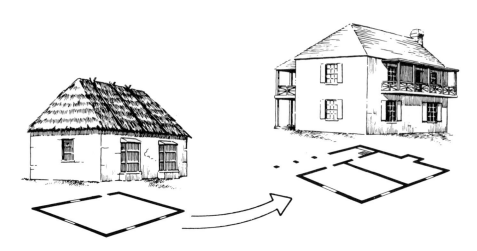

7–15 The St. Augustine-plan house probably evolved from a single, one-room, thatch-covered cottage. (From Ma Ma!ncy)

to the street until British influence began to be felt. Most houses of this type were two-stories high, so that a roofed balcony projected over the loggia of the ground floor. On the opposite side of the houses, facing the street, there was often a second, unsupported balcony.

St. Augustine-plan houses were most often oriented with the porches and loggias facing south or east, so that the prevailing southeastern breezes of summer provided maximum cooling.[6] The adjustment is reminiscent of that of the Charleston single house, except that the house's orientation was such that complete privacy of the porch was achieved by having it open upon the garden or backyard.

Several other features of St. Augustine houses facilitated climatic adjustments. Loggias and porches were roofed or re-cessed, so that cooling shade was provided. However, roof overhang was limited and during the brief winter season, light and warmth from the lower sun angle was available. Recessed porches and loggias were sheltered from winter's chilly breezes and could be quite pleasant on all except the coldest days.[7] Few of the early houses had any heating system and even cooking was done in separate buildings. Chimneys were uncommon before the middle of the eighteenth century, with heat in winter provided by small, portable braziers of charcoal.

Windows were always few and small in size, with those facing the hot afternoon sun being especially small.[8] Those windows that faced the street at ground level, however, were larger than the others. These windows were often covered by a projecting, close grating of wood called a *reja* (see fig. 7–15). Window shutters in the Spanish period were inside the window, folding back against the thickness of the wall.

Tabby as a building material

Walls of houses in St. Augustine were constructed of a variety of materials, the most common of which were wood, stone, and tabby. Walls both of vertically set posts and board walls using a timber frame were employed. The most distinctive material, however, was tabby, which is the name given a masonry construction composed of an aggregate material such as shells, gravel, or bits of stone held in a mortar of lime and sand. The most commonly used aggregate consisted of shells obtained from kitchen middens of early Indian villages, from more extensive natural shell beds close to the sea, or from deposits of lightly cemented shell rock called *coquina*. Throughout the coastal areas of southeastern United States, tabby was employed as a building material in both English and Spanish settlements.

Walls built of tabby were constructed in successive layers about a foot high by pouring the mixture between forms, tamping it extensively and allowing it to set for several days (fig. 7–16). The tabby hardened very gradually, but once covered with lime stucco or plaster it proved quite durable. Tabby walls were typically between one and two feet thick and could rise as high as twenty-five feet.[9] Often to strengthen the walls and especially to provide support for the roof, vertical wooden posts were embedded within the tabby at about five- or six-foot intervals.

65

Not only was tabby used as wall material, it also was employed for floors, in thicknesses of about four inches, and for roofs, although the advantage of its impermeability was counterbalanced by its great weight. Tabby roofs were, of course, virtually flat and usually laid on a wooden plank base. Finally, it may be noted that tabby has continued to the present to be used as an important road building material in coastal areas.

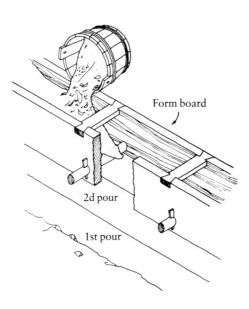

7–16 Building a tabby wall. A method of construction used by the Spanish in southeastern United States. (From Mauncy)

Form board

2d pour

1st pour

Colonial housing in summary

The colonial housing of eastern North America shows a surprising basic unity across the entire area. Dwellings are rarely anything except oblong shapes, either singly or in combination. Because most structures normally housed only one family and were the residences of the common people, they rarely exceed one-and-a-half or two stories. The gable roof, and less frequently the gambrel, covers most structures. Although other materials were used when locally present, timber and logs were widely available at low cost and hence came to be the most used construction materials.

Despite basic similarities, sufficient differences occur to enable identification of at least twenty distinct house types. In each instance the house is associated with a particular cultural group that has introduced elements derived from foreign origins, or the houses have evolved from earlier, more distinctly ethnic forms. Quite clearly, house building is an activity that carries the stamp of cultural identity. On the other hand, house styles change with time as imported original types prove to be unsuited to new climatic conditions, as family size alters, as various cultural groups come in contact with one another, and as fashion and taste shift when both family and society evolve. All these circumstances can be observed in the colonial housing of North America.

The study of folk and popular housing offers an opportunity to geographers to evaluate the impact of different ethnic groups on the landscape within an area. To date, however, only a few such studies have been made.[10] The diffusion of house types also provides clues to the movement of various peoples. Cultural geographers thus have a tool available that can partially unmask the secrets of the landscape of each region.

Western America provides a greater range of environmental challenges than does the eastern part of the continent. The West is composed of several macroregions and in each one a different environment functioned to limit the kinds of dwellings that were built. Great stretches of the interior were virtually treeless, lacked good lime deposits for mortar making,[1] or were essentially devoid of outcroppings of building stone, so early residents were forced to utilize materials for their housing that were not commonly employed elsewhere in North America. On the Great Plains, for example, not only was timber limited, but the abundant grass vegetation provided a ubiquitous food to support the roaming buffalo and antelope herds, which necessitated a portable Indian dwelling. At a later stage, breaking the sod facilitated cultivation of the soil for pioneer farmers.

The even greater aridity in southwestern United States encouraged use of earthen dwellings, both excavated and erected, as well as combinations. Adobe structures predominated in this area until the arrival of the railroad, well after the middle of the nineteenth century. In contrast, the Pacific Northwest is so humid and forest vegetation there is so prevalent that no building material but log and lumber was used from the start, and these still are the dominant materials for domestic building.

In the various environments of the West, the level of technology achieved by each ethnic group determined the mode of adjustment. Thus, the earlier Indian groups, generally but not always, employed more primitive methods of construction or less-finished materials than later settlers. This chapter will be devoted to examining several groups and their particular response to creating shelters adequate to the challenges of the environment and to using materials available within each area. In the rainy, heavily forested Pacific Coast, Indians and Russians built quite different structures by using the same material in different ways. On the interior plains, the Indians and the American pioneers reacted quite differently in constructing shelters because their economies were quite different. Finally, in the Southwest, certain Indian groups, the Pueblos, responded much as the later Spanish-Mexicans did, while other Indians, the Navajos, found different solutions to obtain shelter based upon ancient traditions.

Russians and Indians in the North Pacific Coast

Western North America has been subjected to cultural influences from two groups whose centers or hearths lay outside the area (see fig. 1–5). Of these, the Russian penetration provided the least lasting influence. It was restricted in area and limited in consequence. Only parts of the coastal regions from central Alaska to northern California were affected. Throughout this area, settlement was confined to a few trading sites and military outposts, which were never staffed by more than a few Russians at any time.

These Russians employed log construction, which was a logical approach given the abundant forest resources along the Pacific Coast. Virtually nothing has been written specifically about Russian-American building, although some structures existed well beyond the middle of the nineteenth century. Today, only the reconstructed buildings of Fort Ross in northern California provide any trace of Russian building techniques.

Most of the effect of Russian penetration was in style and employment of log construction and has had very little impact upon subsequent building in North America. Perhaps a contributing reason for such modest impact is that the rate of deterioration for unpainted wooden structures was very high in the damp climate of this area. The Russian-American Trading Company buildings, for example, were depreciated over the rather short period of just twelve years.[2]

Rapid deterioration may account as well for the almost complete disappearance of Indian plank houses, although by all indications these were substantial structures. Quite unlike other Indian dwellings elsewhere, the Pacific Coast Indian plank houses were built of cedar, spruce, Douglas fir, or redwood. Although the trees were massive (i.e., up to twelve feet in diameter), they could be split fairly easily with simple wooden, stone, and elk-horn tools.[3]

In some instances, the beams and posts of the houses were interlocked by an ingenious tenon device (fig. 8–1). More often, the impressive gable facade of the house was structurally independent from the roof beams that rested on interior posts.[4] The walls were of split planks laid either horizontally or vertically, and flush rather than overlapping. Vertical wall boards normally were inserted into a heavy plate. Horizontal boards were kept in place between heavy interior posts and lighter exterior poles.

Roofs were extremely low pitched and also covered by planks. Except for the Puget Sound and Frazer River delta areas, where a shed roof predominated, Indian plank house roofs were ridged. In houses with shed roofs, the side wall containing the main entrance customarily faced the sea, but over most of the coast the chief entry was in the gable wall, which in these instances also faced the sea.[5] Among certain groups, the door opening was through a large and elaborately carved totem pole; in some other cases, the entry was through the body or mouth of an effigy elaborately painted on the gable wall. Thus, entrance to the house symbolized acceptance within the tribe or clan.

Most houses were communal, sheltering as many as six families. In plan they were either square or oblong and they had a central pit in which cooking fires were laid. Some houses were excavated in the center to a depth of six feet or more. Mats and boards covered the ground around the sides and on narrow terraces leading down into the fire pit. Virtually all traces of these elaborate structures, with their magnificent carving and painting, have been lost, despite the fact that some were inhabited up to the beginning of the twentieth century.

8–1 Structural frame of a Northwest Pacific Indian plank house

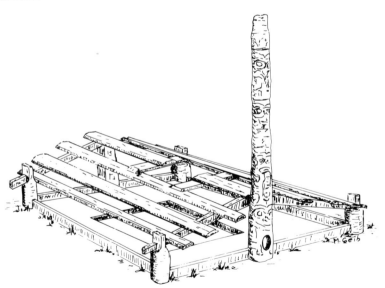

Other Indian dwellings

The role of American Indians in determining the cultural landscape in North America is multifaceted and complex. Not only did Indians successfully implant features of their own invention, they also were among the important adopters of European forms, especially those of the Spanish.

Earlier in eastern North America, Indian culture had been shattered by contact with the expanding European settlement. The bark-covered lodges of the forest-dwelling Indians disappeared fairly quickly from the eastern landscape.[6] In part, this was a result of the Indians' migration westward beyond the reach of European settlement or onto tiny reservations where they were encouraged to build "proper" houses of log, timber frame, or lumber following the European design. At the same time, by a process of acculturation, other Indians were adopting European building practices by their own free choice.

The disappearance of Indian folk dwellings also was partly due to the fact that Indian inhabitants were always few

and, as the land filled up with Europeans, the Indians became less and less conspicuous. Finally, the devastating effects of diseases, such as smallpox, caused Indian populations to drop precipitously in many areas.

The result of all these circumstances was the disappearance of the wigwam, the bark-covered, arch- or hemisphere-roofed lodge, and other types of Indian dwellings in eastern North America, and the substitution of wooden, gable-roofed, European structures among Indians. Only in the swamps of Florida did a few cheekees of the Seminoles survive the onslaught of European settlement.[7] Today, a few of these remain merely as tourist curiosities. Throughout eastern North America, Indian structures have exercised virtually no influence upon subsequent buildings. Even on the reservations, little evidence of earlier dwellings is perceptible.

8–2 The Plains Indian tipi

The Plains Indian tipi

A similar situation exists over the plains of central North America, where forests give way to prairie and steppe grasses, broken here and there by fingers of gallery forest along the major water courses. In these areas, partly because of the lack of available wood for building purposes, Indian dwellings were quite distinct from those of eastern North America. Also, the economy of the Plains Indians, which was oriented to hunting, involved a migratory existence, which demanded a light portable structure. Apparently, the effective occupation of the central plains roughly coincided with the importation of horses from Mexico, a change that provided the plains hunters with greatly increased mobility enabling them to find and follow the great bison herds upon which their existence came to depend.[8]

During the winter season, the Plains Indians grouped their habitations in small clusters, usually along stream courses where both water and firewood were available. In spring, summer, and fall, however, the Indians followed the game herds, camping in large circular encampments and moving every few days. The tipi (fig. 8–2) was admirably suited to this type of existence. Light, easily dismantled, and portable, it still was durable and efficient, both in the heat of the plains summer and in the bitter cold and biting winds of the winter season.

The frame of the tipi consisted of either three or four poles, each roughly twenty to twenty-five feet long. Within the entire expanse of the plains this kind of pole was available only along a few water courses or in small, scattered mountain ranges, such as the Black Hills, and they were highly prized. The lightest woods were most sought after, especially cedar or lodge-pole pine, whose use in tipis gave the tree its Anglo name. Once the basic frame of the tipi was established, somewhat lighter poles, as many as twenty per structure, were added by leaning them into the crotch of the original three or four, and placing the butt ends so as to form a large circle between twelve and twenty feet in diameter.[9] Over this frame was stretched a covering of buffalo skins sewn together. The skin covering was held together in the front by thin wooden or bone skewers.

The frame was erected in such a fashion that a tilted cone was created, more perpendicular in the back and more sloping in the front where its circular or oval door opening occurred. By tilting the structure, the smoke opening could be fashioned in front of the vertex of the cone and still be placed above a more or less centrally positioned fire pit. Smoke rose directly to the opening at the top, whose size could be altered by opening or closing two smoke flaps or "ears," each attached to a long pole outside the tipi (fig. 8–3). The bottom of the tipi cover was weighted down along the ground with whatever stones were locally available. Stone rings, left after the tipi was struck and moved, are a common relict feature in many areas of the plains.[10]

8–3   An Indian tipi at Old Fort Sill Museum, Oklahoma. Notice the ventilator flaps controlled by poles. (July 1974)

8–4   Area within which the Plains Indian tipi was used. From *The Indian Tipi: Its History, Construction, and Use* (2d ed), by Reginald and Gladys Laubin, p. 203. Copyright 1957, 1977 by the University of Oklahoma Press.

Perhaps the most important feature of the tipi, as far as providing comfortable living quarters, is the interior lining, which was originally of light skins and later of canvas or other lighter textile materials. This lining was hung from the poles and effectively created an insulating air space between the outer covering and the inner, so as to keep the tipi cooler in summer and warmer in winter.

The lining also helped create a draft to assist the central fire and it provided a screen so that the inhabitants of the tipi were not silhouetted against the outer covering. More important than the privacy that this gave was the security thus attained. A potential enemy would not have an obvious target.

The tipi was widely utilized until just before World War I (fig. 8–4). By that time the frontier had closed, the great bison herds had disappeared, and most Indian tribes had themselves been herded onto reservations where their life style was effectively altered.

Sod structures on the plains

The American and European settlers who advanced into the largely treeless prairie plains of central North America also had to adjust, and for them it was to an environment in which familiar building materials were largely lacking. Their needs were rather different from the Indians, however, since they were seeking permanent settlement sites. Therefore, unlike the Indians, they could employ heavy and bulky construction materials. These settlers also had the advantage of a higher level of technology and they had among their implements the steel plow. By using a specially designed "grasshopper plow," which instead of a mould board had a set of adjustable rods, a feature that prevented the turf from being turned over and destroyed,[11] they could cut furrows in the prairie surface. This process yielded sods subsequently cut into blocks. These sod blocks, which were sometimes referred to as "Kansas bricks," became the earliest standard

8–5 Probable extent of sod dwellings in North America

building material of white settlers on the plains.

Cass Barns suggests that the Mormons were the first to employ sod construction because, when they were thrown out of Nauvoo, Illinois, and began their westward migration, "they had only what they had been able to carry with them and they had only a few months to construct make-shift shelters and gather meager stores of supplies."[12] However, the widespread use of sod construction among Russian-Germans, who knew such techniques in Russia, strongly argues for a different origin. As westward movement of Mormons and other peoples continued, sod shelters were erected throughout the central plains wherever grasses were the dominant vegetation (fig. 8–5). Log, timber frame, and lumber, the chief building materials of eastern North America, also continued to be used, especially along the forested water courses, and, later on, along the railroads.[13]

Sod as a building material

Sod structures were built of necessity because other building materials were mostly lacking on the great expanses of prairie plains. In addition to availability and, hence, low cost, sod construction had other advantages. First, sod possessed excellent insulating qualities. Sod houses were cool in summer and quite warm during the bitterly cold winters typical of the prairies. Sod was a good fortress material "stopping arrows and slowing bullets." Sod structures could withstand the frequently violent winds of tornadoes and severe thunderstorms. Sod was a relatively easy material to

use; little more than average skill was needed to build a dwelling. Finally, sod structures were more or less safe from fire, especially if they were provided with a fire break. Such fire barriers were constructed by plowing seven or eight furrows around the property, leaving a space of ten to twelve feet and then plowing seven or eight furrows again. The grass in the space between was then carefully burned on a windless day.[14]

But sod structures suffered from important disadvantages, too. Because the entire building was of sod and dirt, the dwelling was alternately muddy or dust covered. Dirt kept filtering down from the ceiling, and most sod roofs leaked when it rained, which is not surprising considering the large number of capillary tubes and root channels that interlaced the sods. Unless the insides of the walls were plastered, the structure was not entirely weather-proof and the winter winds whistled through. Because sods were natural materials, they harbored mice, insects, and occasional snakes. Unless carefully made, walls settled unevenly and wooden structural members, such as ridge poles and rafters, were always put in "green" because settlers rarely could afford the luxury of waiting for them to season.[15] Therefore, these timbers might twist enough to encourage leaking or even to bring the structure down.

Time and money were of the essence for the pioneer immigrant. A sod house could be put up in about a week of hard labor; a sod dugout in just a few days. The sod house would cost considerably

71

8–6 The sod dugout

8–7 The sod house

less than five dollars, excluding labor costs; the dugout even less.

Sod dugouts and houses

It is not surprising then that sod dugouts were built by the thousands by pioneering settlers. Once a land claim was located and staked, the first task was to build some type of shelter. During the period of construction, a wagon usually served as a temporary house. Most critical was the locating of a suitable water source, but this seldom preceded the building of the dugout, sod house, or frame shack. Often quarters laboriously dug or built had to be subsequently abandoned in order to use a more convenient water supply.

The sod dugout (fig. 8–6) was a primitive affair, dug into the bank of a ravine, with luck above the limit of flood waters. The front of the structure was built up of sod blocks or, less often,

made of logs or poles.[16] Typical dimensions were eight to nine feet deep and perhaps twelve feet wide, often with only a single door to illuminate the interior. Whenever possible, dugouts faced eastward, away from the prevailing winds.[17]

The ridge line normally was at right angles to the slope of the land so that the major sod or log wall was the gable. The house entrance was through this wall in a major departure from earlier house building. Roofs were often ridged, but single-slope shed roofs slanting back into the hill were not uncommon. In fact, the dugout roof was often difficult to distinguish from the adjacent hillside itself. Roofs were comprised of poles, upon which a layer of brush was spread, which was then covered with additional layers of prairie grass, thick enough to hold a final covering of soil. Frequently, grasses, flowers, and weeds grew upon the roof, further obscuring its artificial nature.

Just how difficult it was to distinguish dugout roofs from natural hillsides is revealed by this early account:

After a time I saw something in the darkness that I took for a post, and believing we had come to a fence, I walked up to it and felt on both sides for the wires, but finding none, I put my hand on top of the supposed post and discovered to my dismay that it was a stovepipe, and still warm.

By the time my investigations had resulted in this warm discovery, Morrison had driven the team up quite close to me and demanded a reason for my stop. I explained the nature of my find, and suggested a careful backing up of the team for fear of a tumble through the roof, which would be likely to disturb the sleepers below. I had seen enough of "dugouts" to know that we had discovered one, but just how to get inside I did not know. After getting the team out of all possible danger, I started on a voyage of discovery. The problem of the lay of the dugout was soon solved to the satisfaction of all concerned. Of course it was dug out of a bank, but just where the bank ended and the house united with it I could not make out in the darkness; but I soon discovered that there was a space of about four feet between the end of the dugout—which had a wall of logs at the end —and the bank which sloped towards the house. The way I discovered this opening was by the happy one of falling into it, and the way I gained admittance into the house

72

was by rolling down the sloping bank and in at the window, and the way I aroused the household was by alighting on a promiscuous collection of tinware, which made noise enough to stampede a bunch of plow horses.[18]

There were three great problems of the dugout. First, they were poorly illuminated and ventilated. This condition resulted from their largely below-ground position and the consequent lack of door and window openings. Second, the structures were always small because of the immense labor required to excavate earth materials to obtain anything but a limited interior area. Finally, and most distressing, was the difficulty of maintaining dry interiors. Not only did roofs leak, underground drainage often permitted water to enter the dugout. The sod house, erected above ground, reduced or eliminated most of the problems associated with the dugout.

The sod house (fig. 8–7), nevertheless, was still a primitive structure. Most were small, averaging between twelve and sixteen feet wide by between fourteen and twenty feet long, consisted of only one or two rooms (fig. 8–8), and were rarely more than a single story in height. As with the dugout, the sod house normally was located along a valley or ravine, where it was protected from the more or less constant prairie winds. Such locations also had other advantages.[19] Drinking water was easier to find in the valleys, where the higher water table also provided the best sod for building. Finally, if timber were available anywhere, the valley was the most likely site and, therefore, the hauling of the timbers necessary for the roof was reduced.

The best time to break sods for build-ing purposes was when the prairie was thoroughly wet by either rain or snow.[20] Buffalo grass was the preferred sod because of its superior toughness,[21] but blue stem and slough grass also were widely used. Oxen were preferred for cutting sod-block furrows because their slow pace permitted straight furrows to be cut, and these produced the most uniform blocks or bricks.[22] The sod strips, which varied from twelve to eighteen inches, were cut into blocks eighteen to thirty-six inches long. These were hauled to the house site and usually laid in regular courses, the lowest placed directly on the ground. Rarely were footings of any kind used to secure the structure; sod buildings were universally viewed as temporary structures. Although Roger Welsch in 1968 called attention to the fact that "several

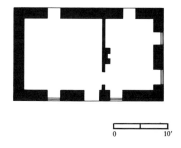

8–8 Floor plan of a sod house. Note the thickness of the walls.

sod houses remain standing in most counties of central and western Nebraska,"[23] the average life of a "soddy" as a dwelling was only six to seven years.[24]

The sod-block walls were laid up much as brick wall, with staggered joints. About every third course consisted of blocks laid endwise (headers). Hence, sod-house walls were between one and a half and three feet in depth. As the walls were raised, light lumber frames for a door and one or two window openings were placed in position. The frames were held in place by wooden dowels driven through the frame and into the surrounding sod.[25] The outside wall was frequently tapered but the inside wall was always as true as possible. The crevices between the sod blocks were carefully filled with soil. Sometimes wooden posts and strands of barbed wire[26] were used to protect and strengthen the corners, the weakest features of the building. Barbed wire had the added advantage of discouraging stray animals from rubbing against and weakening the corners of the house.

Also a potentially weak point, and always a vexing problem, was the roof, which because of its weight had to be stoutly supported. "When the roof was well soaked its weight was immense. The heavy rafters sank deeper and deeper into the soggy walls until occasionally the roof caved in or the walls collapsed, burying people underneath the ruins. To prevent this kind of accident, heavy posts were placed in the house to support the roof; these were a

73

great nuisance because they took up so much room."[27] The roof itself might be single slope, ridged, or hipped, although a low-gable form was most common. The ridge pole and the rafters were of whatever wood was available, but cedar, because of its straightness, strength, and light weight, was preferred. Several modes of roof covering were employed. The most common in the early period was a brush-and-pole roof. Light rafters were laid between the center ridge and the sod walls. At right angles over these was placed a layer of branches from plum, chokecherry, or other bushes, which in turn were covered by hay or dried wild prairie grass. The final covering was either sod with the grass side up, or sod, grass side down with a final topping of clay or alkali mud plaster. The latter version was more desirable because the reversed sods permitted less dirt to drop down from the ceiling and the mud plaster helped to seal the roof from water. Other roofing modes utilized vertical planks with battens, horizontal planks, lapped, rabbeted, or butted, and thin planks covered with shingles, tar paper, and/or canvas.[28]

The adjustment of the pioneer settlers to the demands of the plains environment was quite different from that of the Indian. The settlers' economy required a permanent abode, whereas the Indians needed a light, easily portable habitation. Ultimately, however, because of the higher technology that was available to them, the settlers were able to employ materials transported from outside the prairies and thus to establish their more efficient economic system. The Indians, who followed an economy far more primitive (although in many respects more in harmony with the prairie environment), simply could not compete for space, and after a series of violent clashes they were defeated and broken.

The Navajo hogan and ramada

At least two major Indian cultures, however, have persisted, and many of their members still inhabit traditional dwellings. The Navajo[29] represent the more primitive one with simpler dwellings, befitting the needs of the more mobile society.[30] Although the specific origins of the Navajo are obscure, they probably originated somewhere to the north as evidenced by the linguistic connection of Navajo with the Athabascan Indian languages of northwestern Canada.[31] The Gobernador Canyon in northwestern New Mexico appears to have been the cultural hearth from which the Navajo spread outward over much of the Colorado plateau (fig. 8–9). The domain occupied today by people of Navajo culture stretches from the Rocky Mountains to the Colorado River and is centered roughly over the

8–9 The probable hearth and domain of the Navajo tribe

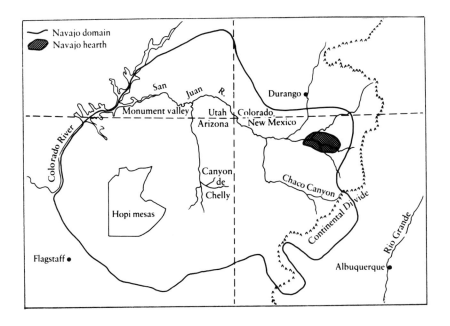

8–10 The Navajo ramada

8–11 Ruins of a primitive Navajo hogan of the leaning-log type. One of the main forked posts holding a roof beam can be seen in the wall gap on the right side of the structure. (Near Canyon de Chelly, July 1974)

four-corners intersection of New Mexico, Arizona, Colorado, and Utah.

Throughout this often desolate, arid region, building materials are in short supply, except, of course, for the clay that can be formed into adobe walls. Natural stone deposits from which rough blocks can be extracted are limited to specific sites, but they appear to have been used by the Navajo from early times. Because of the weight of stone, the difficulty of splitting it into smaller, more convenient pieces, and the lack of high-quality mortar, the use of stone was restricted to specific areas where, however, it may have been extensively employed as a building material.[32] In intermediate elevations, where rainfall is somewhat greater and piñon pine and juniper forests thrive, rough timbers were available. Heavier logs were used in mountainous areas for walls as well as for framing. Lighter timbers were transported greater distances[33] and often served as framing members and roof supports, both at higher and lower elevations.

With the changing seasons the Navajo economy also changed and so there was a need for two quite distinct dwellings. The ramada (fig. 8–10), which was easily erected and often lacking in sides to permit maximum air circulation, was the common shelter of the summer season.[34] During this period, the shelter might be shifted every few weeks as flocks migrated to new grazing grounds. The ramada was of light construction and was essentially a collection of poles tied together for the primary purpose of providing shade from the blazing summer sun of the Colorado plateau. Light branches, brush, and, sometimes, cut grasses usually provided the roofing materials. A light ladder might give ac-

cess to the roof, which could be used to store feed and to keep human food supplies safe from both grazing flocks and prowling wild animals. Very frequently, the side of the ramada that faced the prevailing wind was blocked by a combination of light poles, branches, and shrubby bushes to provide a modicum of protection from the wind-blown sand of daytime winds, as well as from chilly breezes during the typically cool nights of the plateau.

At the end of summer, the Navajo sought a different shelter. In earlier periods and over most of the domain, the sheepherding Navajos returned to the lower elevations of secluded valleys and canyons, which offered environments more conducive to grazing animals during the winter season. Water was usual-

75

ly available nearby, at least in limited quantities, and thus these valleys and canyons came to be occupied for the entire season. In other parts of Navajo territory where the economic emphasis was at least partly based on farming, an opposite seasonal migration pattern operated. In these areas the Navajo occupied the better-watered valleys and flood plains in the summer season but moved toward somewhat higher locations in the intermediate altitude piñon-pine and juniper zone as winter approached.[35] In both of these wintering areas, shelters were erected in small groupings that facilitated social intercourse.[36] Clearly, a more substantial and permanent building was called for during the winter.

The Navajo hogan is a building derived from an ancient stick house. Indeed, a few primitive forked-stick structures, largely in ruins (fig. 8–11), can still be found in the region, mostly in the more inaccessible western parts of the Navajo reservation.[37] Often these early hogans contained a dirt floor dug one or two feet into the ground.[38] A frame of three forked poles, interlocked to support the lighter sticks, branches, and earth that were piled up to form the rough walls was firmly anchored by having the butt ends of the poles slightly buried in the earth.[39] Sometimes, additional forked poles supported a lintel and formed a projecting doorway structure,[40] which broke up the conical surface of the rest of the hogan.[41]

More substantial hogans, usually built at later dates, were assembled from

8–12 The Navajo hogan, stone mode

8–13 A Navajo summer shelter, partially excavated, partially erected of stone and roofed with earth over piñon poles. The door and doorframe are of sawn lumber. (Near Zion National Park, 1969)

8–14 Floor plans of Navajo hogans

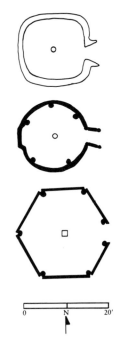

roughly cut stone blocks (fig. 8–12). Such hogans are common in certain parts of the Navajo domain where outcroppings of easily broken sandstone occur and where timber is absent. These structures are usually capped by a dome-shaped, tamped-earth roof supported by a crib of poles laid on the stone walls. Although Navajo hogans are erected buildings, a rough, partially excavated, summer shelter is often built in valleys where timber is scarce (fig. 8–13). These structures are not given a religious dedication ceremony as is the case with hogans, and in their construction, less attention is paid to form.[42] All the structures discussed above usually maintain the traditional circular or nearly circular floor plan (fig. 8–14).

Most recent hogans either are of timber frame covered with sawn plank walls or are entirely of rough-cut logs chinked with mud, stones, and small branches (fig. 8–15). The timbers, normally of piñon pine or juniper, are often

8–15 The Navajo hogan, log mode

twisted and irregular. Simple saddle notches hold the logs in place (fig. 8–16). In these two types of hogans, the floor plan is polygonal, its shape dictated by the desire to replicate the original circular shape, but restricted by the less-flexible nature of the building material. Six, eight, or nine is the most common number of sides. Whether round or polygonal, the typical hogan consists of a single room measuring roughly fifteen to twenty-five feet in diameter and rising five or six feet at the eaves.

The doorway usually faces east in order to catch the first rays of the rising sun.[43] In recently constructed hogans, a small gable may break the conical slope of the roof to provide additional height to the door and somewhat greater protection from the weather. Roofs may be in the form of a low dome if they are covered with earth or sod (see figs. 8–12 and 8–15), or they may be pyramidal if they are constructed of plywood, planks, or timber.

Recent features include tar-paper roofing and/or siding, stucco wall coating held in place underneath by chicken wire,[44] and a centrally positioned stove vent, which replaces the original smoke

8–16 Close-up of saddle notching of piñon-pine logs in the ruins of a hogan (near Canyon de Chelly, July 1974)

hole. The use of an iron stove for cooking as well as space heating is a distinct improvement over the traditional open pit fire, only a small part of whose smoke found the smoke vent quickly.

Originally intended to be occupied only during the winter season, many Navajo hogans gradually have come to be full-time dwellings, as Navajo Indians have modified their life style and economic pursuits and have become more sedentary. As a consequence, the ramada and the hogan often complement one another on a single building site. At the same time, of course, many Navajo have adopted house types derived from Europeans who have penetrated this area, or they have begun to modify the Navajo structures to incorporate European features.[45]

The Indian adobe pueblo

The second major Indian group that has
maintained much of its earlier culture
and that continues, at least in part, to
inhabit traditional dwellings is the
Pueblo. The modern-day Pueblo Indians live in areas that are vestiges of a
much larger domain occupied in the period prior to Spanish penetration (fig.
8–17). The hearth from which Pueblo
expansion began has not been studied
carefully or located accurately, but appears likely to have been near the four-
corners area, probably in the drainage
basin of the San Juan River. The contraction of the Pueblo culture area and
the migration to presently occupied
areas resulted from a variety of influences which are still not clearly under-
stood. The various explanations given
for the successive abandonments of
early settlement sites from the end of the
thirteenth century onward may be
grouped under six headings: droughts,
disastrous arroyo cutting that ruined
previously productive lands, feuds between and within settlements, epidemic
diseases, adverse ecological changes
that upset the local environmental
balance, and the depradations of nomadic raiders. Although individual
causes may have been most important
at particular locations, the effect of
nomadic raiders clearly had an impact
on the form of the habitations everywhere.[46] The early, scattered, one-room
structures came gradually to be replaced by multiple dwellings, which
were easier to defend because more de-

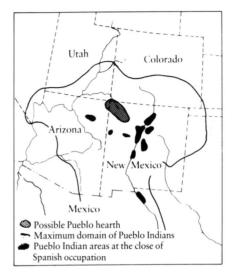

8–17 Areas influenced by Pueblo Indian
culture

Possible Pueblo hearth
Maximum domain of Pueblo Indians
Pueblo Indian areas at the close of
Spanish occupation

fenders were available to oppose the
nomadic attackers.

The word *pueblo* is Spanish and refers
to a village, town, or inhabited place.[47]
Thus, the term by which the Indian culture is known is intimately connected
with its settlement pattern. The earliest
dwellings of the Pueblo Indians were
one-room, rectangular or oval, pit habitations, dug between two and six feet
into the earth and covered with a roof of
saplings, brush, twigs, and mud, supported on rough poles. The only entrance was through a small opening,
usually in the middle of the roof and by
means of a ladder. Later dwellings were
more elaborate and built above ground,
but the early pit form has survived as a
special ceremonial structure, the *kiva*
(fig. 8–18).

First supplementing and then succeeding the early and individual pit houses,
rooms began to be constructed above
ground from about A.D. 700 onwards.
In a sense, these adobe or stone structures, which had no door or window
openings, were simply pit houses raised
up above ground level. Entrance was
from the roof by means of a ladder.
Thus, one had to climb to the roof and
then use the same ladder to descend
through the smoke hole into the interior. Needless to say, these buildings,
one or two rooms wide and several
rooms long, served admirably as defensive structures.

After A.D. 1000, pueblos grew considerably in size; as time passed and in response to the need for protection
against raiders, some pueblos added
fortifications and others retreated to inaccessible cliff-side locations, such as
those in Mesa Verde (fig. 8–19). Ultimately, most of the early settlement

8–19 View of the ruins at Mesa Verde. The circular structures are roofless kivas. (June 1967)

8–18 Wooden ladder projecting from the entry way of an underground kiva (Mesa Verde National Park, June 1967)

sites were abandoned and new sites were occupied in the Rio Grande valley and on mesa summits to the west. Individual pueblo settlements continued to expand, although the area of Pueblo cultural influence steadily was diminishing in the fourteenth and fifteenth centuries.

The typical adobe pueblo (fig. 8–20) in existence during the Spanish and American periods consisted of two or more large, elongated buildings, usually set roughly parallel to one another. The courtyard or plaza between the two buildings contained one or more kivas (Spanish: *stufas*), and the courtyard was sometimes limited by a right-angle extension of one of the buildings to form a third side of the courtyard.[48] The scale of these structures is often impressive. The northern block at Taos Pueblo, for example, is ten rooms deep and five stories high (figs. 8–20 and 8–21). A. F. Bandelier provides mea-

surements for the ruins of Pecos Pueblo, estimating one block to have been 460 feet by 65 feet, containing 517 rooms on four floors, while the second block measured 490 feet by 245 feet and contained 585 rooms on five floors.[49]

The basic unit of construction of the pueblo is the single room, normally measuring from seven feet by nine feet up to nine feet by eleven feet, although Victor Mindeleff indicates some rooms to have been considerably larger.[50] The room illustrated in figure 8–22, which is taken from Mindeleff, has a projecting adobe buttress dividing one side of the room into two work areas. That to the left contains a triangular bin faced with a thin stone slab, while to the right are three *metate* stones for grinding corn. The corner fireplace has a circular hood and chimney and the adobe floor has been paved with close-fitting, thin slabs of stone. Upper-level rooms, such as this

79

8–20 The Indian pueblo

8–21 Floor plans of the Indian pueblo illustrated in fig. 8–20

8–22 Plan of a one-room unit of a pueblo (after Victor Mindeleff)

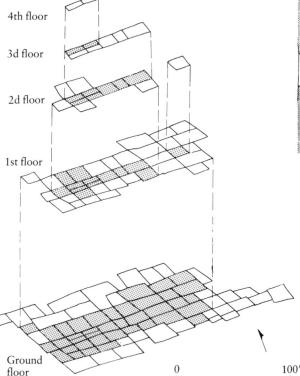

4th floor

3d floor

2d floor

1st floor

Ground floor

0   100′

one, often had more than one door.

Each family in the settlement occupied one or two rooms, sharing common walls with other families. Families were organized into matrilineal clans, which tended to cluster together within the pueblo. The rooms were roughly rectangular and built either of sandstone blocks with mud mortar to hold them in place, or of puddled-adobe construction. After contact with the Spanish, adobe bricks increasingly were employed.[51]

Apparently the need for defensive strength and a growing population were the impetus for upward growth. As units were added, creating upper floors, the entire structure became easier to defend. At the same time, lower units became less accessible, harder to light, and less well ventilated, so these rooms often came to be used for storage or were abandoned. The method of providing light and air to an interior room was by means of an oblique opening, which ran from the lowest part of an outside terrace wall into the highest part of the wall of an interior room (fig. 8–23). Generally, each succeeding floor was set back, especially on the east and south sides, by terraces on which cooking and other household activities were performed.[52]

Several distinctive minor features occupied the terraces (fig. 8–24). Ladders protruded from square roof entrances surrounded by low flat stone ridges to keep rainwater from draining into the opening. Roof drains pierced the otherwise unbroken parapet, and the parapet itself was protected from erosion by a coping of flat stones. Chimneys, often consisting of burned-out pots stacked upon one another and plastered with

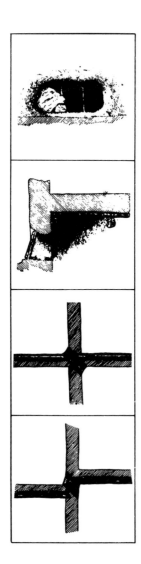

8–23 Frontal view and three cross sections of a typical oblique window opening for an interior room (from Victor Mindeleff)

adobe, provided outlets for the smoke of fires in rooms below.[53]

Although pueblo buildings are elongated, a cubic structure is readily apparent. The adobe walls, unbroken by windows or doors, combined with flat roofs and irregular terrace setbacks, emphasize the cubic block appearance, which has considerable aesthetic appeal.

Once the Pueblos were no longer forced by fear of attack to live on the upper levels of their community houses, they began to utilize ground floor rooms with windows and doors, or they built new blocks of unfortified houses, generally of only one story. . . . The pueblos are rapidly losing their architectural integrity as foreign materials (concrete block, aluminum windows, wrought iron porch supports, brightly painted hard stucco or even Permastone wall surfaces, hollow core doors, and ridge roofs covered with tar paper or metal sheets) disrupt the old harmony of adobe and timber that was so simple and so beautiful. The widespread introduction of fenestration employing large, undivided sheets of glass destroys the scale

8–24 Certain minor features were quite characteristic of the terraces of an Indian pueblo. Stacks of burned-out pots functioned as chimneys, *vigas* protruded through adobe walls which were often capped by stone copings, wooden *canales* led off rainwater which dripped against sloping stone slabs. Wooden ladders gave access to different levels.

of the building and nullifies its solid geometric character. Similarly the extension of house fronts to a common building line in imitation of American practice diminishes the lively modular character of the pueblo which was one of its most important visual assets.[54]

The influence of Anglo building is steadily becoming more pervasive among the Pueblo Indians. In the early years of the twentieth century, squarish,

81

8–25 Taos Pueblo, perhaps the best remaining example of an Indian adobe pueblo. The beehive-shaped ovens are of Spanish origin. Windows and doors are late additions. (June 1967)

single-room, detached stone houses with pyramidal roofs began to be built on the perimeters of the pueblo. After World War II, cement block replaced cut stone, and the pyramidal roof gave way to the gable roof. Furthermore, houses assumed a rectangular form and began to contain two, three, or four rooms.[55]

In the final analysis, the character of the Indian pueblo is, in large part, the result of using adobe as wall and roof material. It provides, at one and the same time, a smooth, straight, regular surface and a moulded, irregularly textured surface (fig. 8–25).

Adobe as a building material

Adobe is the term applied to clay used in an unfired condition for building purposes. The clay is mixed with water, shaped in the desired form, and permitted to dry. Once dried, the adobe will retain its form and strength unless exposed to moisture. Adobe structures are especially prevalent in desert or near-desert areas. However, even in humid areas, mud can be plastered against a frame to form a wall (the *daub* of wattle and daub), if it is protected sufficiently from falling rain and splashing water.

Moisture is the great nemesis of adobe buildings.[56] Not only can water splash upward after falling on the ground as rain or eave runoff, thus rapidly eroding and undercutting the structure, but also moisture can spread more slowly and insidiously, softening by capillary action and thus weakening adobe walls.

Roofs are also critical areas. Although the typical pueblo roof is a complicated affair consisting of at least five layers, the basic roof material is earth or clay (fig. 8–26). In general, the adobe roof is composed of large rafters of round, straight poles over which a layer of much thinner poles is laid at right angles. Over this a covering of thin branches, brush, reeds, or grass is placed.[57] Upon this, wet mud is poured and finally a top layer of firmly trampled earth is formed. Sometimes the underside of the roof (i.e., the ceiling) is chinked with small stones to reduce the constant sifting of dried earth.[58] Since

8–26 Exposed adobe roof construction (from Victor Mindeleff)

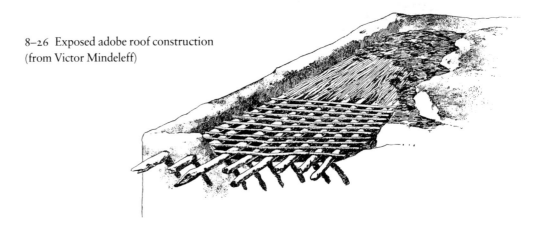

the major roof covering is earth, any leak in the roof is stopped by plastering the offending area with another layer of mud.

Because major roof beams were scarce and hence particularly valuable, they were taken from ruined or abandoned buildings and used over and over again. The Indians lacked iron tools, such as axes or hatchets, and they did not bother to trim beams to fit smaller rooms. As a result, beam ends projecting through the adobe walls became a common feature of pueblos.[59]

Adobe roofs baked under the blazing sun normally provide adequate protection from the widely spaced desert rains. The capillary action that weakens walls also permits adobe roofs to absorb considerable rainwater. During heavy rains, the excess water must be removed from the flat roof by wooden or stone drains projecting through the parapets. Figure 8–27 shows several types of roof drains, or *canales*, used in Indian pueblos. The areas surrounding these drains represent potential trouble spots. Water spilling over or penetrating under the canales can rapidly destroy a large wall section if it is not kept under repair.

Adobe has much to recommend it as a building material. It is cheap, readily available, and reasonably durable in dry climates. Normally it is quite easy to repair and only simple skills are needed to manipulate this material. Modification of existing structures is readily accomplished. Finally, it provides good thermal insulation. The Indian utilized adobe widely as *puddled adobe* in which form walls were painstakingly built up, layer by layer, by applications of wet mud. The Spanish-Mexican tech-

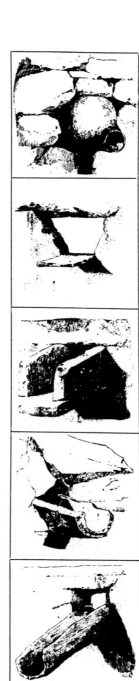

8–27 Types of roof drains, made of wood, stone, or old clay pots (from Victor Mindeleff)

8–28 A new wall being constructed in Taos Pueblo in 1967. The Spanish-derived adobe bricks are being used rather than the puddled-adobe Indian technique. Wooden window frames are also a late innovation.

nique of adobe construction was different in that it involved the use of rough bricks, formed in a wooden frame and well dried before they were made into a wall (fig. 8–28). Straw was often added as a binding material to provide greater strength and to lessen the effects of contraction upon drying.[60]

83

The Spanish-Mexican building techniques

Of the two cultural groups whose centers or hearths lay outside western United States, the Spanish were by far the more important. Highly significant in its cultural thrust was the expansion of Spanish material settlement forms, which ultimately spread across the entire southwestern quarter of the United States. Not only were Spanish features brought by migrants moving northward from the cultural hearth located in the southern part of the Mexican plateau, but also many features were popularized through their adoption by the Indian inhabitants of the American Southwest.

Spanish influences in what later became southwestern United States began at the very close of the sixteenth century with the introduction of settlers into the middle Rio Grande valley, although earlier Spanish exploratory thrusts already had occurred.[61] The important Spanish penetrations into California and Texas did not take place until the middle of the eighteenth century.[62] Eventually, however, Hispanic culture came to influence a vast segment of the American southwest (fig. 8–29), in the process providing a distinctive approach to building that utilized local materials thoroughly adapted to the rigorous climate of the region.

The Spanish used adobe mostly in the form of roughly made bricks, though they employed it in some plastering, both exterior and interior. In higher elevations a Mexican log building technique, probably evolved from techniques introduced in the sixteenth century by German miners in central Mexico,[63] utilized the more abundant forest resources. Rough quarried sandstone also was employed for selected buildings in locations near stone deposits, but this material was never widely used, probably because of its cost and the skills needed to cut and dress it. The overwhelming number of structures built by the Spanish-Mexicans in southwestern United States were either of adobe or *jacal*.

Jacal is the Spanish term for a type of construction quite similar to wattle and daub, and it also refers to the flat-roofed building in which such construction is employed. The term is derived from the

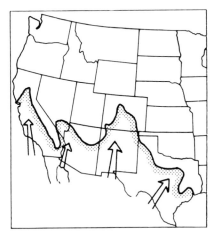

8–29 Limits of the Hispanic domain in southeastern United States (after Nostrand)

Aztec, *xa-calli* which means "adobe house or house of straw, a humble dwelling." The English term *shack* apparently is also derived from these Indian and Spanish words.[64] In jacal buildings, poles or branches of wood are held in place vertically by fastening them to a framework of heavier wooden pieces, consisting of corner and side posts and sometimes a sill and plate. Horizontal girts, also of light poles, keep the vertical poles in line. This light frame is covered over with adobe plaster. Because jacal construction is light, and hence quite perishable, little of it has survived except in interior house partitions and in recent animal shelters and storage buildings.[65]

A later method of construction, also sometimes called *jacal*, closely resembles the French *poteaux-en-terre*, consisting of light upright posts fitted into a groove in a horizontal log that functions as a plate. This method of building may very well have been derived from French sources. Little serious study has been devoted to it to determine its extent and its antecedents.

The Spanish-Mexican contribution to American building types is limited primarily to two examples, the Spanish adobe house and the Monterey house, an amalgam of Spanish-Mexican and Anglo ideas.

The Spanish adobe house

Adobe is the standard building material of the Spanish-Mexicans and the flat-roofed, earth-colored, rectangular dwelling is the standard early housing structure of the Hispanic domain (fig. 8–30). Still, because adobe is essentially a perishable material, and an even more easily modified material, little remains of early domestic structures.

The earliest Spanish-Mexican dwellings were single-room houses constructed of adobe. Later, houses of two, three, or more rooms were built, but they were normally arranged in a line to produce a markedly elongated, rectangular building. Ultimately, the Spanish adobe house evolved in which rooms surrounded an open courtyard, the whole being termed the *casa*. Adjoining the dwelling was another, rather similarly arranged structure, the *corral*, in which light storage buildings and animal shelters, often of jacal construction, combined with adobe stables and cow houses to surround the open central area. Access to both corral and casa was through a covered entrance, as deep as the file of rooms and secured by a stout gate (fig. 8–31). In California the same house was built without the attached corral. Since all these structures generally were only one story high and the roof was flat or very gently sloping, the silhouette was very low, blending in with the surroundings.

The roof of the Spanish adobe house was formed of larger wooden beams, called *vigas*, which were normally about fifteen or sixteen feet long, thus determining the width of Spanish-Mexican rooms and houses. The viga rafter beams, spaced two or three feet apart, supported lighter materials, such as aspen, willow, or cottonwood poles, or split cottonwood or cedar, laid diagonally (to form a herringbone pattern) or at right angles. Over these materials, called *latias*, was the outer coating of adobe mud.

Distinctive fireplaces occupied the corners of the more important rooms, with the less significant rooms remaining unheated. The fireplaces were not deep, but projected into the room and were covered by a hooded adobe flue to catch the smoke.

8–30 The Spanish adobe house

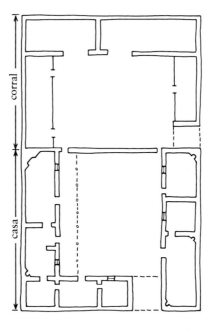

8–31 Floor plan of the fully elaborated Spanish adobe house

Window and door openings were few and small. Wooden shutters kept out the chilly night air, as well as the heat of midday.[66] Not until the American period was much window glass available. Windows usually opened out into the central courtyard of the Spanish adobe house. Since penetration of the structure could normally only be accomplished at the two gates, and since the entire structure was fireproof, the building served a defensive function quite well in the early Spanish-Mexican period.[67]

85

The Spanish adobe house gradually declined after railroads penetrated the Southwest, making dimension lumber available for housing. Furthermore, the widespread use of barbed wire after the 1880s encouraged range fencing and corrals located away from the homestead.[68]

The housing in southwestern United States that has been derived from Spanish sources has not been adequately studied and additional house types, or at least variants of already recognized types, may be identified in the future. A. W. Conway, for example, has suggested the presence in northern New Mexico of an adobe house capped with a gable-roofed, loft storage area.[69] This *alto*, which is entered from the outside through a small door in the wooden gable end and not from inside the dwelling, is a later addition to the adobe house. The steeply pitched roof is placed directly upon the adobe parapet rather than on the floor, so as to secure additional space and to provide maximum headroom in the loft. Northern New Mexico, with higher elevations and more abundant forest resources, is also the location of a Spanish-Mexican log building tradition.[70]

The Monterey house

The other major house type associated with the Spanish-Mexican tradition is the Monterey house (fig. 8–32). It evolved, as its name suggests, around Monterey, California, at the end of the

first third of the nineteenth century and combines Spanish-Mexican building techniques with American ideas.[71] The combination was surprisingly successful and produced an attractive, well-proportioned building that fitted the Mediterranean-like climate of California very nicely.

The Monterey house is comprised of two stories, built of adobe brick, and finished with an exterior plaster of adobe, lime, or stucco. The floor plan consists of three, four, or more rooms arranged in a file in the normal Hispanic pattern. A distinctive feature of the house, and one that helps create unity in the structure, is the long balcony supported on the extended vigas of the first-floor ceiling. Each room has at least one door opening onto the balcony, which thus serves as a hallway. A second balcony often was added at the rear of the house. In some instances, the overhanging balcony is supported by slim wooden pillars and is used to cover a long verandah.

The roof of the Monterey house follows American rather than Spanish-Mexican practice. The roof style may be either hipped or a rather low-pitched gable, but almost always the roof material is baked tile, burned to a dull red or orange hue.

Low one-story wings frequently extended to the rear, often enclosing a garden in the best Mediterranean traditions, and, incidentally, establishing the precedent upon which generations of later California ranch houses would be built, not only in California, but throughout the rest of the country after World War II.

8–32 The Monterey house

The Mississippi River knits the Great Lakes to the Gulf of Mexico, providing a great natural routeway to the interior of the North American continent. The French were the earliest to appreciate the full significance of the Mississippi and they made valiant, if unsuccessful, efforts to secure dominion over it.

Ultimately, however, the tide of settlement moved, not along the river, but across it, although the routes of the Mississippi's major east-west tributaries, the Ohio and the Missouri, were advantageously used. Americans of Anglo stock, together with newly arrived European immigrants, streamed westward throughout the late eighteenth and nineteenth centuries. The tide was stemmed only briefly by the War of 1812 and the resistance of determined Indian groups fighting for survival.

The advancing American pioneers carried concepts about houses and other structures from the East. Some of the routes of movement and some of the modifications that occurred over time and distance are considered in chapter 10.

Those settlers who arrived directly from Europe, or in some instances via the Caribbean, introduced new house types. To be sure, a number of these houses shared common characteristics of buildings found in the Atlantic seaboard hearths. Thus, some French houses in Louisiana resembled houses in the St. Lawrence valley, certain German structures in Missouri and Wisconsin are related to houses of the early Germans in eastern Pennsylvania, and so on.

This chapter discusses the houses erected by the French, one of the three most important early European groups to settle central United States. The French initiated settlement of the Gulf Coast between 1699 and 1722, ultimately establishing a cultural hearth in the eighteenth century along the lower Mississippi River in the vicinity of New Orleans.[1] The French subsequently attempted, via the Mississippi River basin and the Great Lakes, to establish a link with the other, earlier French hearth, that of the St. Lawrence valley. Much later, German settlers, responding in the early and mid-nineteenth century to the lure of cheap land and free institutions, created a much less cohesive cultural landscape, which is most apparent in Missouri and Wisconsin. Still later in the nineteenth century, other Teutonic settlers, the German-Russians, flooded the western plains as the last of the migrating Europeans to occupy much territory in North America. These latter two groups will be discussed in chapter 10.

French settlement in the Mississippi valley and delta

The European group making the earliest cultural impact in central United States was the French, whose long occupation of the Mississippi valley was interrupted for about forty years (1762–1800) by Spanish control. The Spanish, however, failed to impress their stamp of culture as strongly here as they did both to the east in Florida (see chap. 7) and to the west in Texas and beyond (see chap. 8). Although modest numbers of Spanish settlers were drawn to New Orleans, elsewhere in the valley "with the exception of officers and soldiers to represent authority, less than a dozen Spaniards took up their abode . . . in the forty years it belonged to Spain."[2]

With the initial establishment of French authority around New Orleans, a great natural interior routeway fell under their influence. French fur trappers and traders, pushing westward from the St. Lawrence hearth via the Great Lakes, could, by a series of easy

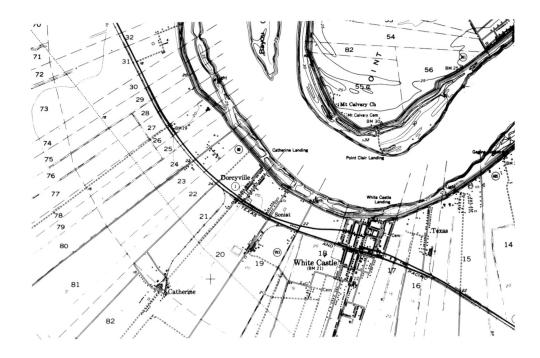

9–1 The French connection. French settlements and routes of communication in the seventeenth century. (1) Maumee-Wabash rivers; (2) Chicago-Illinois rivers; (3) Wisconsin-Fox rivers; (4) St. Croix River.

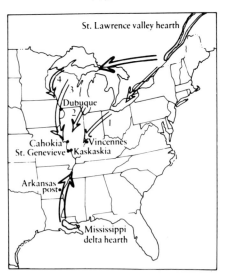

9–2 The French land system appears clearly on a USGS topographic map of White Castle, Louisiana. Whenever possible the lot lines are perpendicular to the river.

portages, cross over the Great Lakes drainage to that of the Mississippi system. At least four important routes were used: the Maumee-Wabash rivers; the Chicago-Illinois rivers; the Wisconsin-Fox rivers; and the St. Croix River. The large number of surviving French names is indicative of these early movements throughout the area. At least six important early French outposts were still thriving when, at the beginning of the nineteenth century, American settlement met and overwhelmed them (fig. 9–1).

French occupation of New Orleans provided the control over the mouth of the Mississippi that might have secured that river for the French and restricted American expansion to the eastern third of the North American continent. The early failure of the French to successfully encourage emigration and their later impotence stemming from defeat in the Seven Years War combined with the Napoleonic preoccupation with the East and the bitter memories of the Haitian rebellion to seal the fate of their hopes for empire in North America.

The French left behind them in the Mississippi valley material traces of their occupation, as they had to a greater extent in the St. Lawrence valley. Undoubtedly, the most significant French settlement feature, and the easiest to identify, is the long-lot system of land division along the Mississippi flood plain (fig. 9–2). Here, in contrast to the St. Lawrence valley, transverse roads frequently do not coincide with the *rang* boundary and, hence, the elongated rang-settlement form never developed extensively. Only in the Cajun country west of New Orleans, where French settlement is most concentrated, is the suggestion of the rang village found.

Within the area of southern and western Louisiana a quite distinctive settlement landscape has evolved, partly as a result of French-Cajun influence and partly in response to the natural environment of poor drainage, swampy forests, and the high salinity of the ground water. The Cajuns, so named because they originated in Acadia (French-settled Nova Scotia), entered the bayou country of Louisiana after being expelled from their former home by the British in 1755. A few Acadians came directly to Louisiana from Nova Scotia, but more were first sent to other British North American colonies. An even larger number fled first to the French colonial possessions in the Caribbean, such as Santo Domingo, or to France itself.

The grenier house

The Acadian settlers established their own culture upon the foundation of earlier French and German settlements.[3] Among the more distinctive cultural features within the Cajun landscape is a building that has been called the *Acadian house*.[4] In the Louisiana delta and farther eastward along the Gulf of Mexico coast, the structure is known as the *Creole house*.[5] To complicate the situation further, an unnamed but almost identical house type is reported in black settlements along the Mississippi River between Baton Rouge and New Orleans.[6] It seems likely that these are all subtypes of a basic structure that may be termed the *grenier house*, the name derived from the French designation for its oversized loft, which projects forward over the open, front *galerie*, or verandah.[7]

The grenier house (fig. 9–3) is the standard French house of rural Louisiana. Among other early ethnic groups, the front porch is usually clearly added as an afterthought, tacked on to the main structure and having a separate

9–3 The grenier house

roof of different pitch from the main roof. The *grenier*, however, is an obvious part of the original design of the French house, as is the *galerie*. Together they provide a profile that distinctively marks this structure. Originally used as sleeping quarters for the bachelor members of the family,[8] in which instance it was referred to as a *garçonnière*, the grenier functions today mostly for storage of such things as grains, pelts, and animal traps.

These buildings are usually of frame construction and covered with cypress siding. In the earliest period, the roof was either palmetto leaves or cypress shingles. Structures were raised several feet off the ground, originally on cypress stumps, later on cypress posts, and finally on cement blocks or pillars. One reason for elevating the building is that better cooling is made possible by permitting air to circulate under the structure. Another reason that is cited is that it offers protection—against flood waters (which are always a hazard in the low-lying delta), against rotting from contact of the timbers with the constantly moist ground, and against termites. Finally, the elevation permits an enhanced view of the surrounding flatness of the delta.[9]

Perhaps the most easily recognizable characteristic of the grenier house is its built-in porch. The porch, or more properly the galerie, is deep, defined by several wooden pillars, and spreads entirely across the front of the house, providing a living area shaded from the sun, sheltered from the frequent rains, and yet open to whatever cooling breezes may blow.

The front wall of the house, at the back of the galerie, normally is treated differently from the other walls. Sometimes it is even made of different material, perhaps coated with mud plaster or stucco, and either whitewashed or painted, which the rest of the house is not.[10]

Another important diagnostic feature is the narrowness of the roof overhang, which gives these houses a clipped appearance, as if they had been cut off prematurely (fig. 9–4). The pitch of the roof is quite steep, adding to the distinctive appearance of these houses. The chimney is usually in the center of the ridge line, although in early and very small examples of this house, the chimney, which was often made of mud with Spanish moss serving as a binder, was located outside the gable wall. Jay Edwards has suggested that exterior gable chimneys are a borrowing from the Upland South culture.[11]

The most typical floor arrangement has two front rooms, each with a door opening onto the galerie (fig. 9–5). Each room contains a hearth connected to a centrally placed chimney. Behind the main rooms are two smaller ones used as bedrooms. Because all the rooms are small, the outside doors, which are of the French type, i.e., full-length double doors, open outward to conserve interior space. Window shutters also open outward, and both doors and windows were customarily painted only on the inside. Thus, during the daylight hours

9–4 An example of a grenier house in the French Quarter, New Orleans (April 1978)

the doors and window shutters decorated the galerie and the outside of the house, whereas after dark they brightened the interior.[12]

William Knipmeyer has demonstrated, by examining typical floor plans, that an evolutionary sequence exists among grenier houses, from single-room structures with an outside stairway on the galerie to houses of eight to ten rooms with a rear stairway.[13] William Rushton suggests that the former are typical of Cajun buildings, whereas the latter are of Creole origin.[14]

Construction materials also are different in the two groups, which again serves to emphasize the difference in af-

9–5 Floor plan of a grenier house

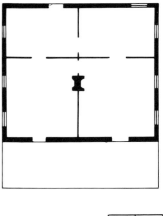

fluence between Cajuns and Creoles. Cajuns, who lived on the river levees but close to the bayou swamps, used a mixture called *bousillage*, which was made of Spanish moss, mud, and sometimes calcined seashells as an infilling between hewn, vertical timbers. As their economic levels increased, Cajuns turned to the abundant resources of the bayous for cypress wood to use as cladding. Creole builders, on the other hand, may occasionally have employed bousillage in the very early times, but were much more likely to use soft bricks as wall nogging.[15] Furthermore, their houses might be raised on brick foundations or brick piers. Often the more elaborate examples had full lower stories of brick. Many of the later, and most of the larger, grenier houses had prominent hipped roofs, whereas the Acadian houses primarily employed the gable roof.

Additions to the basic grenier house are made in a variety of ways. One of the more unusual is made by erecting an attached similar but, generally, smaller house at the rear of the original structure. Unlike virtually all building additions elsewhere, the ridge line of the addition is parallel to that of the original house, which creates a roof valley between the two parts.[16]

A unique minor characteristic of grenier houses in the Cajun bayou country was the kitchen tablette, a shelf built outside a kitchen window so that the housewife could place a dishpan on it and wash dishes or do other wet work outside while remaining inside. A small roof sometimes sheltered the tablette from the sun or rain.[17]

Few studies have been made of the grenier house outside Lousiana, al-though it undoubtedly has diffused over a wider area. Many grenier features are found on French-derived houses in Missouri, for example. The grenier house's most distinctive feature, the built-in porch, is typical of other houses, especially those built where German influence is known to have been operating.[18] Although it is possible that such a feature is of German origin (early German settlers were also well established in those areas of Louisiana where the grenier house was most common), it is much more likely that the grenier house is a derivation of Yoruba housing, modified by intermediate transferal to Haiti.[19]

Mississippi Valley French houses

Elsewhere in the Mississippi valley, two other house types were built that are indisputably French, or at least French-Canadian, in origin. Because French settlement was insignificant after the end of the eighteenth century, only a handful of these early structures still exist, except in the French Quarter and the Creole faubourgs of New Orleans. Elsewhere the greatest concentration is in the small village of Ste. Genevieve, Missouri.

The houses built in the mid-Mississippi valley by the French are derived from earlier French structures in the St. Lawrence valley,[20] modified by French contact with influences from the Caribbean.[21] So few structures have survived that generalizations must be made with extreme caution and must be somewhat tentative.

On the basis of overall plan and exterior form, two subtypes of Mississippi Valley French houses may be recognized. The first subtype (fig. 9–6) is clearly related to the Norman cottage of the St. Lawrence valley (fig. 9–7). The plan consists of two main rooms, usually flanked by small bedrooms at the ends of the structure. In the earliest houses the chimney was centered, as in Canada, but later the chimneys were constructed at the ends of the building.

The basic hipped roof of the Norman cottage was retained, although it was modified by the addition of a deep galerie on two, three, or all four sides. A Caribbean connection for this house is confirmed by the term *St. Dominique house*, the name sometimes earlier applied to it in the mid-Mississippi valley,[22] although the exact nature of that connection has not been investigated. Typical roof pitches measure roughly fifty-two degrees, with the end slopes inclined about seventy-two degrees. The galerie roof pitches are, of course, much lower.[23] The roof was covered originally with thatch, but as time went on, wooden shingles were used increasingly. Shingles had several advantages over thatch: easily split wood from which they were made was more plentiful than suitable reeds; they were less susceptible to fire; they were more durable, needing replacement less frequently; and they formed a roof better able to shed moisture, especially melting snow.

The overall effect of the wide galleries is to give the house a hooded appearance that makes it appear much larger than it really is. As in the grenier house, the galleries are normally eight or nine feet deep, in order to provide maximum shade. The posts frequently rest directly on the ground or on very small stone pilings.

Wood in contact with the ground, termed *poteaux en terre*, was also characteristic of wall construction employed by the French. In this method, a trench marking the line of the wall was dug. Squared hewn logs were placed upright in the trench and secured with a heavy plate beam. The trench was backfilled and the chinks between the logs filled with a mortar of mud and grass or lime mortar and stone fragments.[24] Mul-

9–6 The Mississippi Valley French house (type 1)

berry, red cedar, and cypress were the woods usually used because they were most rot resistant.

The exterior of the house frequently was left to weather gradually, or it may have been covered with a white lime wash. Few houses were painted. The recessed walls in the galerie, in any case, were whitewashed to reflect the heat and because it was "healthful."[25] Interiors were normally plastered and covered with whitewash, which must have been a constant nuisance because it rubs off on the slightest contact. The dooryard of the house was enclosed by a palisadoed wall, affording both protection and privacy (fig. 9–8). Within the villages, the advantage of having all the private lots enclosed is obvious. By merely barricading the ends of the street in an emergency, it would be possible to enclose the entire village for defense.[26]

The second subtype of the Mississippi Valley French house (fig. 9–9) may be a derivative of the Quebec cottage of the

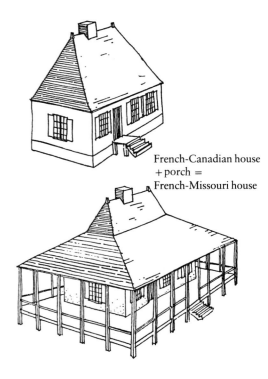

French-Canadian house
+ porch =
French-Missouri house

9–7 Probable derivation of the Mississippi Valley French house, type 1 (from Peterson, "Early Ste. Genevieve and Its Architecture," p. 227)

St. Lawrence valley. The floor plan is two rooms deep, sometimes with a central hallway. A high percentage of early French houses were squarish, a shape that may be partly due to the abundance of long straight timber for rafters that permitted a wider house, and partly to the severe winters that favored a compact plan with peripheral heating sources.[27]

The basic roof is gable rather than hipped, a modification that, because it allows windows, permits better second-story ventilation and lighting.[28] In contrast to the first subtype, which has only one story, the second subtype has a finished upper half story, to which dormers have been added for better headroom and light.

On these houses, the galerie might surround the structure, but just as often it

9–8 The Bolduc House in Ste. Genevieve, Missouri. An example of a Mississippi Valley French house, type 1. Note the enclosing palisade fence. (November 1979)

masked only the front and rear (fig. 9–10). The lower pitch of the galerie roof provided a broken silhouette when viewed from the gable. The second subtype also was apt to be raised upon a stone basement. In all instances, the timber frame of these buildings was placed upon some sort of foundation so that the upright posts did not come into contact with the damp ground (*poteaux sur solle* construction), a distinct advantage in the periodically moist climate of the Mississippi valley.

9–9 The Mississippi Valley French house (type 2)

Finally, although a large number of stone houses were built in St. Louis and elsewhere in the region, none has survived. It is understandable that urban growth in St. Louis and other early centers has erased the first buildings, but it is strange that no stone structures survived in the smaller settlements and countryside, unless stone was too expensive to be used except in the most cosmopolitan center. Perhaps because good building stone was available and timber was plentiful and cheap, no brick structures were erected by the French in the mid-Mississippi valley.

9–10 An eighteenth-century Mississippi Valley French house, type 2. Located in Ste. Genevieve, Missouri. (December 1979)

9–11 The Louisiana plantation house

The Louisiana plantation house

In Louisiana and elsewhere in the lower Mississippi valley, building stone was not available because rock outcrops were buried under accumulated riverine sediments. As a consequence, large prestigious houses utilized walls of *colombage* (wood posts with brick nogging between). Because bricks were soft and porous, they were normally covered by cement or board siding.[29]

The Louisiana plantation house (fig. 9–11) has a number of characteristics that distinguish it from other structures. The main floor is raised a full story on brick piers as a concession to the damp ground. The brick ground floor is used for the kitchens, store rooms, and other service areas.

Galleries normally are placed on the front and rear of the house, and, less often, on the sides. The basic plan of the house consists of two files of rooms, with frequent door and window openings onto the galleries (fig. 9–12). Beginning about 1820, a central hallway was introduced, together with a large, centrally situated stairway from the ground level to the front galerie.[30] Double French doors and hinged casement windows, also frequently double, are typical. Small bedrooms break the line of the galleries at the rear corners of the house.

The immense roof is the most conspicuous feature of the house. Three distinct forms are used. Probably the earliest was similar to roofs of the Mississippi Valley French houses, with a hipped central area flanked by roofs of lower pitch over the galleries. A second simpler type, in which a hipped roof of one single pitch covered the entire structure, appears to be the most common. The expanse of the roof was, more often than not, broken by a series of gable roof dormers, sometimes on all four sides. The third roof variant is that of the front-to-back gable,[31] resembling the roof of the grenier house.

The Louisiana plantation house is a large and impressive structure, rising a full two stories and often measuring forty by sixty feet, although smaller structures also were built. Much less pretentious are other French houses that belong to the "shotgun" family.

9–12 Floor plan of a Louisiana plantation house

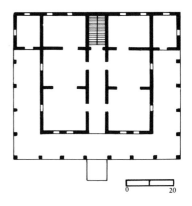

94

9–13 Two versions of the shotgun house

was solved in some houses by incorporating a narrow front-to-rear hallway along one side of the building. Such an arrangement is particularly common in Ohio valley shotgun houses.[35] In such houses, the facade is broken by two windows and an off-center doorway. Other shotgun houses may have one or two windows and the door may be centered or not, although the uncentered door is more common.

Both gable and hipped roofs covered shotgun houses (see fig. 9–13). The hipped roof was used before the gable and wide overhanging bell-cast eaves

9–14 Floor plan of a shotgun house

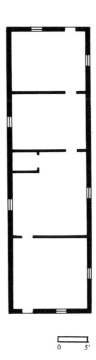

The shotgun, double shotgun, and corner-porch shotgun houses

Shotgun houses obviously owe something to the French, but this connection is indirect. John Vlach has shown that the shotgun house is derived from structures built in and around Port-au-Prince, Haiti, and introduced into New Orleans and southern Louisiana by free Haitian blacks about the beginning of the second quarter of the nineteenth century.[32]

The shotgun house (fig. 9–13) is unmistakable because of its narrow facade and extreme length, a configuration produced by the front to rear arrangement of a single file of rooms. Linearity and depth are the hallmarks of this house type. The name, by agreed folk traditions, refers to the alignment of all doorways within the house, "so that a shotgun blast fired in the front door would exit through the rear door." It is

much more likely that the term is a corruption of the west African word *to-gan* (place of assembly).[33] Whereas some of the earlier houses had such a door arrangement, later houses tend to have nonaligned doorways (fig. 9–14). In certain instances, the rear of the house contains an entryway added on to the side of the structure (fig. 9–15); in other cases, such an addition may have been made later and contains a bathroom.

The earliest shotgun houses were two rooms deep, following the Haitian pattern almost exactly. Vlach found both inside and outside dimensions of houses in the two areas to correspond.[34] However, with time, a third and even a fourth room was added to the rear of the house. The rear room is invariably the kitchen and the front room is the living room, with bedrooms between. The lack of privacy encountered when three or more rooms adjoined one another

95

were also common in the early period. After the mid-nineteenth century, a roofed front porch replaced the wide roof overhanging the gable.[36]

The form of the shotgun house was well designed for the hot humid climate of the lower Mississippi valley. Cooling and drying generally were more important considerations than heating. The single file of rooms permitted cross ventilation and the high ceilings helped keep the room temperatures bearable in the sultry summers. Rural shotgun houses were raised on cypress or cedar blocks and the urban shotgun houses, on brick piers to assist in keeping dampness from the structures.

Stove or fireplace chimneys either were placed along the ridge line, in which case back-to-back hearths or stoves were likely,[37] or they occurred singly, in line along one side wall of the house. In rural areas, shotgun houses made of sawn lumber could be erected quickly and cheaply. Hence, they rapidly came to be used as slave quarters on plantations. Much later in the twentieth century, for the same reasons, shotgun houses found favor in the oil boom towns of Texas and Oklahoma.[38] Gradually, shotguns began to be built as urban residences, primarily for blacks, throughout the southern part of the country. As blacks migrated to the North in the middle of the twentieth century, they introduced a few modified shotgun houses into the primarily black wards of northern industrial cities. Several can be identified in Akron, Ohio, for example.

9–15 A single shotgun house, with a rear ell containing the kitchen (Louisville, Kentucky, October 1979)

9–17 Floor plan of a double shotgun house

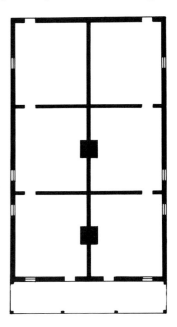

9–16 The double shotgun house

In New Orleans and other river cities the shotgun house was often constructed of brick and became a substantial dwelling for both blacks and whites. Part of its popularity undoubtedly was due to its suitability for narrow urban lots, which consequently reduced property taxes based on front footage. The Mississippi River was an important routeway for the dispersion of this house type. Virtually every important river town has a collection of shotgun houses, with Louisville, Kentucky, as perhaps the outstanding upriver example.[39]

As happened with most other simple houses, the basic structure of the shotgun house was modified over time to suit changing conditions. Growing family size and gradually increasing prosperity called for more elaborate houses. One response to these conditions was the development of the double shotgun house (fig. 9–16), which is essentially two shotgun houses with a common center wall (fig. 9–17). In many double shotgun houses no interior connection exists between the halves of the house. Indeed, in some urban neighborhoods these houses function as duplexes, which suggests another possible origin of this variation. It is possible that the

9–19 A corner-porch shotgun house located in Lincoln Parish, Louisiana. Note open louver in gable and raised foundation. (October 1975)

double shotgun house arose as a way of reducing building costs in poor, black neighborhoods of southern cities. However, not all urban double shotgun houses sheltered two families. In rural areas such houses are rarely occupied by more than one family.

Besides the plan, three features identify the double shotgun house. The facade invariably is balanced and has two doors and two windows. The pitch of the roof is much lower than that of the single shotgun house and lower than that of the California bungalow (cf. figs. 9–16 and 11–42). Finally, the double shotgun house does not have an upper half story as the bungalow does. Unfortunately, many double shotgun houses are locally referred to as *bungalows* in Louisiana. Researchers have often not noted the difference.

A further modification produces the corner-porch shotgun house (fig. 9–18). Basically similar to the double shotgun house, this structure usually contains five rooms rather than six. One front corner of the building is left open to serve as a recessed porch (fig. 9–19). Corner-porch shotgun houses are common in northern Louisiana and may occur elsewhere.

9–18 The corner-porch shotgun house

The North Shore house and the camelback house

Other modifications of the basic shotgun house took place. Adding two rooms across the rear of the house to form a T-plan produced the North Shore house, whose distribution is apparently limited to the area north of Lake Pontchartrain. This house "was spread by well-to-do New Orleanians to the North Shore, where they kept summer homes in the higher, cooler, fresher Ozone Belt of the Southern Florida Parishes." In rural and small town settings, the basic house acquired wide galleries on the three sides of the shotgun portion.[40]

Quite in contrast, the camelback house (fig. 9–20) acquired its distinctive form largely because of the limited size of urban lots.[41] Basically, the camelback house is a shotgun, single or double, with a two-story section behind, and a shed-roofed addition at the very rear, which does indeed give it a humpbacked appearance (fig. 9–21). In Louisiana, the camelback house is generally small, with a one- or two-room shotgun portion backed by a two-story part consisting of two rooms on each floor. The rear part of the house is no wider than the front part (fig. 9–22a).

In Louisville, Kentucky, there is another important concentration of camelback houses. Here, however, the front part of the house is often three rooms deep. The front room of the house is the parlor. The second room is the living room, which opens onto a

9–20 The camelback house

small recessed side porch, secluded from the street (fig. 9–23). If there is a third room, it may be a bedroom or a dining room. The rear of the house consists of four main rooms, two over two, often placed sideways so that they extend beyond the line of the side walls of the front part of the house. A bathroom and a small rear porch complete the house (fig. 9–22b). In some cases, the front of the house is only two rooms deep, and a large shed-roofed kitchen has been added behind the two-story part of the house (fig. 9–22c).

Much additional scholarly study needs to be given to all these houses. The relationship of these types to one another and the diffusion of the type through the Mississippi valley and throughout southern United States would be a particularly rewarding study.

9–21 An example of a camelback house, located in the French Quarter, New Orleans. Note the Victorian abundance of decoration, the hipped-roof construction, and the French-style doors and window shutters. (April 1978)

The southern pyramid-roof house

The range of domestic structures, derived at least in part from the French, extends to a widely distributed house that may be termed the *southern pyramid-roof house* (fig. 9–24). Widely encountered throughout the entire southern section of the United States, and almost always built of lumber, this house appears to have evolved in the nineteenth century from the combining of various essentially French architectural elements from New Orleans.[42] More or less square in plan, the southern pyramid-roof house possesses one of two floor plans. The first consists of four more-or-less equal-sized rooms with no interior hallway. This plan appears to be more common in Louisiana and hence may be the earlier of the two plans. The second variant, which is widespread throughout southeastern United States, follows a Georgian format with two rooms on either side of a central hallway and interior paired chimneys (fig. 9–25). Henry Glassie feels that this later plan "arose early on the Carolina-Georgia coast" but offers no documentation.[43] Further work is obviously needed to sort out the typology and to establish relationships existing among the southern pyramid-roof houses.

The dominant characteristic of this house is the steeply pitched roof, which sometimes is fully pyramidal, but more often than not terminates in a short ridge. The simple roof lines associated with the early period of this building

9–22 Floor plans of camelback houses:
A. New Orleans type, B. Ohio valley type,
C. Louisville type

9–23 A Louisville, Kentucky, camelback house, showing the recessed side porch (October 1979)

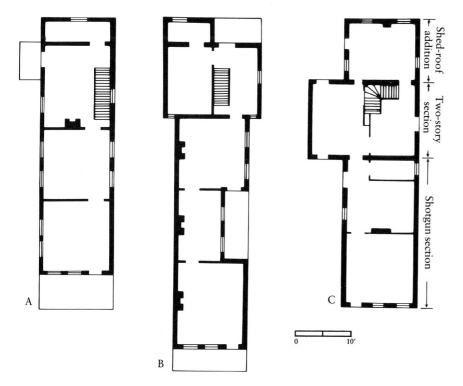

Shed-roof addition

Two-story section

Shotgun section

A

B

C

0   10'

9–24 The southern pyramid-roof house (early)

became more complicated as the house type matured. Thus, a middle phase may be identified in which the basic plan is augmented by a series of bays, ells, alcoves, and gables, as well as by larger porches (fig. 9–26).

The process can be traced to its logical conclusion in a late phase, which began by the end of the nineteenth century. Prominent wings, dormers, gingerbread embellishments, and even Queen Anne–style towers were added (fig. 9–27), but close inspection reveals the basic lines of the original house form.

It is surprising that the southern pyramid-roof house, which extends over the entire southeastern quadrant of the United States (at least from Virginia to Missouri), has never been seriously studied. In many parts of this area, it is the dominant house type, yet its origin, characteristics, and evolution have never been investigated.

The evolutionary sequence that can be

9–25 A southern pyramid-roof house of the Georgian-plan type. The chimneys mark the positions of interior paired hearths. A prominent front dormer and a wide porch are typical features. Located near Fancy Gap, Virginia, on the piedmont. (January 1981)

9–26 The southern pyramid-roof house (middle)

illustrated so nicely with southern pyramid-roof houses applies to other house types in other parts of the continent as well. A particular type of house gradually will be modified in response to environmental, economic, social, and stylistic influences. The same factors may also cause one house type to succeed another, so that a series of structures can be traced. Generally speaking, although not in every instance, the association of particular ethnic groups with distinct house types was less and less perceptible as westward migration and consequent mixing of peoples took place. The next two chapters discuss the later succession of houses.

9–27 The southern pyramid-roof house (late)

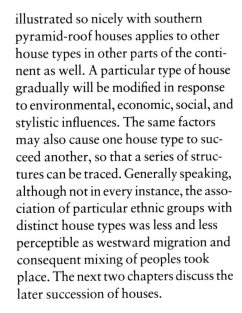

PART FOUR
Evolution of Later Houses

10   The Diffusion and Modification of Eastern Houses

The early chapters of this volume discussed the establishment of house types in the various cultural hearths strung along the eastern seaboard of North America. Each hearth had at least one significant ethnic group and a distinctive ensemble of early house types.

For various reasons, chief among which was a failure to sustain a sufficient level of emigration from the European source areas, certain of the cultural hearths were not successful as bases for the spread of their ethnic and cultural components. The most conspicuous of such restricted cultural hearths was that of the Dutch in the Hudson valley and northern New Jersey (see chap. 4), where limited numbers of Dutch settlers, a great admixture from other ethnic groups, and the early loss of political control to the British combined to reduce the effectiveness of Dutch cultural expansion to an area not much beyond the boundaries of the original hearth.

In other areas, to a greater or lesser degree, expansion of settlement occurred and a series of cultural domains and spheres grew up (see chap. 1). As would be expected, with expansion of settlement, cultural domains and spheres grew together. As they did the settlers began to exchange or borrow cultural elements and ideas. For example, the English, who did not customarily build two-story barns, after contact with Germans, who typically had banked barns, began to construct basement or raised barns, although these were distinct in several respects from the barns of the German settlers.[1] A probable origin in central New York for the North American basement or raised barn has been proposed.[2]

The ultimate architectural result of such intermixing of ethnic groups and their cultural elements is that as one moves westward in eastern North America, in many instances the structures closely associated with a particular ethnic group or cultural hearth undergo modifications. In almost all cases, the result is a more complex structure, as the basement or raised barn is more complex than the English three-bay barn, for example.

At the same time, the simpler structures that were derived at an earlier period also were carried along by the migrating people. Thus, in Ohio, for example, English three-bay barns, German bank barns, and basement or raised barns are all encountered in relatively high proportions (see the chapter in volume 2, entitled "Diffusion of the Farm Barn in Northeastern North America"). Such a combination is, in part, a reflection of the influence of time on domestic building. In virtually every region of human habitation, buildings of earlier design coexist with structures evolved at a later period. The demands of society and economy are constantly changing, and hence architecture is always being modified. Furthermore, some individuals are innovators and others are cultural conservatives, holding on tenaciously to earlier forms and concepts.

Society also responds to fashion changes. As the frontier of settlement progressed westward across the country, different types of houses tended to dominate in each of the various geographic areas. The first scholar to articulate this principle, which he termed the *principle of dominance of contemporary fashion*, was Fred Kniffen, who studied the postcolonial sequence of dominant house types in northeastern United States.[3] It seems quite surprising that virtually no scholars subsequently have seen fit to examine this sequence, since it forms the major line of evolutionary development of house types in northeastern United States.

The balance of this chapter will attempt to sketch this connection of house types, as well as examine parallel but quite distinct sequences for other parts of the continent. Northeastern United States experienced a sequence of timber frame house types drawing their original inspiration from New England. By contrast, in Appalachia the log mode of building was most commonly employed, and one can trace both Anglo-Saxon and Germanic influences. In Canada, later English cultural elements largely replaced the early French, and French building practices themselves were modified as time passed and settlement progressed across Canada.

The evolution of houses in northeastern United States

The last of the house types to evolve in colonial New England, the New England large house (see chap. 3), had appeared and been accepted somewhat before the Revolutionary War. However, relatively few such houses were erected outside New England.[4] New Englanders began to drift westward, and, following a route across Massachusetts to the Albany area and then either up the Mohawk valley or along a parallel route slightly to the south skirting the Catskill Mountains and via the Cherry Valley Turnpike, reached approximately halfway across New York state, at which

point their further progress was blocked by the powerful opposition of the Iroquois Indians. Not until well after the Revolutionary War was the power of the Indians broken and a flood of westward-bound Yankee settlers released to sweep across New York, along the south shore of Lake Erie, and on into the central and northern parts of the Midwest (fig. 10–1).

In upstate New York, the tide of migration was in full spate in the late eighteenth century when ideas of classical architecture from England were beginning to penetrate this country. Such concepts stressed harmony, balance, and bilateral symmetry, producing houses often referred to as *Georgian*, a

10–1 The path of migration from New England in the nineteenth century

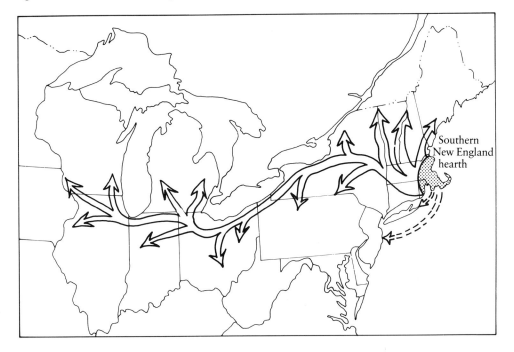

term derived from the time of George I, George II, and George III. In fact, Georgian architecture introduced to Britain the building styles of the Renaissance, which had been adopted earlier on the European continent, and which were introduced still later to the British colonies in North America. Georgian ideas pervaded folk building (by far the dominant mode of construction), as well as academic architecture (i.e., the formal mansion houses and public buildings).

Another factor to be considered in upstate New York was the influence of Germans from the Palatinate who were settling in the Mohawk valley by this time. Classical building styles were already familiar to these settlers, although they did not always use them, and a tradition of building in stone was embedded in their culture. The houses of upstate New York, built in the latter half of the eighteenth century, often reflected both English Georgian concepts and German classical traditions.

The Georgian double-pile house

One of the dominant house types being built at this time was the Georgian double-pile house (fig. 10–2), partially named from its internal form.[5] Rooms and hallways on the second floor have exactly the same size and position as those on the main floor. Hence, an upstairs room plus a downstairs room can be conceived of as a "pile." The four rooms on each floor were separated by a central passageway creating two double piles (fig. 10–3). Such is the intricate yet quite logical way in which some structures received their names.

The central passageway, which is one of the hallmarks of Georgian buildings, required a radically different approach to house building from that of the colonial structures of New England. By employing the hallway, an internal formality was achieved, which was expressed externally by the balanced form and the bilaterally symmetrical facade

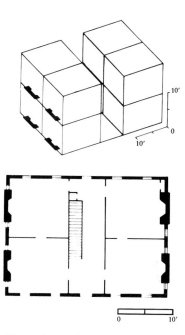

10–3 Floor plan and isometric view of a double-pile house

(fig. 10–4). The central hallway also made it necessary for the facade to always possess an uneven number of openings on each floor. Finally, the center passage required that the centrally positioned chimney of earlier New England houses be relocated. Shifting the chimney, however, required that two chimneys be used, both for heating efficiency and to maintain the balanced symmetry of the house. Paired interior chimneys with back-to-back hearths were sometimes used, especially in southern New England. More common was the placement of hearths on the gable ends. Such an arrangement was

10–2 The Georgian double-pile house

10–4 A double-pile house. The heavy decorative elements are in the Georgian style. (Akron, Ohio, January 1981)

far more efficient for heating than the central chimney. The roof of the Georgian double-pile house also demonstrates a modification from earlier house types. The pitch was usually quite a bit lower and the amount of roof overhang, both at the eaves and at the gable, was reduced. The gambrel or curb roof began to appear, since such a roof could more easily and economically span the two-rooms-deep structures.

The Georgian double-pile house accommodated growing families, and its use was an indication of developing prosperity. But as its size expanded, this house type became more and more unsuitable for families of ordinary income and social status. Perhaps in response to this situation, the turn of the nineteenth century saw a resurgence of much smaller houses.

The one-and-a-half New England cottage

By the opening of the nineteenth century, the wave of New England settlement had swept across New York state and northwestern Pennsylvania into Ohio. In northeastern Ohio, the one-and-a-half New England cottage (fig. 10–5) reaches its maximum development, although examples occur in areas of earlier settlement, especially in the upper Hudson valley and its major tributaries, and the type persists as New England settlement continued beyond Ohio.

The one-and-a-half New England cottage is a modest structure, both in plan and elevation, compared to most Georgian double-pile houses. Because it was being built in an era when great interest in classicism was manifest, its facade often incorporates elements of classical architecture. Most common are pilasters, which are flat, false columns with square capitals that generally lack a prominent base (see fig. 10–5), elabo-

10–5 Examples of one-and-a-half New England cottages

rate doorframes (fig. 10–6), and a heavy appearing classical entablature or eave line (fig. 10–7). The elements characterizing the classical revival style of architecture are discussed more fully in the following chapter.

The facades of these houses may be balanced or not, which suggests that their builders were trying to come to terms with classical styles, although not always successfully (fig. 10–8). The unbalanced facades generally mark the earlier versions, while later structures often conform more faithfully to classical ideas. Floor plans also show a similar evolution (fig. 10–9). The first examples, using a central chimney, approximate the floor plans of earlier New England houses (cf. fig. 10–9 with figs. 3–12 and 3–16), but later examples have paired chimneys located on the gables. Still, the arrangement and relative sizes of the rooms clearly show New England origins.

Perhaps the most unusual feature associated with one-and-a-half New En-

10–6 A late one-and-a-half New England cottage, with wing addition. Central chimney plus end chimney, balanced facade, and frets below the entablature distinguish this house from that in fig. 10–7. This house stands on Route 59 in Stow, Ohio. (January 1975)

10–7 An early one-and-a-half New England cottage with a wing addition. Note central chimney position, unbalanced facade, Classical Revival roof and door treatment. This house stands in southern Portage County, Ohio.

10–8 Another version of the one-and-a-half New England cottage, with a shed addition. This particular house is characterized by a balanced but asymmetrical facade, no frets or knee windows, and a single end chimney. Photo taken in December 1975, in Hudson, Ohio.

10–9 Two floor plans of one-and-a-half New England cottages

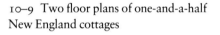

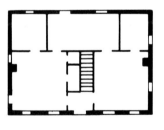

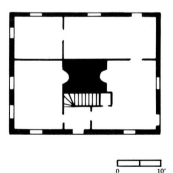

gland cottages is the funeral door. Until after World War II funerals normally were held in the home, with the body "laid out" in the parlor. Because the early houses had a massive central chimney with an adjacent stairway, the entry hall was quite small. The empty coffin could be turned on end and moved through the front door and into the parlor. The ceremonial removal of the occupied coffin in the same fashion, however, would have been undecorous. To provide a means of exit in this eventuality, many one-and-a-half New England cottages were provided with a funeral door on the side of the house (see fig. 10–5) through which a coffin could be moved horizontally by pallbearers. Such a door normally was not used, except perhaps for cross ventilation, and often steps to the doorway were not even provided.

More common than the funeral door as a distinguishing characteristic of the one-and-a-half New England cottage is the use of small windows, variously called *knee windows, lie-on-your-stomach windows*, or *half windows*,[6] to allow better lighting of the upper half-story of the house. In some instances, the windows are replaced by decorative iron work frets (see figs. 10–5 and 10–6). Normally, but not always (as in fig. 10–6), the openings occur in the wide band of the entablature.

10–10 The Ontario cottage

The Ontario cottage

At about the same time that one-and-a-half New England cottages were being built in the United States, across the border in southern Ontario a different small house was being constructed. These structures, called Ontario cottages, were small folk houses, but, as with the one-and-a-half New England cottages, their exteriors frequently reflected currently popular styles.[7] Hence, some Ontario cottages have a Gothic Revival flavor, whereas others are Classical, and a very few are Italianate.

The Ontario cottage (fig. 10–10) is characterized by a one-and-a-half story elevation, a hipped roof, and a generally compact, square, octagonal, or rectangular floor plan. Balanced side wings are typical (fig. 10–11), but not universal. In many instances, especially in houses built in later years, an encircling verandah is encountered. Early versions have simpler lines and internally positioned paired chimneys; later versions (fig. 10–12) have dormers, entry gables,

pyramidal instead of hipped roofs, and a wider eave overhang.[8]

One quite unusual feature associated with the Ontario cottage is the heat hole, which had become common by 1841.[9] The heat hole was an opening, roughly three feet square, which was closed by a decorative panel in the summer and opened in the winter to permit heat from the fireplace to reach an adjacent unheated room or hallway. In figure 10–11 a heat hole is shown located in the wall partition separating the central hallway from the left side room.

The form of the Ontario cottage is rather like that of the German-Russian house (see below) which is scattered across the Prairie provinces of Canada. It is possible that the former may have influenced the form of the latter as it was being introduced into Canada from Europe. Such a connection would be an intriguing subject for a research study.

Regardless of any connection with the German-Russian house, the Ontario cottage surely was the inspiration for the simple prefabricated houses that

10–11 Plan of an Ontario cottage

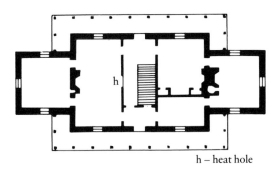

h – heat hole

were erected across the Canadian West between 1900 and 1910.[10] These simple, one-story, wooden-frame boxes had hipped roofs, bell-cast eaves, a front dormer, and a raised foundation. They are conspicuously lacking in stylistic elements, and thus were quite unlike the sequence of houses found as settlement moved across northwestern United States. In this latter area, the employment of classical features became steadily more significant in the early nineteenth century.

10–12 A late Ontario cottage in London, Ontario. Note the "gingerbread" gable, added porch, and central chimney. (October 1980)

The gable-front house

The use of classical architectural elements placed greater emphasis on the gable, or end, of the house than had been the case with earlier structures (fig. 10–13). Furthermore, the gable was generally narrower than the side of a house. Hence, orienting the gable to the street or roadway meant that narrower and thus less-expensive town lots could be utilized (fig. 10–14) at the same time that gable ends were displayed (fig. 10–15). Of course, in an almost revolutionary break with tradition, doorways had to shift from the side of the house to the gable, which caused a major realignment of the floor plan (fig. 10–16). The gable-front house is not truly a folk house but rather a building whose form is largely a response to economic conditions and fashion.

10–13 The gable-front house

Folk houses, popular houses, and academic houses

A most useful distinction, which has been made by some folklorists, architectural historians, and cultural geographers, is that which attempts to classify houses on the basis of their genetic relationship to the culture in which they originate. Folk houses, sometimes called *vernacular buildings*, are those built by an individual who lacked specific training, but who was "guided by a series of conventions built up in his locality, paying little attention to what may be fashionable on an international scale."[11] Tradition determines the size, shape, and methods and materials of construction, although the function for which the structure is intended sets the initial parameters of design.

Quite in contrast are academic houses, sometimes called *elite* or *polite architecture*. Academic houses are designed by professionally trained people who are attempting to set or follow national or international standards.[12] Aesthetic considerations are at least as important as functional ones, and most architects hope to achieve a happy combination of both. Academic houses may incorporate folk elements, but usually as novel design features introduced from a foreign culture. A split-level ranch house that incorporates a Finnish sauna would be an example.

Between folk houses and academic houses lie a very large number of structures termed *popular houses*. Popular houses incorporate elements of folk architecture; indeed, they are derived from folk types. But they also utilize academic design elements, often in a way not intended by the originators of the styles. Popular housing does not have its origins entirely in the traditions of a cultural group nor in the rigid discipline of an architectural style. Popular housing is just that—whatever appeals to and serves the mass of people. The dividing line between folk and popular housing and between popular and academic housing is not always sharply defined or easy to detect.[13] One grades into another.

The one-and-a-half New England cottage is a folk house, as can be seen from its floor plan, which confirms its connection with earlier folk houses of colonial New England. It does, however, often have certain features that could suggest its inclusion as a popular house. The use of classical architectural design, which was enormously popular in the early part of the nineteenth century, is the most obvious.

The gable-front house, which incorporates classical design features to an even greater degree, is clearly a popular house. The floor plan does not follow earlier traditions, being primarily influenced by the necessity of placing the entrance door on the gable (see fig. 10–16). The final building in the sequence of New England–derived houses represents a return from the popular house to one with stronger folk traditions.

10–14 A street of gable-front houses on narrow town lots. Each house facade is treated in a different architectural style. (Boonville, New York, September 1974)

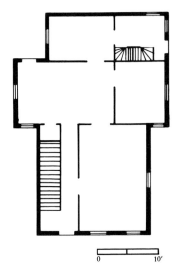

10–15 A gable-front house. Note the Classical Revival features of low roof pitch, entablature, wide cornice moldings, formal doorway. (Randolph, New York, 1978)

10–16 Floor plan of a gable-front house

The upright-and-wing house

The gable-front house was often too small for growing families, especially those on farms. In such locations, there was no need to consider the economic benefits of gables presented to the street on narrow town lots. Hence, expansion of the structure took the form of a one-story wing attached to the side of the one-and-a-half or two-story main structure to produce the upright-and-wing house (fig. 10–17). The house also has been referred to as a "lazy-T house," such designation deriving from the T-form of the plan and the one-story elevation of the wing.[14]

The new addition housed one or two bedrooms, sometimes a pantry, and always a large kitchen, which became the center of family life and the most important room of the house (fig. 10–18). Just how significant the kitchen became can be illustrated by what happened to the main door to the house. In early upright-and-wing houses (see fig. 10–17a), the entry was through the gable of the main wing, but such a main entrance was both inconvenient for the housewife and inappropriate when both farm residents and visitors wore

10–19 A lazy-T or upright-and-wing house (Tallmadge, Ohio, January 1975)

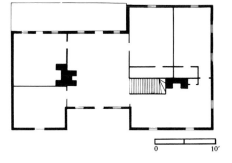

10–18 Floor plan of an upright-and-wing house

mud-covered shoes and boots. In later versions of the house (fig. 10–17b) the main entrance is off the porch, which fronts the side wing, and goes directly into the kitchen. A main entry directly into the kitchen is a break with the popular formality of the Victorian period and a return to the traditional form of folk houses.

The exterior of the upright-and-wing house made use of academic architectural motifs, with classical styles predominating (fig. 10–19). Basically, however, the march of settlement from New England into the Middle West was accompanied by a shift from folk traditions to popular housing. In southeastern United States a different sequential housing pattern was evolving with much stronger folk attachments. It employed logs as the dominant construction material.

10–17 The upright-and-wing house

A. Early version

B. Later version

109

Log as a building material

As already noted in chapter 5, the Swedes, Finns, and Germans independently introduced techniques of log construction into North America. In terms of areal extent, Germanic influences were more significant. Expanding outward from the Delaware valley hearth, Germans and the Scotch-Irish who adopted German log building technology spread log construction to most of eastern United States (fig. 10–20).[15] The southward and westward moving Americans were supplemented by newly arrived immigrants from European centers of log construction, who made their particular contribution.

In time, the log house came to be accepted as the symbol of the American pioneer settler[16] and his resourcefulness, his independence, and his courage. Appropriately, it also became a somewhat romanticized emblem of his strength and stability, for log houses *are* strong and stable.

Although many woods were used, oak and pine were most often chosen. Both are straight grained and whereas oak is more durable, pine is more easily worked. In certain restricted areas other woods predominated. For example, in southwestern Virginia most log houses were of poplar.[17] Green or unseasoned wood was preferred as it was easier to work with an axe and adze.[18] Rarely could logs longer than twenty-four feet be used because of their weight and the problem of natural taper. Hence the log house, generally erected by one or two men, was modest in dimensions.[19] Normally, such logs measured less than a foot in diameter, and were nowhere as impressive as some of the great hewn timber beams in a number of early New England houses. What separates and distinguishes the log house from that of the timber frame is the use in the former of entire tree trunks, more or less modified, to form the exterior walls.

Logs could be left in the round with even the bark adhering, or they could be hewn (fig. 10–21). Round logs tended to be more common in frontier areas, but they were not unknown in more settled regions, especially where pine predominated.[20] Rough-hewn logs were often used because a flat inside wall was more serviceable than a wall of rounded logs and the exterior appeared to be more finished and hence offered greater status to the log house's inhabitants. Rough-hewn log walls also could be chinked more easily than walls of round logs. Materials used for chinking varied

10–20 Extent of log construction in eastern United States

■ Delaware valley hearth

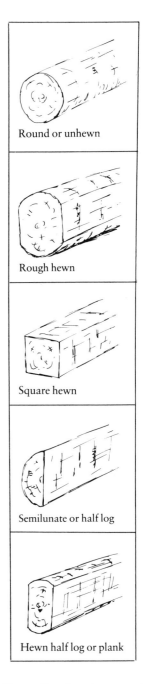

Round or unhewn

Rough hewn

Square hewn

Semilunate or half log

Hewn half log or plank

10–21 Types of logs based upon methods of hewing

widely but commonly included wooden shakes, stones, mud, grass and straw, and moss (fig. 10–22). On occasion, rough hewn logs were so modified that the log almost became a plank (see below, fig. 10–25c). Logs hewn to a square-beam form required considerable labor and thus were not initially very widely used in log structures. Gradually, however, square-hewn logs became quite popular.[21] Logs that were split to produce a semilunate or half-round cross section were used mostly on barns and farm outbuildings rather than on houses. Round logs were often used in barns and outbuildings, even where rough-hewn logs characterized the houses.

The horizontal placement of logs to form a wall necessitates some method of securing the logs and preventing their collapse or shifting.

If any single element can properly be called the key to log construction, it is the corner notch, the joint where logs from adjacent walls are attached to one another. The entire weight of the building exclusive of the sills and floor rests on the four corners and therefore on the notches. Not only is the notching weight bearing, but it also holds the walls laterally in place by preventing horizontal slippage. If the notching is faulty, the entire structure is faulty.[22]

Several types of corner notching have been widely employed throughout eastern North America. The simplest type, usually employed with round logs, is the scoop-shaped saddle notch (fig. 10–23a). The cut may occur only on the under sides of each log, or only on the top, or on both top and bottom. In the first two instances, the notch is referred to as a *single saddle notch*; the third is called a *double saddle notch*. Although occurring throughout eastern United States, saddle notching is most prevalent in the extreme South.[23] Softwood pine forests predominate there and saddle notching is especially employed on barns and outbuildings.

More sophisticated and more stable is the V-notch (fig. 10–23b and d), in which the bottom of each log is cut into a vee, whereas the top is chamfered at ninety degrees from the bottom vee. If the log is round, the visible cross section of the log end is pear-shaped; if the log is square or rough hewn, the cross section looks very much like the gable profile of

10–22 Log wall chinked with wooden shakes. A bit of mud daub also clings to the chinking in the uppermost layer. (Portland, Missouri, November 1979)

A. Saddle

B. V-notch (round)

C. Half dovetail

D. V-notch (square)

10–23 Most common types of log corner notching

111

a house. [24] Because of this, the notch is sometimes called *roof topping* or *steeple notching*. Widely distributed across the country, the V-notch predominates in Pennsylvania and western Virginia,[25] and in Missouri,[26] and is well known in most other parts of eastern United States. One reason for its widespread popularity is the fact that with this notch, logs can be cut to be flush with intersecting walls, permitting corners to be boxed with lumber, and siding to be added quite easily.

The third major type of corner notching is the half-dovetail, in which sloping angles lying in different planes are cut into the log end (fig. 10–23c).[27] This notch is used primarily by those who have some rudimentary knowledge of carpentry. Saddle and V-notches are entirely hewn, but dovetail notches are often partially sawn.[28] The half-dovetail notch is employed primarily with square-hewn or plank-hewn logs. Its areas of dominance are widely scattered and include Alabama, Ohio, Texas, and the Ozarks.[29]

Saddle, half-dovetail, and V-notching are the most important types of log corner notching, but several minor types also occur. The full dovetail (fig. 10–24) requires the most skill to execute and provides the firmest bind. In early structures, it does not occur much outside the Delaware valley hearth, but among late-settling Scandinavians and Finns in the upper Midwest it also frequently is found. The diamond notch also requires considerable skill to execute and has an even more limited distribution, occur-

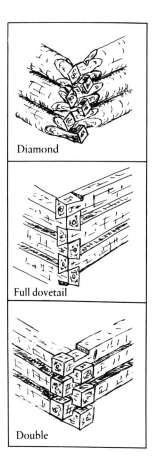

10–24 Less common types of log corner notching

Diamond

Full dovetail

Double

C. Half dovetail, planked

10–25 Additional corner notching: both the square and the half notches require pegging for stability. Walls hewn to plank thickness were quite common.

ring mostly in the vicinity of the Virginia–North Carolina border. It appears to be an English modification of German techniques. The double notch is always cut into square-hewn logs and results in a tightly fitted structure. In North America it apparently is restricted to the upper Midwest, where it was introduced well after the opening of the nineteenth century by Fenno-Scandinavian immigrants.

In addition to these minor notch types, two other methods of corner timbering have been widely employed. These, however, are not true notches because they are not self-binding. The most common is the square notch (fig. 10–25) in which both the top and the bottom corners of the log are removed. It has been suggested that the square notch is a degenerate form of corner timbering, but it is just as likely that the popularity of square notching is related to the increased use of the saw instead of the axe. The square notch requires only a few straight cuts, but the joint must be secured by wooden pegs or by spikes. Closely related to the square notch is one termed the *half notch*, which requires that only the top or bottom section of the log be cut; spikes or pegs are still required.

As settlement proceeded westward and southward, the wide variety of notching types gradually became simplified. Half-dovetail notches gave way to square, and V-notches to saddle.[30]

Although logs had been employed in the earliest settlements in the Delaware valley hearth, not until westward settlements began to be established did logs come to be regarded as the dominant construction material. Part of the reason for the popularity of log buildings

lay in the abundant forest resources. Trees, after all, had to be cut and the land cleared for cultivation. Use of some of the trees for shelter was common sense. Logs also required a minimum of labor in their preparation and sturdy buildings could be erected quickly. As frontier settlement pushed southward and westward, wood and especially logs became much more important building materials than they had been earlier and further east.[31]

Two major streams of southern- and westward-moving settlers carried log construction methods throughout southeastern United States (see fig. 10–20).[32] One major route led southwestward from Pennsylvania on either side of the Blue Ridge to northern Georgia, Alabama, Mississippi, and southern Tennessee, and thence westward to the Ozarks and Texas. Subsidiary streams made use of the natural route-

10–26 The Upland South cultural hearth and domain

Hearth   Domain

ways of the Kanawha, Big Sandy, Licking, and Cumberland rivers to gain entrance to the interior of Appalachia. In the north, another major routeway carried settlers across Pennsylvania, the central parts of Ohio, Indiana, and Illinois, and on to northern Missouri. Tributary to this routeway were branches along the Ohio and Wabash rivers. Together, these two predominant pathways generally defined the limits, not only of major log construction, but of a cultural area termed the *Upland South*.

The Upland South culture area

Though without a doubt one of the three or four dominant subcultures of eastern United States, the Upland South has never received the detailed discussion and analysis that it deserves. Its existence has long been recognized by cultural geographers, folklorists, and others,[33] but many of its salient characteristics have not been clearly identified and studied.[34]

The Upland South culture appears to be one largely diffused by Scotch-Irish immigrants and to be composed not only of Ulster cultural phenomena, but also a mixture of at least German, Swiss, Bohemian, and English elements. The combination of these earlier cultural strains may have taken place in a hearth centered upon the southern Blue Ridge, and adjacent Tennessee valley (fig. 10–26), where the Scotch-Irish appear to have been the dominant group.[35] The existence of such a hearth has been suggested indirectly by a number of scholars,[36] and directly by Newton and Pulliam-DiNapoli, whose hearth boundaries, however, appear to be very much too generous.[37] The idea of such an Upland South (or perhaps Scotch-Irish) cultural hearth could explain the variance that has been observed by several scholars between the log houses from the Delaware valley hearth (see chap. 5) and those of the southern Appalachians.[38]

The rectangular log pen house of the Scotch-Irish appears in both areas, confirming the importance of this ethnic group in the diffusion of log architecture throughout eastern United States. The major variation is the addition in the South of an external chimney, a feature derived from contact with the English of tidewater Virginia and Maryland.[39] The dimensions of the rectangular log pen house averaged about sixteen or seventeen feet by twenty-one through twenty-four feet. Other typical characteristics included a rear shed addition housing the kitchen, half or Dutch doors, a trait found in Ulster houses,[40] doors centered on the house sides but somewhat displaced toward the chimney gable, and a one- or two-room plan. The two-room division was formed by a light interior partition of whitewashed vertical boards, placed so as to create rooms of unequal size. The larger room contained the doors and the fireplace.[41]

The continental log house, on the other hand, did not spread much outside of Pennsylvania, except in the Moravian settlements on the piedmont of North Carolina, where it is usually found in a half-timber or *fachwerk* mode of construction. In place of the continental log house there evolved a log structure from the combination of cultural traditions in the Upland South hearth.

The square log cabin

The square log cabin (fig. 10–27) differed in several important respects from both the log pen house and the continental log house. First, it was square in plan, usually sixteen or seventeen feet on a side (fig. 10–28). Although built primarily by Germans, the cabin plan adopted the dimensions of single-bay houses of English settlers of the tidewater.[42] A sixteen to seventeen foot length had long been a standard dimension in both English houses and barns. It formed the basis of measurement termed the *rod* (sixteen and a half feet).[43] Another important characteristic of the square log cabin, which is more clearly German in origin, is an elevation of one-and-a-half stories with loft joists projecting three to five feet below the wall plate. The loft thus has considerable head room, giving the cabin a tall silhouette. Rectangular log pen houses, of Scotch-Irish derivation, characteristically had loft joists resting directly on the plate,[44] and, consequently, a lower silhouette.

Other characteristics of the square log cabin include an interior gable chimney, the lack of a rear door, a front door on the side of the house but displaced away from the chimney gable, shed-roofed additions to the gable (an English tradition) about as common as rear additions, and the lack of front porches.[45] All in all, the square log cabin is a remarkable blend of German, English, and Scotch-Irish features.

10–27 The square log cabin

10–28 Floor plan of a square log cabin

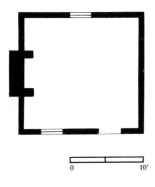

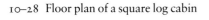

0   10'

10–29 The saddlebag house

The evolution of houses in southeastern United States

Eugene Wilson and others have identified log-building traditions in southeastern United States, but from somewhat different perspectives.[46] Included within one tradition is the use of V-corner notching, loft joists placed between wall logs without any mortising, partly hewn walls, and a small window in the front side wall. The second tradition involves building with half-dovetail notching, loft joists mortised into front and rear walls, planked walls, and small windows in the loft gable.[47]

Wilson also has suggested that as time passed the changes that occurred in folk houses were sufficient enough so that three distinct generations of houses could be identified.[48] First-generation houses contained oblong rooms and were taller than second-generation log houses. These latter houses also were constructed of smaller logs because by this time most virgin forest had been removed and only second-growth timber was available. Third-generation houses resembled those of the second, but were built in lumber frame rather than log.

Not only did log cabins or houses change in form with time, but so also did the need for larger buildings become manifest. Log constructions generally were more difficult to expand than constructions of timber frame, lumber, stone, or brick. Adding an upper floor was even more difficult because of the weight of the logs, the height to which they had to be raised, and the need to unroof the entire structure during the construction period.[49] Thus, the normal process of expansion involved adding rooms to the gable of the original structure.

The saddlebag house

One solution was to add a room to the chimney gable of the original structure, creating a two-room, central-chimney house called a *saddlebag* (fig. 10–29). The great advantage of this arrangement was that the heat source was centrally located, but to be most effective the chimney-fireplace had to be rebuilt to provide a hearth opening into the new room. Because log walls cannot be expanded easily except by using half notches, the new room was often built as a separate cabin adjoining the chim-

115

ney, but separated from the original cabin by the width of the chimney (fig. 10–30). The gaps thus created were covered by planks or boards (fig. 10–31) to conserve heat, and a doorway was often subsequently cut through both log walls beside the chimney.

In many instances the addition was of frame construction because such a structure was much easier than a log addition to incorporate into an earlier log building. Eventually, the concept of a two-room, central-chimney saddlebag house caught on and these structures began to be built as complete houses (fig. 10–32), recognizable by the combination of central chimney and two front doors, even when camouflaged by Classical Revival decorative facades (fig. 10–33).

10–31 A saddlebag house reportedly built by Abraham Lincoln and his father in Goose Nest, northern Kentucky. Photo taken in 1891. From the Thruston Photograph Collection, courtesy of the Filson Club, Louisville, Kentucky.

10–30 Floor plans of saddlebag houses

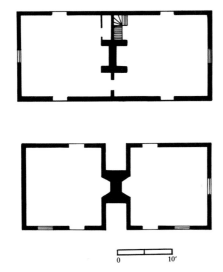

10–32 A frame saddlebag house in Ghent, Kentucky. The rear addition contains the kitchen. (October 1979)

10–33 A saddlebag house with a Classical Revival facade. Situated in Mahoning County, Ohio, near Orangeville. (March 1973)

116

The double pen house

A second alternative available when expanding the log cabin or house was to make the addition to the gable end away from the chimney, thus producing a double pen house (fig. 10–34). The addition consisted of one room, usually the same dimensions as the original building with opposed front and rear doors. An interior door was cut through the adjacent log walls of the two pens and the original roof was extended to cover the second pen. A second chimney was added to the new pen on the gable farthest from the original chimney gable. Although the double pen house is often remarkably similar to the saddle-bag house in having two doors on each side and roughly the same dimensions, it is distinguished from the latter by the presence of chimneys at the gables (fig. 10–35). The double pen house, which does not appear to have been especially popular, is different from the hall-and-parlor, which does not have two front doors. Frame double pen houses are much more common than those built in log and occur widely throughout eastern United States.

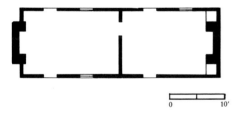

10–34 A double pen house in Ghent, Kentucky (October 1979)

10–35 Floor plan of a double pen house

10–36 The dog-trot house

The dog-trot house

A third solution to the problem of expanding the log cabin or house produced the dog-trot house (fig. 10–36). A second pen, similar or identical to the original pen, was erected in line with the original, but separated by an open space of eight to twelve feet. The gable roof was then extended to cover not only the two pens but the open passageway between, which became known as the *dog trot, dog run, possum run,* or *breeze-way.* Chimneys are centered on the outside gables as in the double pen.[50] The roof frequently is extended to also enclose the exterior chimneys, thereby confirming the earlier use of primitive mud and stick chimneys susceptible to rain damage in early dog-trot houses.[51] The roof is also sometimes extended forward to enclose a porch that runs the length of the front side of the house. Such a porch facilitates communication in rainy weather between the two separate pens whose front doors open onto the porch.

Later dog-trot houses were built with the doors opening onto the open passageway (fig. 10–37) and the pens were more apt to be squarish than oblong (Wilson's second generation).[52] With this door arrangement, the open passageway became the focal point for family life. It offered a cool yet protected place to carry on household chores and for evening gatherings and recreation (fig. 10–38).

Additions to the dog-trot house usually involve a rear shed extension of just

117

one pen.[53] However, to the south and west, the dog-trot house assumes a form that suggests a quite different type (fig. 10–39). It has been given the name of *bluffland house* by Milton Newton.[54] To the basic dog-trot house is added a rear extension running the width of the house and a front porch incorporated within the width of the structure by projecting loft joists. Although similar to the porch of the grenier house of the French, this feature appears in this instance to have been contributed by Germans.[55] Such a recessed, integrated, or incorporated porch is widely distributed in German buildings in the Midwest.

10–37 Floor plan of a dog-trot house

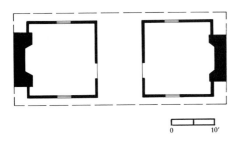

10–38 A dog-trot house in the Ozarks, north of Little Rock, Arkansas (October 1975). In this cabin, vertical boards cover the log structure.

10–39 The bluffland house

German houses in Texas, Missouri, and Wisconsin

As settlement proceeded westward, German material traits, which had first been introduced to North America in Pennsylvania (see chap. 5), remained important. Indeed, the Germanic contribution was strengthened and complicated by the continual infusion of new elements directly from Europe which supplemented, and in some instances combined with, earlier Germanic elements. The newly introduced influences were especially noticeable in south-central Texas, Missouri, and Wisconsin, areas where German settlers were most numerous.

Terry Jordan has suggested that in Texas no distinctive house was created by Germans, but that it is rather the methods of construction that reveal the Germanic contribution.[56] In both Missouri and Wisconsin a similar situation obtains, up to a point. In Texas, German settlement is reflected in the use of stone and half-timber construction, in which oak timbers were supplemented by wall filling of stone. This construction is a slight modification of the traditional German *fachwerk* method of building.

Fachwerk building evolved in those parts of Europe where, by the sixteenth century, building timbers had become scarce as a result of continued population growth, consequent agricultural expansion, and forest depletion.[57] Although familiar to, and used by, many ethnic groups in North America,[58] half-timber building became especially the hallmark of German settlers, particularly later groups, for whom the log structures of early Germans were considered primitive. Throughout the eastern United States, but especially in Pennsylvania, Ohio, North Carolina, Missouri, and Wisconsin, fachwerk building techniques were employed by various German groups (fig. 10–40). Normally, the framework consisted of heavy squared timbers held in place by mortise-and-tenon joints and wooden pegs. The wall spaces were then filled by brick *nogging*, sometimes bound in mortar and sometimes not (fig. 10–41). Often the bricks were covered with plaster and/or whitewash (fig. 10–42).

Although widely and persistently introduced, fachwerk construction never was accepted into the mainstream of American building.[59] One reason, of course, was the abundance and low cost of timber. Another reason was the early establishment and spread of sawmills, which provided a convenient source of clapboards for siding.[60] A third reason may have been that buildings entirely of brick were of higher status, and, hence, prosperous settlers frequently opted for all-brick construction. Such was the prestige of brick that it became the predominant material of later German houses in Missouri towns, and for the most prosperous of rural dwellings.[61] Brick houses also were widely built by Germans in Wisconsin (fig. 10–43).

In Texas, however, stone substituted for brick as a building material. This variation was not the only departure from traditional architecture for these German settlers. Roof pitch was lowered since cypress shingles were substituted for the thatch that had required a

10–40 The Single Brothers House, Old Salem, North Carolina. An example of a fachwerk building. (August 1978)

10–41 Close-up of brick nogging and hewn structural timbers. (Old World Wisconsin Museum, Wisconsin, October 1979)

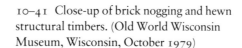

10–42 A black-kitchen house, Old World Wisconsin Museum, October 1979. Note the whitewashed half-timbering. (Photo by Martin Perkins)

10–43 A German brick farmhouse near West Bend, Wisconsin. Note the decorative brick work along the eave line. (October 1980)

high pitch to shed rainwater. Porches, verandahs, and covered, open breezeways were added to the basic structure to accommodate the warmer drier weather of Texas. Houses were smaller than in Germany because communication between parts of the structure, as well as certain household functions, could be carried on largely outside.[62] Thus, small, porched, one-room houses with a rear lean-to kitchen addition, typically have outside stairways to the loft.[63]

An outgrowth of these German building practices was the development in the late nineteenth and early twentieth centuries around Fredericksburg, Texas, of Sunday houses (fig. 10–44). These were quite small, stone or timber dwellings erected in town and initially used by farmers who lived in the surrounding countryside and stayed in town only on weekends when marketing and attending church.[64] Some have only a single ground-floor room, but most have two. The distinguishing feature of the building is the half-story sleeping and storage loft reached by an outside wooden stairway. "The use of the outside stairway, an unthinkable feature in northwestern Europe, is a valuable space saver in the warmer climate" of Texas.[65]

In parts of Wisconsin, a quite different climatic adjustment is encountered. Winters are long and cold and the northern European tradition of a centrally located hearth is preserved. Such houses have been termed *black-kitchen* houses, because the main hearth is an open space in the center of the house en-

10–44 Two Sunday houses showing the outside stairways to the lofts (Fredericksburg, Texas, April 1982)

tirely surrounded by other rooms (fig. 10–45). A corner fireplace within the kitchen provides for normal cooking needs, but the central hearth functions as both a house heating source and a smoke house. The brick walls of the *schwarze Kuche* "taper up toward a central chimney in pyramid fashion, and charred oak cross beams are fragrant reminders of the hams, sausages, and sides of meat that were smoked here."[66]

The black-kitchen house, which evolved in Pomerania, was introduced in the mid-nineteenth century to eastern Wisconsin, but there were never very many. Despite their unmistakable floor plan, the exteriors of black-kitchen houses (see fig. 10–42) are not so distinctive that they form an identifiable type. In this respect, they are like the German houses of Texas.

10–45 Floor plan of a German black-kitchen house. Drawing by Richard W. E. Perrin. Reprinted by permission of the State Historical Society of Wisconsin.

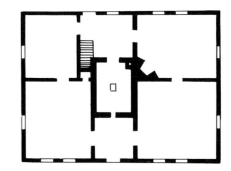

The piece-sur-pièce construction of the French

Other ethnic groups in Wisconsin and other places also are notable for their building methods rather than for particular types of houses. The French are a good example. In Wisconsin and elsewhere in the upper Great Lakes country, a method of log building called *pièce-sur-pièce* was employed by the French. In eastern Manitoba, a variant of this type of construction is called *Red River frame*.[67]

A framework of hewn timber is erected by mortising upright posts into both sill and plate (fig. 10–46). Horizontal logs are roughly squared and a tenon is cut into each end. These logs are then inserted into grooves cut into the sides of the upright posts. Houses erected by this method are more weather tight than most log houses and certainly neater in appearance (fig. 10–47). However, some chinking of

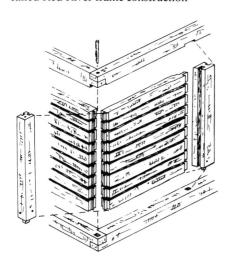

10–46 Pièce-sur-pièce construction, also called Red River frame construction

10–47 Example of the French pièce-sur-pièce log construction. The horizontal logs are held in place by tenons that fit into slots in the upright posts. Heritage Hill State Park, Green Bay, Wisconsin, October 1980. (Photo courtesy of William Laatsch)

moss or clay daub is required.

The origins of pièce-sur-pièce log construction are not at all clear. It apparently had no antecedent forms in France, but the earliest reports of its use in French North America date from the mid-seventeenth century. Peter Moogk has suggested that this method of construction originated in New France because of three circumstances. First, good building timber was more widely available than it had been in France. Second, wood is a better insulator against cold than stone or brick. Third, extreme temperature variations in eastern Canada would cause rapid weathering and disintegration of the bond between the structural timber and the wall

filling if the more traditional colombage construction were used.[68]

In any event, pièce-sur-pièce construction caught on quickly in the middle and upper St. Lawrence valley. Eventually, from this strategic base location, it was carried by early French fur traders and trappers across the Canadian Shield and into the eastern and northern prairies.[69]

Fenno-Scandinavian log building techniques

The Finns and the Scandinavians, who also settled in the upper Great Lakes area in the nineteenth century, approached the problems of log construction differently from the French and Germans. Logs were hewn so that the top of each was convex, the bottom concave, and the sides flat (fig. 10–48). The resultant snug fit was not only weather tight, but was also very sturdy, since the entire length of each log was locked in place. These distinctive methods of log shaping were made possible by the use of an instrument called a *vara* (fig. 10–49), a two-pronged, iron scriber. One prong traced the top contour of the lower log, while the other, sharper prong etched a corresponding contour line into the bottom of the upper log. Etching was done on both sides of the log and then the wood was hewed to the line, after which the bottom of the upper log was further scooped out to fit the unhewn top contour of the lower log.[70] Another characteristic was the

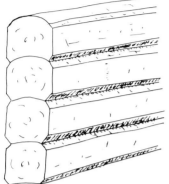

10–48 The Fenno-Scandinavian method of log hewing

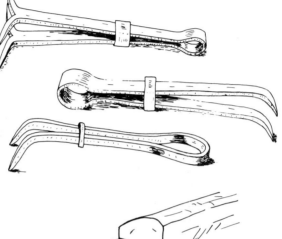

10–49 Examples of the Finnish log scriber (after Kaups)

10–50 The tooth notch

chamfering of the bottom edges of the logs (see fig. 10–48) to create a V-profile along the contact between the logs. This made it easier to cover them with chinking or wooden lath and it also was quite decorative if it was not covered.

The use of full dovetail-corner notching or double notching appears to have been associated with Finns and Scandinavians, who also employed a number of notches not found among other peoples. The tooth notch (fig. 10–50), which provides an unusually rigid and firm joint, illustrates the sophistication of Finnish and Scandinavian log building techniques.

Fenno-Scandinavian structures are much less common than those of the major ethnic groups, i.e., German, French, Anglo, and Scotch-Irish. A high

standard of workmanship and skill in manipulating timber may be seen in many Fenno-Scandinavian buildings. Most of these houses did not have fireplaces and chimneys but used cast-iron stoves for both cooking and heating. This reflects in part the later period of their construction. The second volume of this book contains a further discussion of Norwegian and Finnish buildings in the chapter entitled "The Settlement Landscape."

The Baltic three-room house

Some Scandinavian and Finnish houses fit into the group of structures having an elongated, three-room plan. In Scandinavia these have been called "Nordic hearth houses"[71] and in Russia they have been identified as the *izba* (*izbah*).[72] The first term is not appropriate for such houses in Finland or Russia and the second is clearly not suitable for Scandinavia or Finland. Because the basic plan is found throughout the Baltic Sea region, it appears reasonable to classify these houses and their close descendants in North America as *Baltic three-room houses*.

A centrally located hearth is one of the oldest and most basic traits of early housing in all colder climates. Around the shores of the Baltic Sea, the central hearth was combined with an elongated floor plan of three rooms in a row (fig. 10–51). Very few of these old houses have been identified or studied in North America. The Old World Wisconsin Museum has a Finnish house, first described by Richard Perrin,[73] which, although complicated by later modifications, is in both form and plan a Baltic three-room house. Matti Kaups also has recorded a limited number of these structures from Finnish areas of the upper Midwest.[74] Additionally, Alvar Carlson has identified such houses in western North Dakota, although he called them German-Russian houses,[75] a term better reserved for another house type discussed below. Some Mennonite farm houses in Manitoba[76] and Slavic houses in Alberta and Saskatchewan may also be closely related (see the chapter entitled "The Settlement Landscape" in the second volume for a more complete discussion of these structures).

The Baltic three-room house (fig. 10–52) is usually built of logs, although timber-frame and mud-brick examples are not unknown. The three rooms are usually of very similar proportions. When constructed of log, the three pens are normally independently built but connected by common interior walls. Roofs are usually of gable form, but hipped roofs also occur. Originally, thatch was about as common as wood shingle. Of the three rooms, the middle one generally functions as the kitchen

10–51 Floor plan of a Baltic three-room house

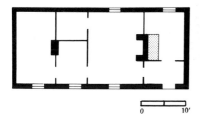

and the hearth thus remains centrally positioned.

The Baltic three-room house is worthy of additional study. It may prove to be one of the most significant of late introductions, associated as it is with Russian, Polish, Finnish, Scandinavian, and German immigrants across a wide area of central North America.

10–52 A Baltic three-room house near Sheffield, North Dakota. The walls are of fieldstone. Note the opening for the stove chimney. (Photo by Alvar Carlson)

10–53 The German-Russian house

The German-Russian house

As settlement expanded out onto the Great Plains, other German groups came into prominence. Among the most important were those Germans who had migrated originally to Russia and who, beginning in 1873, settled throughout the prairies of North America.[77] Some of these settlers, especially in the eastern, wooded section of the Plains, erected log cabins. Others resorted to the *semeljanken*, a half-dugout, half-sod house.[78] The semeljanken, also called a *semlin*, differed from the American sod house in being excavated about three feet into the prairie surface. Still other immigrants

10–54 Floor plan of a German-Russian house

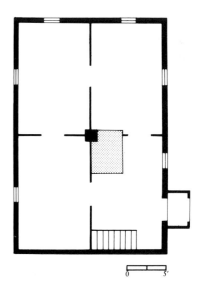

123

erected the *izba* and other houses of the Baltic three-room house type. Finally, some settlers, primarily from the Volga River and Black Sea German settlements, erected squarish houses derived from a German-Russian antecedent type called the *khata*.[79]

The German-Russian house (fig. 10–53) is much more compact than the Baltic three-room house. Construction material consisted of lumber frame, cut stone, or unfired clay bricks called *kohlsteine*, or some combination of these materials. In a few areas, walls of poured mud or rammed earth were used.[80] Houses were rarely more than a single story or a story and a half, with a rather low silhouette. Roofs were generally hipped with simple dormers breaking the roof line.

The floor plan consists of four rectangular rooms of roughly equal size. The bedrooms are situated at the front of the structure adjacent to the street or road.[81] Windows originally were covered by heavy shutters. Entrance to the house is from the rear, directly into the kitchen. A small entry often provides protection and insulation from cold in the winter and from dust and flies in the summer. The kitchen originally contained a large brick oven used not only for baking and cooking, but also for heating the entire dwelling (fig. 10–54).

The western bungalow

The German-Russian house appears to be the predecessor of a small house that has spread across the entire Great Plains and beyond. The western bungalow (fig. 10–55), constructed of lumber, is so numerous in Nebraska, Kansas, and Iowa as to be the dominant house type in many small towns. It occurs as far east as Wisconsin and as far west as Washington and British Columbia, although it is decidedly uncommon in these latter areas. The basic four-room plan of the German-Russian house is re-

10–55 The western bungalow

tained, but the simple dormer is usually missing. Very often a prominent but low porch covers the facade (fig. 10–56).

Superficially, the western bungalow resembles the southern pyramid-roof house (see chap. 9), although it rarely contains a central hallway. Furthermore, the roof pitch is very much higher in the southern pyramid-roof house. Thus, the resemblance is probably coincidental.

No one has yet investigated the western bungalow despite the fact that it is likely that it is the link between the German-Russian house and the most typical prairie house type, the Cornbelt cube.[82]

10–56 Typical western style bungalow, with central chimney. Note especially the asymmetrical facade with off-center door. (Beatrice, Nebraska, July 1974)

10–57 The Cornbelt cube house

The Cornbelt cube

Here again, one encounters a house type that has been all but ignored by serious students of domestic architecture. Such avoidance may be because the Cornbelt cube (fig. 10–57) is so common. It frequently dominates the countryside and small-town landscape of the northeastern interior and central parts of North America. On the basis of both form and plan, the Cornbelt cube appears to be related to the western bungalow. However, certain features raise questions about this connection. The floor plan of the Cornbelt cube, which is also called the *four-square house*,[83] the *two-story pyramid*, or the *prairie square house*,[84] usually consists of four rooms per floor (fig. 10–58), but some other aspects are often quite different from the plan of the western bungalow. For example, the sizes of the rooms may vary and a central hallway is often introduced. Furthermore, the Cornbelt cube may have

10–59 A Cornbelt cube, west of Des Moines, Iowa. Note the large dormers that add third-story headroom and light. (October 1980)

10–58 Floor plan of a Cornbelt cube house

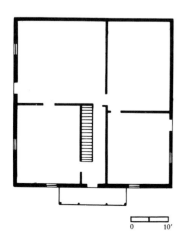

as many as four quite prominent dormers. Decoration of the Cornbelt cube is usually minimal; indeed, the house type is notable for its exterior simplicity and lack of decoration (fig. 10–59).[85] Aside from a plain, one-story porch across the front of the house, perhaps the most common embellishment of the Cornbelt cube is its roof brackets at the eave line. This, together with the basic cubic form of the house, suggests some sort of connection with Italianate houses (see chap. 11). Finally, the Cornbelt cube is most typically found in the eastern Midwest,[86] whereas the western bungalow occupies a more westerly area. Given the generally westward drift of settlement, it is difficult to see how the Cornbelt cube evolved from the western bungalow. Recently, Thomas Hanchett has suggested that the Cornbelt cube developed as part of a "stylis-

tic movement" called the *rectilinear*.[87] This style occupies a middle ground between the ornate Queen Anne and the simple, angular Prairie style. The rectilinear style has not been accepted by most architectural historians, however.

Complicating the matter still further, the form of the Cornbelt cube house is strikingly close to that of several precut, mass-produced, popular houses marketed by mail order by Sears, Roebuck in the 1920s.[88] Undoubtedly, many Cornbelt cube houses identified in the field as true folk structures will turn out, on closer inspection, to be of the Sears, Roebuck genre. Whether the Cornbelt cube is a folk house, a popular house, or an academic house remains an open question.

For the most part, this chapter has been concerned with folk houses, either those that have strong ethnic associations or those derived from earlier ethnically connected structures. Throughout the nineteenth century, newly arriving groups introduced into different sections of the continent house types that had previously been unknown in North America.

At the same time, in other areas, increasing prosperity and sophistication permitted the employment, first of professional builders and later of professional architects, to design and construct fashionable houses. With the passing of time, one style was quickly superseded by another, as the next chapter reveals.

11 Style and Fashion: The Sequence of Nineteenth-Century Houses

In earlier times, houses were mostly built by carpenters or professional builders, or by the prospective residents of the structures themselves. Hence, building followed traditional lines of development, and folk structures that were closely connected to ethnic groups predominated. To assist untrained or partially trained builders, handbooks containing patterns that could be duplicated were widely used throughout North America (fig. 11–1). By this method, new ideas of classical architecture were gradually introduced in a large number of places at roughly the same time. A Renaissance style of building began to supplant the medieval forms used up to this time. Folk houses gave way to popular houses. In the preceding chapter, the difference between folk and popular housing was explored. This chapter emphasizes the growing importance of academic styles of housing during the nineteenth century.

By the eighteenth century, professional architects were firmly established in most of Europe, although their work was largely restricted to the design of important public buildings and the spacious homes of the wealthy. In North America, too, public buildings were the first to receive the attention of professional architects. Not until after the Revolutionary War were architects much employed for domestic building and not until after the beginning of the nineteenth century was the impact of the architect felt in North America on any considerable scale.

A question of style

The growing importance of academic architecture and popular housing at the expense of folk structures meant that style became a steadily more significant component of building as the nineteenth century progressed (fig. 11–2). The concept of *style*, as applied in architecture, is difficult to define; it is an attempt by an architect to express a point of view or a set of relationships.[1] Some styles succeed and are widely accepted; others wither away quickly. To a considerable extent, the success of a style depends upon how responsive a chord has been struck in society, and not always upon how suitable the style is for its surroundings. For example, the exceptionally low-roofed Italianate style was popular throughout northeastern

11–1 Title page of a nineteenth-century builder's handbook

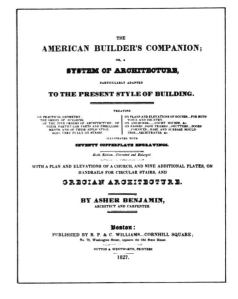

THE
AMERICAN BUILDER'S COMPANION;
OR, A
SYSTEM OF ARCHITECTURE,
PARTICULARLY ADAPTED
TO THE PRESENT STYLE OF BUILDING.

TREATING

ON PRACTICAL GEOMETRY.
THE ORIGIN OF BUILDING.
OF THE FIVE ORDERS OF ARCHITECTURE, OF
THEIR PARTICULAR PARTS AND EMBELLISH-
MENTS AND OF THEIR APPLICATION.
ALSO, VERY FULLY ON STAIRS.

ON PLANS AND ELEVATIONS OF HOUSES....FOR BOTH
TOWN AND COUNTRY.
ON CHURCHES.....COURT HOUSES, &c.
ON SASHES...SASH FRAMED ...SHUTTERS....DOORS
...CORNICES... BASE AND SURBASE MOULD-
INGS...ARCHITRAVES, &c.

ILLUSTRATED WITH
SEVENTY COPPERPLATE ENGRAVINGS.

Sixth Edition....Corrected and Enlarged.

WITH A PLAN AND ELEVATIONS OF A CHURCH, AND NINE ADDITIONAL PLATES, ON
HANDRAILS FOR CIRCULAR STAIRS, AND
GRECIAN ARCHITECTURE.

BY ASHER BENJAMIN,
ARCHITECT AND CARPENTER.

Boston:
PUBLISHED BY R. P. & C. WILLIAMS....CORNHILL SQUARE;
No. 79, Washington Street, opposite the Old State House.

DUTTON & WENTWORTH, PRINTERS.

1827.

United States from about 1850 to almost 1890, in a region experiencing heavy snowfalls.[2] Consequently, considerable efforts have been required to keep these flat or low roofs free of heavy snow accumulations during the long winter season (fig. 11–3).

The responsive chord that different successful styles strike is not always the same one. Thus, one hears the attraction of Greek democracy and Roman virtue and greatness connected with the Classical Revival styles. A religious emphasis is associated with the Gothic Revival style, as is an era of prosperous pomposity with the Second Empire style. The effective blending of horizontal building lines and the concepts of the wide open prairie plains characterizes the Prairie style.

Styles have a natural life. They grow in popularity and evolve in the process, so that early examples of the style may appear significantly different from the late examples. Styles also become diluted in their application, especially in the more modest buildings designed by nonarchitects. Such houses, which sometimes combine elements of several styles, are termed *eclectic* (fig. 11–4).

In many respects, style is most often best expressed by exterior structure. The form, and hence the floor plan, may not be a particularly distinctive nor significant aspect of the style. For this reason, and because floor plans vary widely within each style, no discussion of them is included in this chapter, which, in any case, must be regarded as only an introduction to the subject. To demonstrate the strong association of style with the exterior appearance, two illustrations are offered. In the first example, a symmetrical building, consisting of a two-

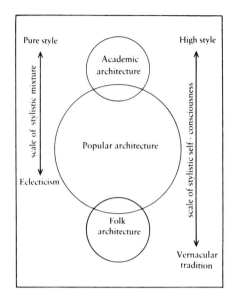

11–2 Model of domestic architecture

11–3 Shoveling snow from the low sloping roof of an Italianate house (Boonville, New York, January 1976)

11–4 An example of an architectural hybrid. This house combines a mansard roof, Italianate roof brackets and window lintels, Gothic Revival roof pitch and gable decoration, with a number of other stylistic features. Such houses are often referred to as *eclectic.* (Rootstown, Ohio, January 1973)

127

story center section flanked by one-story wings, is presented alternatively in Federal style and in Greek Classical Revival style (fig. 11–5). In the second example, the asymmetrical bulk of a house may be expressed either in the Italian Villa or Second Empire styles (fig. 11–6).

Prior to the nineteenth century, style was consciously expressed in only a few houses, most noticeably in the Georgian double-pile structures that marked the beginnings of the shift in North America from medieval buildings to Renaissance buildings. Characteristically, houses of the eighteenth century were severely plain and often totally lacking in decoration, whereas nineteenth-century houses were distinguished by a great variety of decorative features (fig. 11–7). Almost every decade of the nineteenth century saw the introduction of a new style that was to dominate domestic architecture for a time (fig. 11–8). With some justification the nineteenth century has been characterized as the "battleground of the styles."

Even widely recognized writers on American architectural history do not always agree upon the subject. Figure 11–9 lists the various architectural styles as identified by five recent writers[3] and compares their classifications with that used in this chapter. What is clearly and immediately apparent is that only the most general agreement has been reached in the matter of American domestic architectural styling. Certain styles seem to be generally recognized,

11–5 An expanded gable-front house in the Federal mode, with a balanced symmetry, and an expanded gable-front house in the Greek Classical mode, with a balanced symmetry

11–6 A house built in the Italianate style and a house built in the Second Empire style

although both terminology and chronology often vary. Part of the difficulty is that architectural styles are not static entities and while they grow and develop, their exact points of birth are often difficult to identify. By the same token, architectural styles, like old soldiers, "never die; they just fade away," submerged into newer styles.

In this chapter, only those residential architectural styles that received widespread popular approval are discussed. Not examined are those styles, such as Egyptian Revival, High Victorian Gothic, Commercial, or Sullivanesque, which were predominately applied to nonresidential buildings. Furthermore, our concern is not with the academic underpinnings of these styles, but with their popular impact. Thus, for example, the bungalow is discussed for its mass appeal, rather than because of its original artistic pretensions.

11–8 Duration of the popularity of residential architectural styles in North America

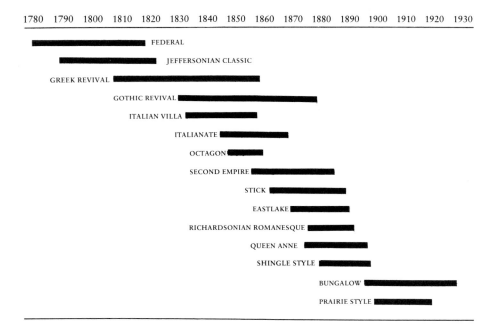

11–7 Two houses in Old Salem, North Carolina, illustrate the basic differences between (left) eighteenth- and (right) nineteenth-century design. (August 1978)

129

11–9 Variation in the classification and terminology of nineteenth-century architectural styles. Five recent studies are compared with the classification used in this volume.

NOBLE	BLUMENSON	POPPELIERS	RIFKIND	ROTH	WHIFFEN
Georgian	Georgian	Georgian Spanish Colonial	Georgian	Georgian Jeffersonian Classicism Gothic	Georgian
Federal	Federal	Federal (Adamesque)	Federal	Adamesque Federalist Federalist	Adam (Federal)
Jeffersonian Classical	Roman Classicism Colonial Revival	Jeffersonian (Roman) Rev.			Jeffersonian Classicism
Greek Revival	Greek Revival Egyptian Revival	Greek Revival	Greek Revival	Greek Revival Early Medieval Revival	Greek Revival Egyptian Revival
Gothic Revival	Gothic Revival Victorian Gothic	Gothic Revival	Gothic Revival Romanesque	Gothic Revival Egyptian Revival Renaissance	Early Gothic Revival Romanesque Revival
Italian Villa	Italian Villa		Italian Villa	Italian Villa	Italian Villa Ren. Revival (Romano-Tuscan) Ren. Revival (North Italian)
Italianate	Italianate Renaissance Revival Second Ren. Revival Victorian Romanesque Richardsonian Romanesque	Italianate Exotic Revival-Egyptian Exotic Revival-Moorish	Italianate Vernacular Victorian	Italianate Romanesque Downing-Davis Cottage	
Octagon	Octagon Chateau Second Empire		Victorian Gothic	Octagon Second Empire Baroque	Octagon High Victorian Gothic High Victorian Italianate
Second Empire Stick Eastlake	Eastern Stick Western Stick Eastlake	Second Empire Stick	Stick	High Victorian Gothic Stick Eastlake	Second Empire Stick Eastlake
Queen Anne Shingle Richardsonian Romanesque	Queen Anne Shingle	Queen Anne Shingle Richardsonian Romanesque	Queen Anne Richardsonian Romanesque Shingle Chateauesque	Queen Anne Shingle Richardsonian Romanesque Francois 1er Chicago Commercial Renaissance	Queen Anne Shingle Richardsonian Romanesque Chateauesque (Francis I)
	Sullivanesque Beaux-Arts Classicism	Beaux-Arts		Beaux-Arts	Beaux-Arts Classicism Second Renaissance Revival Georgian Revival
Prairie	Neo-Classicism	Classical Revival Chicago Schools	Classical Revival Colonial Revival	Gothic	Neo-Classical Revival Late Gothic Revival Jacobean Revival Commercial
	Bungalow Prairie	Prairie	Prairie School	Craftsman Bungalow Prairie School	Sullivanesque Prairie Western Stick Mission
Bungalow			Bungalow		Bungaloid

130

The Federal house

The Federal style, also sometimes called Adamesque, Adam, or Federalist, was introduced into North America from England about the time of the Revolutionary War.[4] Encompassing a wide range of variations (figs. 11–10 and 11–11), Federal houses invariably exhibit a lightness combined with a clarity of form. Such houses can never be mistaken for the earlier, heavier-looking Georgian structures.

In New England, Federal-style houses are usually three stories high with a low-pitched roof, hidden by a wooden balustrade. The principal ornamental feature of the facade is an elaborately designed doorway, which often is set behind an equally elaborate porch. The door normally is framed by side lights and is crowned by a semi-elliptical fan light. Recessing of the door is also sometimes encountered, often with dramatic results (fig. 11–12).

Outside New England, and especially in New York and Ontario, houses built in the Federal style exhibit greater facade decoration (fig. 11–11). Sometimes, but not always, a gable carries a full pediment, and pilasters (false pillars) supplement the elaborate but off-center doorway. Shallow arches often connect the pilasters (see fig. 11–5b). The proportions of the Federal house are elegant and refined.[5]

While not exclusively limited to the northern sections of the country, Federal houses tend to be concentrated there. In the South, a greater early emphasis on classical structures can be perceived.

11–11 This two-story Federal house is located in Randolph, New York. The half eliptic fan light, the elaborate pilasters, and the classical gable form are typical features of Federal-style houses. (June 1978)

11–12 A recessed Federal-style doorway (Hudson, Ohio, February 1978)

11–10 The three-story New England Federal house

131

The Jeffersonian Classical house

Much of the responsibility for introducing a classical orientation to southern domestic architecture rests with Thomas Jefferson, whose talents and force of personality were sufficient to impress Roman architectural forms on a generation of American houses.[6] The model of the Roman temple, however, did not adapt itself easily to houses. In consequence, many Jeffersonian Classical houses were quite simple and plain, but had a heavy, elaborate facade appended to the structure (fig. 11–13). Such houses often are referred to as *temple-form houses.*

The hallmark of the Jeffersonian Classical house is always the gable, with a projecting pediment supported on sturdy Doric or Tuscan columns. The portico thus created lends an aura of dignity and solidity to the structure. It is understandable that the style was meant to translate ideas of Roman greatness and virtue to the American idiom.

The southern sections of the United States seemed to lend themselves to Jeffersonian Classicism better than the North. In the South, a more traditional system of landed estates prevailed and an emphasis on monumental Roman architecture lent an air of presumed authority and permanence to the plantations and to the urban residences of the planters. Indeed, the antebellum colonnaded mansion became the symbol of southern society. The characteristic portico was extended to surround the structure on three sides, and occasionally on all four.

The Greek Revival house

Closely related to Jeffersonian Classicism was the Greek Revival style, which was introduced somewhat later. Its popularity was related to the great upsurge in interest in classical civilization resulting from the Mediterranean archaeological explorations and discoveries of the late eighteenth and nineteenth centuries.

The eclipse of Roman forms by Greek ones was due to several complex developments that occurred among the intellectual groups in both Europe and America and illustrates quite nicely how academic the nineteenth-century building style had become. One reason for the initial popularity of Roman styles was the erroneous and naive belief that the Romans had originated classical forms. Subsequently, European scholars discovered that Roman styles were essentially derivatives of earlier Greek ones. Furthermore, the empire of Napoleon had adopted and modified Roman forms and promulgated the "Empire style." Thus Roman architecture becomes equated with imperialism, autocracy, and despotism in England and English North America. Finally, "the Greek War of independence against the Turks had made 'Greece' synonymous with liberty to romantic minds."[7]

The Greek Revival style was enormously popular in North America and that popularity was sustained longer for it than for any other style (see fig. 11–8). Much of the prolonged interest in Greek Revival style was related to the perception that an architectural style associated with the original bastion of democratic government would serve as an appropriate model for the democracy of Andrew Jackson and the New World. Philosophically, the Greek Revival style was an attempt to link the newest republic with the world's oldest republic.[8]

Part of the problem for folklorists and cultural geographers who study academic architecture is that the familiar frame of reference of house *type*

11–13 The Jeffersonian Classical house

11–15 The Greek Revival house

changes to that of house *style*. What is important is no longer the tradition of the group as reflected in floor plan, form, and construction materials, and ultimately, house type, but rather the decorative, design, and stylistic characteristics of the house style. Therefore, one finds not just *a* Greek Revival house, but many, each one identified by its use of Greek Revival design features. In addition to the modest, one-story Greek Revival, small-town or rural house of northeastern and midwestern United States, the style may be extended to include the ornate mansions of the piedmont of southeastern United States. In this latter area, Wilbur Zelinsky has identified the basic characteristics as a

11–14 A Classical Revival house in Boonville, New York. The roof brackets, the round porch arches, and the window frames show Italianate influences. (January 1976)

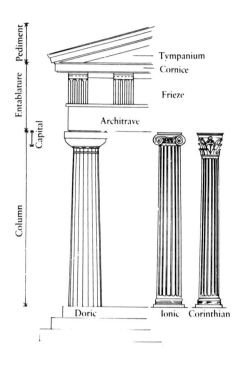

11–16 Elements of Classical Greek architecture

nearly square plan, high-basement story, wood or brick construction (if wood, it is invariably painted white), unusually low roof pitch, and high, broad porticoes across the front and, often, along the sides.[9]

In the Midwest and Northeast, the Greek Revival house is usually symmetrical in composition, although its main entry is typically off center (see fig. 11–15). In addition to the "monumental type of house with a two-story central body fronted with a pedimented portico and flanked by one-story wings" (fig. 11–14), commonly encountered Greek Revival houses were small "cottages with nearly flat roofs and low frieze windows with decorative cast-iron grilles for the upper floors [fig. 11–15], or story-and-a-half gabled cottages" (see chap. 10).[10]

The doorway of the Greek Revival house retains the side lights of the Federal period, but substitutes a rectangular transom for the earlier semi-elliptical one. Roof pitch is very low, eave overhang is restricted, and the facade is ornamented with Greek architectural orders, consisting of vertical columns or pilasters, complete with bases and capitals, and a horizontal entablature divided into an architrave, a frieze, and a cornice (fig. 11–16). The wide entablature is often broken by small windows or by decorative frets.

Despite its attempt to emulate a temple, the Greek Revival house is almost always built in wood; painted white it can be an impressive structure (see fig. 11–14).

The Gothic Revival house

Impressive in quite a different way is the Gothic Revival house (fig. 11–17), which in many design respects was the antithesis of the earlier Classic Revival house. Despite its democratic pretensions, the Classic Revival house was essentially intellectual and aristocratic in its associations. The Gothic Revival style was a movement away from secularism toward a religiously inspired architecture, a conscious attempt to recall the great Christian heritage of the Middle Ages.

In design, Greek Revival simplicity, symmetry, and balance between vertical and horizontal lines gave way in Gothic Revival to "picturesqueness," asymmetrical masses, and a strong predilection for the vertical. Picturesqueness was achieved by an emphasis on intricate detail, by the use of corbeled chimneys, window tracery, finials (a decorative, upward terminal projection at the gable), pendants (a downward projection at the gable), intricately carved porches (see figs. 11–17 through 11–19), and elaborately cut verge boards (fig. 11–20). So successful and popular were the last, which also were called *barge boards*, that they came to be applied to all sorts of houses that were not Gothic Revival style at all (fig. 11–21). Similarly, the perfection of the scroll saw and the lathe permitted elaborate decoration, sometimes called *gingerbread*, to be added to porches and other parts of the house. In the words of

Henry-Russell Hitchcock, gingerbread "spread rapidly . . . like a sort of fungus until the detail of almost all types of domestic architecture was corrupted."[11] Although overstated, it is nevertheless true that the use of ornamentation grew in popularity as the nineteenth century advanced (fig. 11–22), long after the Gothic Revival style was replaced by other styles.

The desirability of asymmetrical massing became more important in the later Gothic Revival buildings. Earlier, especially in smaller houses, the balanced symmetry of the Classical period prevailed. The best known of these early, small structures is that type called the Downing cottage (see fig. 11–18), after Andrew Jackson Downing, although it also owes much to Alexander Jackson Davis, who not only shared Downing's initials but his interest in Gothic architecture as well. It was Davis's design that Downing popularized,[12] in what was probably the most influential book on domestic architecture in the mid-nineteenth century.[13]

11–17 The Gothic Revival house

11–18 A Gothic Revival cottage south of Kent in Portage County, Ohio. Note especially the fine corbeled chimney, vertical batten board siding, and the elaborate portico. (February 1974)

11–19 A Gothic Revival house in Chaumont, New York. Note the elaborate window and door frames and the intricate vergeboard.

134

11–20 Examples of Gothic Revival vergeboards

11–21 A house with Gothic Revival features. Note especially the high pitch of the roof, the elaborately carved vergeboard, and the roof finials. The wide porch, the large windows, and the horizontal clapboards are not Gothic Revival features and lend an air of incongruity to the structure. (Hudson, Ohio, February 1974)

Verticality is one of the hallmarks of the Gothic Revival house. Its effect is achieved by a very steep roof pitch, a large number of narrow dormers, often emphasized by finials or pendants, by vertical board-and-batten siding, and by long narrow windows whose length is exaggerated with even narrower panes and pointed hoods. Vertical siding represented a radical departure from all earlier sheathing and was both possible and necessary because of the popularization of lumber as a building material and the introduction of house framing systems using dimension lumber.

11–22 A carpenter-gothic porch, sometimes called "gingerbread" (Harrodsburg, Kentucky, November 1977)

Lumber as a building material

Previously we have noted the importance of wood used as logs or in hewn timber frames. About the end of the first third of the nineteenth century, lumber became established as the premier American building material.

Several technological developments paved the way for the widespread use of lumber. First, the methods of sawing timber were dramatically improved. In the colonial period, the most common method was to use a pit saw, in which a large hand saw was handled by one worker (the sawyer) standing on top of the timber and another (the pitman) in a large pit up to ten feet deep. The timber was dragged by hand or oxen across the pit as it was laboriously sawed. It is not surprising that virtually all wood in colonial houses was hewn or split!

A considerable improvement came about in the eighteenth century with the introduction of water-driven vertical sawmills. Nevertheless, lumber thus produced was still more expensive than hewn timber. Furthermore, lumber required handmade nails, which were extremely costly. Hewn timbers were fixed in place with wooden treenails or pegs. Most log construction required no securing at all.

The circular saw was invented in 1814 and it permitted the rapid and low cost preparation of lumber,[14] cut much more exactly and precisely than the vertical saw could manage. And finally, nails became cheap and abundant! First, a nail-cutting machine was in-

vented. Later, nails began to be made from thin rods or wires of steel produced in large quantities in nail mills.

These technological advances more or less coincided with the exhaustion of large size, abundant, hardwood timber supplies in eastern North America. Concurrently, settlement was extending into areas of vast softwood forests, whose lumber could be cut and nailed with much more ease than that of hardwood timbers. Finally, as settlement extended westward onto the Plains grasslands, timber resources virtually disappeared at first (see chap. 10). Lumber could be handled more easily than timber and it could be shipped more cheaply by rail to supply the growing settlements of the prairies. Ultimately, the great softwood forests of the Far West were reached and they offered still another bountiful source of lumber.

Six varieties of softwood trees are particularly important as sources of lumber. Both white pine and redwood are used primarily as siding. Neither wood is especially strong, but both are straight grained, permitting wide, long boards to be cut easily. Lumber used for framing is often Southern yellow pine, Douglas fir, spruce, or hemlock.[15]

All these woods are cut into standardized lengths, widths, and thicknesses producing dimension lumber. After the lumber is cut at the sawmill, it is seasoned (or kiln dried in modern days) to drive off the moisture and then smoothed by planing. Hence, the actual dimensions are always less than the designation of the lumber. A two-by-four stud actually measures about 1½ by 3½ inches, for example.

All wood retains some moisture, even after seasoning, and this is one principle

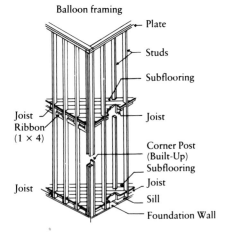

Balloon framing

Plate
Studs
Subflooring
Joist
Ribbon (1 × 4)
Joist
Corner Post (Built-Up)
Subflooring
Joist
Joist
Sill
Foundation Wall

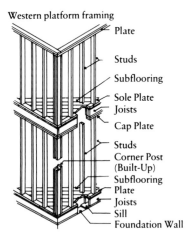

Western platform framing

Plate
Studs
Subflooring
Sole Plate
Joists
Cap Plate
Studs
Corner Post (Built-Up)
Subflooring
Plate
Joists
Sill
Foundation Wall

11–23 Examples of lumber framing

upon which the lumber framing introduced in the nineteenth century was based. Reductions of both temperature and humidity in winter favor framing systems with as many vertical members as possible.[16] A framing system replicating hewn timbers by nailing lumber pieces together to form structural members as thick as timbers still continued to be used in many houses. Such structures are said to have *braced frames*. However, new framing systems, more suitable to lumber and using many more vertical members, were developed. The earliest was called the *balloon frame*, because it was entirely composed of light members nailed together. The entire skeleton was necessary to achieve rigidity and strength (fig. 11–23). Furthermore, siding on both sides of the wall studs was used and this also provided structural integrity. Wall studs, posts, and ground joists rest directly on the sills, and both studs and posts extend in one piece to the roof. The joists of upper floors are supported on ledgers or ribbons, which are horizontal lumber pieces cut into and supported by the studs and posts. The joists are fastened to the studs to support and tie the entire structure together.[17]

The balloon frame was succeeded in popularity by the platform or Western frame (fig. 11–23), in which each story of the building is erected as a separate unit. As a matter of fact, each wall is built as a separate entity, with the studs being nailed to the sill and plate and with window and door headers, braces, and other members included. The wall thus assembled is then hoisted onto the floor platform which has already been put in place. The second-floor platform is then placed upon the erected first-floor frame, and so on. The advantage of the platform frame is that walls can be erected in easily handled sections and work can progress simultaneously on different units. Erection of the platform frame is usually safer than that of balloon frame.[18]

The major disadvantages of lumber, i.e., its susceptibility to fire, lack of durability, and poor insulating qualities (compared to stone, brick, or timber), were more than offset by its extremely low cost, widespread availability, and ease of handling and shipment. Consequently, lumber became the premier material of small and medium-sized houses in the nineteenth century. The Gothic Revival house was admirably suited for lumber construction, as was the Italian Villa, which forged into popularity in the late 1830s.

The Italian Villa

The Italian Villa represents a transition from the Gothic Revival to the Italianate style. The vertical elements of the Gothic Revival are retained in the tall, massive, square tower, which is the most characteristic feature of the Italian Villa style. Balancing this feature are horizontal elements, anticipating the later Italianate houses. The overall floor plan is that of an L wrapped around the tower. Roof pitch is low, with that of the gable facing the street often lower than those facing in other directions (fig. 11–24). The overall composition provides an asymmetrical balancing of forms, which retains some of the picturesque aspects of the Gothic Revival style.[19]

One distinctive decorative feature of the Italian Villa, introduced for the first time in North American domestic architecture, is the roof bracket. Used more or less tentatively in the Italian Villa,

11–24 The Italian Villa house

11–25 Facade of a bracketed cottage. Note the ornate roof-bracket pairs, the circular gable window, and the elaborate window frames, all products of Italianate influence. The door, however, is Federal style. (Hudson, Ohio, December 1975)

roof brackets became much more pronounced in later house styles (fig. 11–25). However, before continuing a discussion of evolving nineteenth-century house styles, notice must be taken of the principal aberration, the octagon house.

The octagon house

Although virtually every section of North America has some octagon houses,[20] these intriguing structures occur most often in northeast and north central United States.[21] A few in the South are of early date, modified from classical European models largely through the original influence of Jefferson and, later, of his friends and admirers.[22]

Most octagon houses, however, are derived from the style originated in 1848 by Orson Squire Fowler, an eccentric who supported himself quite handsomely by lecturing on phrenology. Fowler wrote a remarkable treatise promoting the octagonal style, which immediately caught on among social reformers, eccentrics, and nonconformists, and then among a wider population, who built many such houses up to the Civil War period.[23]

The octagon house (fig. 11–26) usually rises two or three stories and often is crowned by a tall, central, octagonal lantern, belvedere, or cupola. Stairways may be centrally positioned or placed in a variety of other locations, depending upon the ingenuity of the builder. Variation of plan is one of the most pronounced characteristics of the octagon style (fig. 11–27). Rectangular and square rooms combine with triangular, trapezoidal, and irregular chambers.[24] The weakness of this kind of house is its awkward rooms, but a number of advantages also can be cited: better lighting through elimination of deep corners; ease of circulation and internal communication; abundant and efficient closet space; better heat utilization,

and, if it contains a central stairwell, natural ventilation more effective than cross drafts; a house structure stronger than a rectangular one; and a building with more internal space for the same length of wall compared to normal square or rectangular houses.[25]

The octagon mode was a reaction, in large part, to the growing influence of formally trained architects, and especially to their penchant for the decorative extravagances of Victorian styles.

Not the least significant of features associated with the octagon house was the initial use of concrete walls in the United States. Although the overwhelming majority of octagonal houses have been built of wood frame construction (fig. 11–28), one of the most appealing original aspects of the octagon house was its elimination of costly framing with newly developed concrete as a wall building material.

11–26 The octagon house

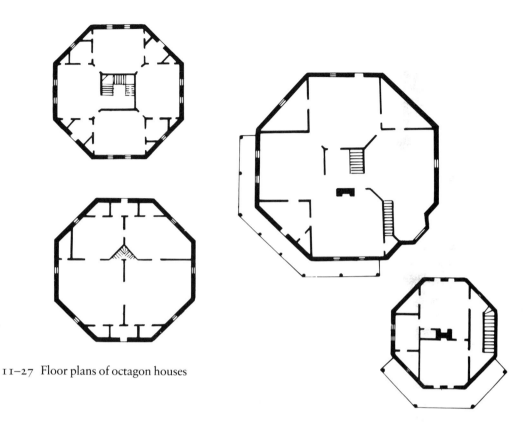

11–27 Floor plans of octagon houses

Mortar, cement, and concrete as building materials

The use of an initially plastic material to bind bricks, stone, or even wood, which ultimately became hard and rigid when exposed to air and dried, is an ancient practice. A lime-sand mortar was a decided improvement in humid areas over the earlier and more basic one of clay. The lime, obtained from limestone, marble, or seashells, was secured by burning (*calcining*) in a kiln to produce quicklime. By adding a controlled amount of water to quicklime, a powder called *slaked* or *hydrated lime* is formed, which later can be combined with sand and additional water to form mortar.

Natural cement is a form of lime that hardens to a maximum degree on exposure. It is *hydraulic* in that it will set and harden under water. Natural cement was first discovered in the United States in the first quarter of the nineteenth century in central New York,[26] but because of its cost it was used only in the finest structures.

In the middle of the nineteenth century, a technological breakthrough of the greatest importance occurred when Portland cement, composed of limestone and cement rock burned together at very high temperatures in a kiln and then pulverized, was perfected. The powder thus produced was cheap, easy to ship and store, and, when mixed with water and an aggregate of sand and/or gravel, produced concrete of great strength, rigidity, and durability. All

11–28 An octagon house in Schoharie County, New York (April 1979)

at once, foundations and even entire buildings could be made of poured concrete.

The first building in North America with walls constructed entirely of concrete was a partly hexagonal hotel erected in Milton, Wisconsin, in 1844. It is a tribute to concrete's durability that the building still stands. The hexagonal inn formed the prototype of construction for a number of other concrete buildings in Milton, which became identified as "a concrete building community for years."[27] By 1880 Portland cement had become a well-established building material throughout North America.[28]

Concrete has several advantages for use as a building material. It is durable and strong. Concrete walls can be two-thirds the thickness of brick and stone walls and still retain an equal or greater strength.[29] Concrete is impervious to rats, mice, and other vermin. Its density provides insulating qualities, both of heat and sound. Its upkeep is extremely low and it does not even require paint. But, above all else, concrete's main advantage is its fireproof quality.

Balancing these advantages initially was the considerably higher cost of concrete over wood, especially for smaller houses where great strength of material was not perceived to be highly advantageous. Furthermore, poured concrete requires lumber forms to hold it in place while it "sets." It was simpler and less costly to use this lumber for the structure itself. Finally, concrete was perceived to be a cold, sterile, harsh mate-

11–29 Examples of the Italianate or Tuscan house

rial without the personality or warmth of wood. Adding decoration to concrete walls requires the services of highly skilled, and thus expensive, masons. Hence, concrete walls were severely plain and unattractive to many in a Victorian age when ornamentation, elaboration, and decoration were highly prized.

The Italianate or Tuscan house

By the middle of the nineteenth century, two circumstances were operating to fundamentally change American life. First, the Industrial Revolution was firmly established. Cities and small towns prospered as manufacturing industries grew. Agriculture, in turn, expanded to supply the growing and wealthy urban markets. Families, both rural and urban, were still large, and substantial houses were in demand, reflecting the traditional society now beginning to pass from the scene.

The second circumstance modifying American life was a widespread rediscovery of Europe and its culture. The Revolution and the War of 1812 had become mostly a faded memory. Newly accumulating industrial wealth combined with a natural curiosity about one's heritage to encourage many Americans to undertake the "Grand Tour of Europe."

Those who couldn't journey to Europe could at least adopt bits of European culture. The Gothic and Classical revivals had offered European house styles, associated with the classical and medieval periods, to earlier American generations. The Italianate or Tuscan style enabled Americans to make a connection with the Italian Renaissance.

The typical Italianate or Tuscan house (fig. 11–29) appears essentially cubic in form, although it usually is rectangular in plan, a little deeper than wide. It frequently also has rear additions that resemble further cubes. The structure is designed to be about as tall as it is wide. Wall surfaces are usually smooth and plain, serving as a neutral back-

11–32 Close-up of massive roof bracket pairs on an Italianate-style house. Notice that the pair over the window are reduced in size in order not to conflict with the ornate window lintel. (Madison, Indiana, October 1979)

ground for windows, doorways, and balconies.[30]

Several other features are characteristic. Windows are tall and usually capped by a gently rounded arch. Shutters are rarely found, but lintels are often profusely ornamented (fig. 11–30). Frequently, the front window lintels are more elaborate than those of the other sides. A half-hexagonal, one-story bay is another feature often present (see figs. 11–29 and 11–31).

When the Italianate house is three stories high the third-story windows are normally much shorter than the windows of the lower stories (see fig. 11–29). When the houses rises only two stories, the structure is usually crowned by a square or rectangular belvedere, lantern, or cupola.

11–30 Decorative details of an Italianate house. Note the delicately carved lintels, the molded window frames, the fine brackets and dentils. The house is in Savannah, Georgia. (August 1978)

11–31 An Italianate house in Boonville, New York. Note the reduced window size on the third floor, the roof bracket arrangement, the heavy lintels over the narrow windows, and the pairing of some windows but not others. (December 1975)

Without a doubt, the most distinguishing and impressive feature of the Italianate house is the roof. Extremely low in pitch, the hipped roof extends far beyond the walls. The exaggerated eave overhang is supported by massive roof brackets, often placed in pairs (fig. 11–32). It is to the eave that the observer's eye is drawn immediately.

The Italianate style was immensely popular and resilient, its vogue lasting fully forty years. Only the Greek Revival gripped the popular imagination for a longer period. The success of the Italianate has been attributed to the fact that "it distorted convention; crashed through the rules of taste, was 'self-made'; it gave an expression of structural frankness, assigning to the ornamental attributes of architecture a subsidiary, merely pretty role."[31]

The Second Empire house

Whereas the Italianate style had strong democratic associations, the succeeding Second Empire style favored a regal or imperial approach. Its inspiration was the reign of the second French emperor, Napoleon III. In America, great public buildings, the visible symbols of government, commercial enterprise, and culture were erected in this style. Because of its monumental aspects, the Second Empire style lent itself usually only to larger houses. The typical Second Empire house (fig. 11–33) rises three full stories. Large, three-story bays and bulky, projecting wings (fig. 11–34)

11–33 The Second Empire house

add to the massive, asymmetrical effect that this style conveys.

Foremost among the features of the Second Empire house was the prominent mansard roof, named for the French architect François Mansart.[32] The roof is composed of a nearly vertical lower or outer slope and a nearly horizontal upper or inner slope, separated by a conspicuous curb, which helps screen the upper roof from view from the street. The roof curb and the eave cornice frequently are elaborated with dentils and roof brackets to make the roof an even more conspicuous and dominating feature (fig. 11–35). The lower roof slope can be straight sloped, convex, or concave,[33] and its covering of slates or tin plates contrasts nicely with the wall surface. The lower roof is

11–34 A Second Empire house in Frederickton, New Brunswick. The dormers and lintels are unusual. (May 1977)

142

11–35 Detail of the tower and roof of a Second Empire house showing the complexity of the structure. The very high-pitched mansard roof is covered with slate tiles. Note also the decorative ironwork on the tower and the corbeled chimney. (Akron, Ohio, March 1977)

broken by conspicuous dormers framed in a variety of heavy moldings (fig. 11–36). Again, the dormer helps draw attention to the roof area. In some instances, a large, square tower with its own mansard roof provides an additional noticeable feature. Finally, corbeled chimneys and cast iron roof cresting (figs. 11–35, 11–37) complete the effect of grandeur.

11–36 Two examples of dormers and window treatment of Second Empire houses. Both houses are on Fir Hill, Akron, Ohio. (March 1977)

11–37 The Hower House on the campus of the University of Akron (Akron, Ohio, March 1977)

143

Stick, Eastlake, Richardsonian Romanesque, and shingle houses

Late in the nineteenth century, several architectural styles arose, which, although academically interesting, generally did not catch the popular imagination, so that in each case their popularity had a rather short reign. The long-lasting Gothic Revival style had developed in response to newly developed techniques in lumber framing. The stick style carried this connection even further, by exposing and emphasizing the framing members and making them obvious decorative features. Particularly conspicuous are the diagonal braces. In other respects, stick-style houses occupy a design position somewhere between the Gothic Revival and Queen Anne styles. They have an asymmetrical form, with an emphasis on height, accentuated by steeply pitched roofs. Large porches and deep verandahs, projecting bays, and prominent gables are standard features. The gables often feature exposed framing or rather elaborate design.

The decoration of the stick style is essentially two-dimensional but that of the even shorter-lived Eastlake style is decidedly three-dimensional.[34] Furthermore, the decoration *is* the style. As Marcus Whiffen notes, "Most Eastlake buildings would be classified as Stick Style or Queen Anne if they were not transmogrified by a distinctive type of ornament. This ornament is largely the product of the chisel, the gouge, and the lathe."[35] What one notices about Eastlake houses is the ornamentation—knobs, circular perforations, lattice work, rows of spindles, spoollike balustrades, tapered posts turned to resemble furniture legs, carved panels, scroll brackets, fan-shaped brackets, and curvilinear brackets.

In contrast to the Eastlake structures, Richardsonian Romanesque houses represent a clear and distinct style, not easily confused with any other. Its major hallmarks include large, hipped roofs, impressive round-arched doorways, short, round, or polygonal towers with low-pitched conical roofs, squat chimneys, and heavy lintels. These structures, named for the influential American architect H. H. Richardson, are invariably built in stone and appear heavy, massive, and solid. As a result, and also because of the cost of stone building, the Richardsonian Romanesque style proved more successful for the construction of public buildings than for private residences.

Closely related to the Richardsonian Romanesque, but less costly, is the shingle style, which received its name from the all-encompassing exterior cover of unpainted wood shingles. Not only are roofs and walls shingle covered, so also are dormers, porches, columns, and posts. Other features of shingle-style buildings are much less distinctive, and include a very narrow eave overhang, narrow pent roofs, broad gable ends, and small-paned windows.

The Queen Anne house

The decorative forces unleashed in the Second Empire style and the movement toward structures of greater and greater exterior complexity and embellishment reached a culmination in America in the Queen Anne house (fig. 11–38).

The style, developed in England to recall buildings arising from medieval origins, should have been labeled Elizabethan Revival, but was mistakenly termed the Queen Anne style, which misnomer became firmly affixed in both England and America.[36] The acceptance of the Queen Anne style in America may be dated from about 1876. Whiffen notes that the Queen Anne style "conjured up a period of the past that was just distant enough to appear rosy in the eyes of an America that had lost so much of its confidence in the future during the financial panic of 1873."[37]

Variety and embellishment are perhaps the two most appropriate terms to

11–38 The Queen Anne house

11–39 A Queen Anne house (Akron, Ohio, March 1977)

describe the Queen Anne house, which rises two full stories and is capped by an enormous third-story attic. Roof pitches are high and roof form may be either gable or hipped. In the latter instances, projecting triangular gables break the slope. Dormers are conspicuous and huge corbeled chimneys are frequently exceptionally ornate. Balconies and recessed porches on upper levels (fig. 11–39) are also characteristic features, as are the great corner-positioned, conical-roofed towers. In composition, the structure of the Queen Anne house is quite irregular, with projecting gables, tower, bay windows, and large attached porches. Wall surfaces are variable. Straight clapboards mix with scalloped clapboards, decorative bricks, and shingles. Much use is made of chiseled woodwork, paneling, carved friezes, and other ornate embellishments. Windows partly done in small, stained-glass panes complete the decorative variations.

Although more popular than most late nineteenth-century American architectural styles, the Queen Anne enjoyed only a brief life—roughly twenty years.[38] The Queen Anne style can be seen as a culmination of Victorian fussiness, ostentation, and formal pomposity. The next significant development in North American architecture carried society in a totally different direction.

The Prairie-style house

In profound contrast with the ornate and fanciful Queen Anne house, with its bulky mass, was a domestic building emphasizing horizontal lines, and called the *Prairie house* (fig. 11–40). Although popularly associated with the wide open spaces of the American Midwest, the style actually originated out of the Japanese interests and experience of Frank Lloyd Wright, the foremost American architect at the turn of the century. The Prairie style thus represented a total break with the European-inspired architecture of North America; nothing like the Prairie style had been seen here before.

Horizontal composition is strong in the Prairie-style house and is achieved by low walls, rows of small windows, low roofs on long, one-story projections from the main two-story structure, and the absence of basement platforms. Roofs may be either hipped or gable, but they are so low pitched as to seem almost horizontal (fig. 11–41). Exaggerated eave overhang also helps to emphasize the horizontality. Even the oblong chimneys are designed for horizontal effect (see fig. 11–40).

The interior room arrangement also represented a sharp break with past architecture. Built-in room dividers instead of solid partitions often separate spaces, creating an atmosphere of greater openness. Interior walls also frequently were not weight bearing, so that upper floor plans were not duplicates of the lower ones. An attempt was made to

11–40 The Prairie-style house

integrate interior and exterior space by the use of large windows, glass doors, patios, covered walkways, walled-in gardens, and other devices.[39]

The Prairie-style house never caught the popular fancy and was never built much outside the eastern Midwest,[40] but the style is significant because it represents such a sharp break with earlier traditions rooted in European revivalist designs. While the Prairie style did not become a major North American fashion, it did produce the climate that permitted rapid and almost universal acceptance of another non-European house style, the bungalow.

The bungalow

Just as the Prairie-style house was a complex creation from the Midwest, the bungalow became initially identified so completely with the Pacific Coast

11–41 A Prairie-style house in Madison, Indiana. Note the very low roof pitch, oblong chimney stacks, and massive porch pillars. (October 1979)

that the term *California bungalow* often is used for all the houses in this category. However, at least two quite distinct structures share the bungalow designation in popular usage.

The popularity of the word, *bungalow,* "was due to its euphony and vagueness of meaning, which made application elastic. In general it may be said to have gradually supplanted the word cottage, eventually taking over many of its duties in our common vocabulary for a period upwards of half a century."[41] The idea of the bungalow may be traced back to Bengal, the country of the Bangla people. The word *bungalow* is a corruption of *Bangla* and originally refers to a gable-roofed,

single-story dwelling of modest dimensions found in Bengal. In the eighteenth and nineteenth centuries, as British administration spread outward from Bengal over the rest of India, a network of sprawling, low, rest houses consisting of wings of bedrooms connected by wide verandahs to a central kitchen-drawing room were established.[42] These *bungalows* were of various designs and thus they transformed the idea of the building, so that the term when introduced into North America really meant little more than a one-story house: "The bungalow was but a cottage given unique expression through the application of certain ideas about the look and purpose of domestic architecture. It displayed no authentic types, but consisted of shared features manifested in a range of styles."[43]

In North America, the antecedents of the bungalow are many and varied. It

11–42 The California bungalow

draws on some of the Japanese ideas that inspired Wright's Prairie-style house. Its roots also appear to include an important Spanish-Mexican heritage and, often, to have some connection with Swiss chalet elements.[44] Clearly, the bungalow demonstrates the maturity of American domestic architecture. Its connections are not merely to European sources, but in a sense to the entire world.

Several factors combined to foster the phenomenal success and popularity of the California bungalow. First, the new style evolved in California, and by this very fact it was perceived in the opening years of the twentieth century to be "modern" and hence acceptable. Second, the house was small, especially in contrast to the gigantic Queen Anne and Second Empire mansions. American families in the urban-industrial society of the twentieth century were growing smaller. Third, the hired girl, the live-in servant, and even the part-time cleaning woman were becoming too costly for many families who earlier

11–43 A small California bungalow in Akron, Ohio (April 1978)

11–44 The dormer-front bungalow

11–45 A dormer-front bungalow with a large shed dormer (Medina County, Ohio, February 1980)

had employed them. Smaller houses were easier and cheaper to maintain and no servants' rooms were needed. Fourth, the small size of the house and its gable-front orientation made it suitable to the tiny town and city lots in new subdivisions. Finally, because the population was expanding in the prosperous teens and twenties, a great demand was created for low-cost housing. The bungalow satisfied this need admirably, since its internal arrangement was simple and its one or one-and-a-half-story elevation permitted rapid, low-cost construction.

The California bungalow (fig. 11–42) is invariably built in wood, the pitch of the gable roof is low and sometimes is broken by a dormer, and decoration and embellishment are mostly lacking. A wide, deep, raised porch, also topped

by a gable roof, covers much of the house's gable end, which is presented to the street or road (fig. 11–43). The main entrance to the dwelling is always on the gable.

A second variant of the bungalow style may be termed the *dormer-front bungalow* (fig. 11–44). This structure is less elongated than other bungalows, the gable is side-facing, and the roof is broken by a conspicuous dormer. In most instances, this dormer is gable roofed, but shed-roofed dormers also may be found (fig. 11–45).

In contrast to the California bungalow, the dormer-front bungalow typi-

147

cally utilizes the upper floor as part of the living quarters of the house.[45] Roof pitch is higher and the large dormer also adds head room to make second-story space quite usable. The large, raised, front porch is attached to the side of the building rather than to the gable, and the roof line of the porch often continues that of the main structure, but usually at a somewhat lower pitch.

Later house styles

An abrupt halt to residential building occurred at the end of the 1920s, with the collapse of business activity. Throughout the economic Depression of the 1930s few new dwellings were constructed. Thus, a great void exists in vernacular and popular architecture for this period.

The conclusion of World War II permitted the capital built-up during the war years to be used in a rash of new construction that attempted to satisfy the demand accumulated during the preceding long period of building inactivity. The demand was so enormous that blocks of identical houses were constructed in virtually every American city. In small towns and the countryside, a similar construction boom took place. Furthermore, the widespread ownership of private automobiles enabled many city folk to escape the perceived evils and disadvantages of the ever-growing urban areas, and to return to the open countryside. The character of rural America was drastically altered in the process.

In the late 1940s, perhaps the most prevalent house style was one termed the *Cape Cod colonial*, popular because it used uncomplicated plans, could be built without a basement on a simple concrete slab, and was small enough to be afforded by large numbers of veterans' families.

The Cape Cod colonial was succeeded in the 1950s by a sprawling, one-story dwelling with attached garage called the *ranch house*. These structures required large building lots that were available in the vast suburbs growing up around American cities or on rural sites in open countryside. The ranch house was a conscious attempt to invoke memories of the western experience of America by recalling low, sprawling adobe houses of the early West.

Having the garage attached to the house was convenient, and at the same time gave the visual impression of a structure much larger than the living area actually was. Because the building was only one-story high, both original construction costs and maintenance expenses were low.

The steadily growing family size during the 1950s and early 1960s favored the growth in popularity of the split-level house typical of this period. The dwelling was designed to maximize floor area without increasing lot size by combining a two-story section with an adjoining one-story section. However, the single-story floor level was placed between those of the two-story section, so that three separate floor levels were used. Such an arrangement provided maximum internal "interest" with a clear separation of household functions. The family room, a bedroom and bath, and utility rooms generally occu-

pied the lowest level. The living and dining rooms and kitchen occupied the intermediate floor. The uppermost level contained bedrooms and associated bathrooms.

Since the 1960s no particular domestic house style has dominated. Rather, a number of revival styles have been utilized. The emergence of severe energy problems coupled with the rapid decline in family size is likely to result in radically altered house designs in the future.

Notes

1 Settlement Landscapes and Cultural Hearths

1 Edward M. Ledohowski and David K. Butterfield, *Architectural Heritage: The Eastern Interlake Planning District* (Winnipeg: Manitoba Department of Cultural Affairs and Historical Resources, 1983), pp. 55–60.

2 Peter O. Wacker, "Traditional House and Barn Types in New Jersey: Keys to Acculturation, Past Cultureographic Regions, and Settlement History," *Geoscience and Man* 5 (1974): 169–71 (special issue, *Man and Cultural Heritage*).

3 Thomas Jefferson Wertenbaker, *The Founding of American Civilization: The Middle Colonies* (New York: Charles Scribner's Sons, 1938), p. 63.

4 Ibid., p. 236.

5 Alan Gowans, *Images of American Living* (Philadelphia: J. B. Lippincott Co., 1964), p. 50.

6 Georges Gauthier-Larouche, *Evolution de la Maison Rurale Traditionnelle dans la Région de Québec* (Québec: Les Presses de l'Université Laval, 1974), p. 234.

7 This address was published as Fred B. Kniffen, "Folk Housing—Key to Diffusion," *Annals of the Association of American Geographers* 55, no. 4 (1965): 549–77.

8 Henry Glassie, *Pattern in the Material Folk Culture of the Eastern United States* (Philadelphia: University of Pennsylvania Press, 1968).

9 Hugh Morrison, *Early American Architecture* (New York: Oxford University Press, 1952).

10 Kniffen, "Folk Housing," p. 558.

11 Wilbur Zelinsky, *The Cultural Geography of the United States* (Englewood Cliffs, N.J.: Prentice Hall, 1973), p. 4.

12 Several specialized bibliographies do exist. Among these are Frank J. Roos, Jr., *Bibliography of Early American Architecture* (Urbana: University of Illinois Press, 1968); Alvar W. Carlson, "Bibliography on Barns in the United States and Canada," *Pioneer America* 10, no. 1 (1978): 65–71; Charles F. Calkins, *The Barn as an Element in the Cultural Landscape of North America: A Bibliography* (Monticello, Ill.: Vance Bibliographies, 1979); Allen G. Noble, "The Farm Silo: An Annotated Bibliography," *Journal of Cultural Geography* 1, no. 2 (1981): 118–26;

Allen G. Noble and Jean M. Danis, "The Literature on Fences, Walls, and Hedges as Cultural Landscape Features," *Pennsylvania Folklife* 33, no. 1 (1983): 41–47; Allen G. Noble, "Sod Houses and Similar Structures: A Brief Evaluation of the Literature," *Pioneer America* 13, no. 2 (1981): 61–66.

13 D. W. Meinig, "The Mormon Culture Region: Strategies and Patterns in the Geography of the American West, 1847–1964," *Annals of the Association of American Geographers* 55, no. 2 (1965): 191–220.

14 Richard Pillsbury, "The Urban Street Pattern as a Culture Indicator: Pennsylvania, 1682–1815," *Annals of the Association of American Geographers* 60, no. 3 (1970): 428–46.

15 Kniffen, "Folk Housing," pp. 549–77.

16 Glassie, *Pattern in the Material Folk Culture*, pp. 35–37, 39.

17 Meinig, "The Mormon Culture Region," p. 215.

18 Ibid., p. 216.

19 Fred B. Kniffen, "Louisiana House Types," *Annals of the Association of American Geographers* 26 (December 1936): 181.

2 French Colonial Houses in the St. Lawrence Valley Hearth

1 Ralph H. Brown, *Historical Geography of the United States* (New York: Harcourt, Brace and Company, 1948), pp. 4–46.

2 R. Cole Harris and John Warkentin, *Canada before Confederation* (New York: Oxford University Press, 1974), p. 40.

3 Ibid., p. 41.

4 Ramsey Traquair, *The Old Architecture of Quebec* (Toronto: Macmillan Company, 1947), p. 52.

5 Gerald Morisset, *L'Architecture en Nouvelle-France* (Québec: Collection Champlain, 1949), p. 32.

6 Georges Gauthier-Larouche, *L'Evolution de la Maison Rurale Traditionnelle dans la Région de Québec* (Québec: Les Presses de l'Université Laval, 1974), p. 233.

7 The term *cottage* is used in this book to refer to a small house. For many house types the term has been retained because earlier authors have used it and, rather than invent new names, it seems better to use existing terminology, even when not precise.

8 Traquair, *The Old Architecture of Quebec*, p. 12.

9 Peter N. Moogk, *Building a House in New France* (Toronto: McClelland and Stewart, 1977), p. 22.

10 Gauthier-Larouche, *L'Evolution de la Maison Rurale Traditionnelle*, p. 233.

11 Ibid., p. 142.

12 Michel Lessard and Huguette Marquis, *Encyclopédie de la Maison Québecoise* (Montréal: Les Editions de l'Homme, 1972), pp. 390–416.

13 Morisset, *L'Architecture en Nouvelle-France*, p. 32.

14 Michel Lessard and Gilles Vilandre, *La Maison Traditionnelle au Québec* (Montréal: Les Editions de l'Homme, 1974), p. 203.

15 William Carless, "The Architecture of French Canada," *Journal of the Royal Architectural Institute of Canada* 2, no. 2 (1925): 142.

16 J. Rawson Gardiner, "The Early Architecture of Quebec," *Journal of the Royal Architectural Institute of Canada* 2, no. 6 (1925): 228–34.

3 English Colonial Houses in the New England Hearth

1 Douglas R. McManis, *Colonial New England: A Historical Geography* (New York: Oxford University Press, 1975), pp. 41–45.

2 Joseph S. Wood, "The Origin of the New England Village," Ph.D. diss., Pennsylvania State University, 1978, p. 178.

3 McManis, *Colonial New England*, p. 59.

4 Edna Scofield, "The Origin of Settlement Patterns in Rural New England," *Geographical Review* 28, no. 4 (1938):656.

5 Richard M. Candee, "A Documentary History of Plymouth Colony Architecture, 1620–

1700," *Old-Time New England* 59, no. 3 (1969):61–62.

6 Fiske Kimball, *Domestic Architecture of the American Colonies and of the Early Republic* (New York: Dover Publications, 1966), p. 5.

7 Martin S. Briggs, *Homes of the Pilgrim Fathers in England and America* (London: Oxford University Press, 1932).

8 Harold R. Shurtleff, *The Log Cabin Myth* (1939; reprint, Gloucester, Mass.: Peter Smith, 1967), pp. 5–6. Reprinted by permission of Harvard University Press.

9 Curt Bruce and Jill Grossman, *Revelations of New England Architecture* (New York: Grossman Publications, 1975), p. 6.

10 J. Frederick Kelly, *Early Domestic Architecture of Connecticut* (New Haven: Yale University Press, 1924), p. 3.

11 Terry G. Jordan, *Texas Log Buildings: A Folk Architecture* (Austin: University of Texas Press, 1978), p. 35.

12 Norman M. Isham and Albert F. Brown, *Early Rhode Island Houses* (Providence: Preston and Rounds, 1895), p. 14.

13 Walter R. Nelson, "Some Examples of Plank House Construction and Their Origin," *Pioneer America* 1, no. 2 (1969): 26.

14 Hugh Morrison, *Early American Architecture* (New York: Oxford University Press, 1952), pp. 30, 16.

15 Anthony N. B. Garvan, *Architecture and Town Planning in Colonial Connecticut* (New Haven: Yale University Press, 1957), p. 89.

16 An extensive discussion of timber framing can be found in Norman Isham, *Early American Houses* (1928; reprint, New York: Da Capo Press, 1967).

17 Antoinette F. Downing, *Early Houses of Rhode Island* (Richmond, Va.: Garrett and Massie, 1937), p. 3.

18 Abbott Lowell Cummings, *The Framed Houses of Massachusetts Bay, 1625–1725* (Cambridge: Harvard University Press, 1979), p. 7.

19 Garvan, *Architecture and Town Planning*, p. 5.

20 Norman M. Isham and Albert F. Brown, *Early Connecticut Houses* (Providence: Preston and Rounds, 1900), p. 6; Antoinette F. Downing,

The Architectural Heritage of Newport, Rhode Island (New York: Clarkson N. Potter, 1967), p. 29.

21 It must be conceded further that the distinct relationship of a particular floor plan with an exterior form is not always as clearly defined as the discussion in this chapter suggests.

22 The problem is compounded by the fact that a few colonial New England houses of massive form that were located on the frontier also have been termed *garrison houses*. These structures were sometimes constructed of log or bricks and they were fortified frontier houses. For a discussion, see Thomas T. Waterman, *The Dwellings of Colonial America* (Chapel Hill: University of North Carolina Press, 1950), pp. 239–40.

23 Garvan, *Architecture and Town Planning*, p. 92.

24 Henry Russell Hitchcock, *Rhode Island Architecture* (New York: Da Capo Press, 1968), p. 13.

25 Ernest Allen Connally, "The Cape Cod House: An Introductory Study," *Journal of the Society of Architectural Historians* 19 (May 1960): 47.

26 Richard Pillsbury and Andrew Kardos, *A Field Guide to the Folk Architecture of the Northeastern United States* (Hanover, N.H.: Department of Geography, Dartmouth College, [1970]), p. 25.

27 Allen G. Noble, "The Evolution and Classification of Nineteenth Century Housing in Ohio," *Journal of Geography* 74, no. 5 (1975): 290.

28 Pillsbury and Kardos, *Field Guide to Folk Architecture*, p. 25.

4 Dutch Colonial Houses in the Hudson Valley Hearth

1 Parts of this chapter originally were published in Allen G. Noble, "A Tentative Classification of Dutch Colonial Rural Houses in New York and New Jersey," *Ohio Geographers: Recent Research Themes* 7 (1979): 31–40.

2 The notable exception to this generalization is the work of Peter Wacker.

3 John Fiske, *Dutch and Quaker Colonies in America* (Boston: Houghton, Mifflin, 1899), p. 116.

4   Ibid., pp. 231, 274.

5   Helen W. Reynolds, *Dutch Houses in the Hudson Valley before 1776* (1929; reprint, New York: Dover Publications, 1956), p. 16.

6   Ibid., p. 22.

7   Thomas Jefferson Wertenbaker, *The Founding of American Civilization: The Middle Colonies* (New York: Charles Scribner's Sons, 1938), p. 64.

8   Several of these early urban houses are preserved in the Stockade district of Schenectady, New York.

9   Harold D. Eberlein, *The Architecture of Colonial America* (Boston: Little, Brown, 1915), pp. 20, 25.

10   Sydney R. Jones, *Old Houses in Holland* (London: "The Studio" Ltd., 1918), p. 21.

11   Wertenbaker, *The Founding of American Civilization*, p. 47.

12   Frank B. Gilbreth, *Bricklaying System* (New York: Myron C. Clark Publishing Company, 1909), p. 209.

13   Joseph S. Sickler, *The Old Houses of Salem County*, 2d ed. (Salem, N.J.: Sunbeam Publishing Company, 1949).

14   Sophia Gruys Hinshalwood, "The Dutch Culture Area of the Mid-Hudson Valley," Ph.D. diss., Rutgers University, 1981, p. 56.

15   Oliver Bowles, *The Stone Industries* (New York: McGraw Hill Book Company, 1939), p. 97.

16   Charles McRaven, *Building with Stone* (New York: Lippincott and Crowell, 1980), p. 13.

17   Bowles, *The Stone Industry*, p. 235.

18   Ibid., pp. 235, 284.

19   Reynolds, *Dutch Houses in the Hudson Valley*, pp. 177–78.

20   Ibid., p. 23.

21   Wertenbaker, *The Founding of American Civilization*, p. 70.

22   Alan Gowans, *Images of American Living* (Philadelphia: J. B. Lippincott Co., 1964), pp. 54–55.

23   Peter Wacker, "Traditional House and Barn Types in New Jersey: Keys to Acculturation, Past Culturegraphic Regions, and Settlement History," *Geoscience and Man* 5 (1974): 169 (special issue, *Man and Cultural Heritage*).

24   Reynolds, *Dutch Houses in the Hudson Valley*, pp. 317–444.

25   Aymar Embury II, "New Netherlands Farmhouses," in *Early Homes of New York and the Mid-Atlantic States*, ed. Russell F. Whitehead and Frank Choteau Brown (New York: Arno Press, 1977).

26   Material in this section is taken from Allen G. Noble, "Variance in Floor Plans of Dutch Houses of the Colonial Period," *PAST: Pioneer America Society Transactions* 3 (1980): 46–56.

27   Information on these house plans has been taken from Reynolds, *Dutch Houses in the Hudson Valley*; Rosalie F. Bailey, *Pre-Revolutionary Dutch Houses and Families in Northern New Jersey and Southern New York* (New York: William Morrow, 1936); Maud E. Dilliard, *Old Dutch Houses of Brooklyn* (New York: Richard R. Smith, 1945); Harold D. Eberlein, *The Manors and Historic Homes of the Hudson Valley* (Philadelphia: J. B. Lippincott, 1924), and *Manor Houses and Historic Homes of Long Island and Staten Island* (Port Washington, N.Y.: Ira J. Freedman, 1928), as well as from the files of the Historic American Buildings Survey, Washington, D.C.

28   Alan Gowans, *Architecture in New Jersey* (Princeton: D. Van Nostrand, 1964), p. 110.

5   Colonial Houses in the Delaware Valley Hearth

1   Thomas Jefferson Wertenbaker, *The Founding of American Civilization: The Middle Colonies* (New York: Charles Scribner's Sons, 1938), p. 321.

2   Stevenson W. Fletcher, *Pennsylvania Agriculture and Country Life, 1640–1840* (Harrisburg: Pennsylvania Historical and Museum Commission, 1950), p. 48.

3   Ibid., p. 51.

4   Robert A. Barakat, "The Herr and Zeller Houses," *Pennsylvania Folklife* 21, no. 4 (1972): 9.

5   Robert C. Bucher, "The Continental Log House," *Pennsylvania Folklife* 58 (1962): 14.

6   K. Edward Lay, "European Antecedents of Seventeenth and Eighteenth Century Germanic and Scots–Irish Architecture in America," *Pennsylvania Folklife* 32, no. 1 (1982): 19.

7   John D. Milner, "Germanic Architecture in the New World," *Journal of the Society of Architectural Historians* 34 (December 1975): 299.

8   Edward A. Chappell, "Acculturation in the Shenandoah Valley: Rhenish Houses of the Massanutten Settlement," *Proceedings of the American Philosophical Society* 124, no. 1 (1980): 55–89.

9   G. E. Brumbaugh, "Colonial Architecture of the Pennsylvania Germans," *Pennsylvania German Society Proceedings*, 1933, p. 30.

10   Robert C. Bucher, "Grain in the Attic," *Pennsylvania Folklife* 13, no. 2 (1963–64): 14.

11   Robert C. Bucher, "The Long Shingle," *Pennsylvania Folklife* 18, no. 4 (1969): 54, 56.

12   Henry Glassie, "A Central Chimney Continental Log House," *Pennsylvania Folklife* 18, no. 2 (1968–69): 35.

13   Robert C. Bucher, "The Swiss Bank House in Pennsylvania," *Pennsylvania Folklife* 18, no. 2 (1968–69): 2–11.

14   Chappell, "Acculturation in the Shenandoah Valley."

15   Robert C. Bucher, "The Cultural Backgrounds of Our Pennsylvania Homesteads," *Pennsylvania Folklife* 15, no. 3 (1966): 24.

16   Bucher, "The Swiss Bank House," p. 10.

17   Henry Glassie, "The Appalachian Log Cabin," *Mountain Life and Work* 39 (1963): 8.

18   Ibid.

19   Thomas T. Waterman, *The Dwellings of Colonial America* (Chapel Hill: University of North Carolina Press, 1950), p. 41.

20   Henry Glassie, "Eighteenth-Century Cultural Process in Delaware Valley Folk Building," *Winterthur Portfolio* 7 (1972): 36–38.

21   Richard Pillsbury, "Patterns in the Folk and Vernacular House Forms of the Pennsylvania Culture Region," *Pioneer America* 9, no. 1 (1977): 27.

22   Henry L. Williams and Ottalie K. Williams, *A Guide to Old American Houses, 1700–1900*

(South Brunswick, N.Y.: A. S. Barnes and Company, 1962), p. 48.

23 Glassie, "Eighteenth-Century Cultural Process," p. 37.

24 Patricia Irvin Cooper, "A Quaker-Plan House in Georgia," *Pioneer America* 10, no. 1 (1978): 14–34, and "Postscript to a Quaker-Plan House in Georgia," *Pioneer America* 11, no. 3 (1979): 143–50.

25 C. A. Weslager, *The Log Cabin in America* (New Brunswick, N.J.: Rutgers University Press, 1969), pp. 158–59.

26 Rosalie F. Bailey, *Pre-Revolutionary Dutch Houses and Families in Northern New Jersey and Southern New York* (New York: William Morrow and Co., 1936), p. 24.

27 Richard Pillsbury and Andrew Kardos, *A Field Guide to the Folk Architecture of the Northeastern United States* (Hanover, N.H.: Department of Geography, Dartmouth College, [1970]), p. 56.

6 English Colonial Houses in the Chesapeake Bay Hearth

1 Dell Upton, "Toward a Performance Theory of Vernacular Architecture: Early Tidewater Virginia as a Case Study," *Folklore Forum* 12, nos. 2–3 (1979): 176.

2 Ibid., pp. 176–78.

3 Henry C. Forman, *The Architecture of the Old South: The Medieval Style, 1585–1850* (Cambridge: Harvard University Press, 1948), p. 15.

4 Paul E. Buchanan, "The Eighteenth-Century Frame Houses of Tidewater Virginia," in *Building Early America*, ed. Charles E. Peterson (Radnor, Pa.: Chilton Book Co., 1976), pp. 54–73.

5 M. W. Barley, *The English Farmhouse* (London: Routledge and Kegan Paul, 1961), p. 98.

6 Forman, *Architecture of the Old South*, p. 121.

7 Dell Upton, "Vernacular Architecture in Eighteenth-Century Virginia," *Winterthur Portfolio* 17, nos. 2–3 (1982): 96.

8 Forman, *Architecture of the Old South*, p. 121.

9 Upton, "Vernacular Architecture in Eighteenth-Century Virginia," p. 96; Henry Glassie, "Eighteenth-Century Cultural Process in Delaware Valley Folk Building," *Winterthur Portfolio* 7 (1972): 38; Ernest Allen Connally, "The Cape Cod House: An Introductory Study," *Journal of the Society of Architectural Historians* 19 (May 1960): 52.

10 H. Chandlee Forman, *Maryland Architecture* (Cambridge, Md.: Tidewater Publishers, 1968), p. 10.

11 Forman, *Architecture of the Old South*, pp. 48–50.

12 Kenneth M. Wilson, "Window Glass in America," in Peterson, *Building Early America*, p. 156.

13 Richard Pillsbury, "Patterns in the Folk and Vernacular House Forms of the Pennsylvania Culture Region," *Pioneer America* 9, no. 1 (1977: 17–19.

14 R. W. Brunskill, *Vernacular Architecture of the Lake Counties* (London: Faber and Faber, 1974), p. 70.

15 Howard W. Marshall, *Folk Architecture in Little Dixie: A Regional Culture in Missouri* (Columbia: University of Missouri Press, 1981), p. 57.

16 Ibid., p. 60.

17 Pillsbury, "Patterns in the Folk and Vernacular House Forms," p. 19.

18 Fred B. Kniffen, "Folk Housing—Key to Diffusion," *Annals of the Association of American Geographers* 55, no. 4 (1965): 551.

19 Ibid., p. 555.

20 Simon Bronner, "The Harris House and Related Structures in South-Central Indiana," *Pioneer America* 12, no. 1 (1980): 15–18, gives measurements for several I houses.

21 Michael Southern, "The I-House as a Carrier of Style in Three Counties of the Northeastern Piedmont," in *Carolina Dwelling*, ed. Doug Swaim (Raleigh: North Carolina State University, School of Design, 1978), pp. 80–81.

22 Ruth Little-Stokes, "The North Carolina Porch: A Climatic and Cultural Buffer," in Swaim, *Carolina Dwelling*, p. 104.

23 Doug Swaim, "North Carolina Folk Housing," in Swaim, *Carolina Dwelling*, p. 43.

24 Kniffen, "Folk Housing," p. 571.

7 Houses of the English and Spanish in the Humid Subtropics

1 Thomas T. Waterman, *The Dwellings of Colonial America* (Chapel Hill: University of North Carolina Press, 1950), p. 79.

2 Hugh Morrison, *Early American Architecture* (New York: Oxford University Press, 1952), p. 171.

3 Henry L. Williams and Ottalie K. Williams, *A Guide to Old American Houses, 1700–1900* (South Brunswick, N.Y.: A. S. Barnes, 1962), p. 58.

4 Waterman, *Dwellings of Colonial America*, p. 79.

5 Albert Manucy, *The Houses of St. Augustine, 1565–1821* (St. Augustine: St. Augustine Historical Society, 1962), p. 49.

6 Ibid., p. 55.

7 Ibid.

8 Ibid., p. 86.

9 Albert Manucy, "Tapia or Tabby," *Journal of the Society of Architectural Historians* 11 (December 1952): 32.

10 Perhaps the best general study dealing with the colonial period is Peter Wacker, *Land and People: A Cultural Geography of Pre-Industrial New Jersey* (New Brunswick, N.J.: Rutgers University Press, 1975).

8 Early Dwellings in Western Environments

1 Arthur A. Hart, "Stone Buildings East of the Cascades," in *Space, Style, and Structure: Building in Northwest America*, ed. Thomas Vaughan and Virginia Ferriday (Portland: Oregon Historical Society, 1974), p. 363.

2 Kyrill Khlebnikov, *Colonial Russian America* (Portland: Oregon Historical Society, 1976), p. 90.

3 George Gibbs, "Tribes of Western Washington and Northwestern Oregon," *Contributions to*

North American Ethnology (Washington: U.S. Dept. of the Interior, 1877), 1:214.

4 Joan Marie Vastokas, *Architecture of the Northwest Coast Indians of America* (Ann Arbor: University Microfilms, 1967), pp. 30–31.

5 T. T. Waterman, "North American Indian Dwellings," *Geographical Review* 14, no. 1 (1924): 20.

6 For a brief discussion of wigwams, as well as other Indian house types, see ibid., pp. 1–25.

7 Alan K. Craig and Christopher S. Peebles, "Ethnoecologic Change among the Seminoles, 1740–1840," *Geoscience and Man* 5 (1974): 91 (special issue, *Man and Cultural Heritage*).

8 Reginald Laubin and Gladys Laubin, *The Indian Tipi* (New York: Ballantine Books, 1957), p. 13.

9 An excellent description of the arrangement of poles and the method of erection of the tipi is given in Stanley Campbell, "The Cheyenne Tipi," *American Anthropologist* 17 (1915): 685–94.

10 Stanley Vestal, "The History of the Tipi," in Laubin and Laubin, *The Indian Tipi*, pp. 1–17.

11 Roger L. Welsch, *Sod Walls: The Story of the Nebraska Sod House* (Broken Bow, Nebr.: Purcells, 1968), p. 39.

12 Cass G. Barns, *The Sod House* (Lincoln: University of Nebraska Press, 1930).

13 John Hudson, "Frontier Housing in North Dakota," *North Dakota History* 42, no. 4 (1975): 6.

14 Sarah Ellen Roberts, *Alberta Homestead: Chronicle of a Pioneer Family* (Austin: University of Texas Press, 1968), p. 41.

15 Howard Ruede, *Sod House Days* (New York: Cooper Square Publishers, 1966), p. 207.

16 Everett Dick, *The Sod-House Frontier* (New York: D. Appleton-Century, 1937), p. 111.

17 Barns, *The Sod House*, p. 58.

18 Solomon Butcher, *Pioneer History of Custer County, Nebraska*, 3d ed. (1892; Broken Bow, Nebr.: Purcells, 1976), pp. 65–66.

19 Welsch, *Sod Walls*, pp. 29–30.

20 Ruede, *Sod House Days*, p. 28.

21 See Hudson, "Frontier Housing in North Dakota," p. 8, for a contrary view.

22 Roger L. Welsch, "Sod Construction on the Plains," *Pioneer America* 1, no. 2 (1969): 14.

23 Welsch, *Sod Walls*, p. viii.

24 Dick, *Sod-House Frontier*, p. 115.

25 Welsch, *Sod Walls*, p. 44.

26 Donald S. Gates, "The Sod House," *Journal of Geography* 32 (December 1933): 355.

27 Dick, *Sod-House Frontier*, p. 115.

28 Welsch, *Sod Walls*, p. 70.

29 The designation of these people may use the Anglicized spelling *Navaho* or the Hispanic form *Navajo*. The terms are used interchangeably in this study.

30 The classic account of Navaho dwellings is Cosmos Mindeleff, "Navaho Houses," *Annual Report of the Bureau of American Ethnology* (Washington: Government Printing Office, 1896). Virtually all later accounts draw on this excellent study.

31 Clyde Kluckhohn and Dorothea Leighton, *The Navaho* (Cambridge: Harvard University Press, 1948), p. 3.

32 Stephen C. Jett and Virginia E. Spencer, *Navajo Architecture: Forms, History, Distributions* (Tucson: University of Arizona Press, 1981), pp. 101, 99.

33 John M. Corbett, "Navajo House Types," *El Palacio* 47, no. 5 (1940): 106.

34 The use of the Spanish term *ramada* is a good illustration of the close connection between Spanish and Indian culture elements. The Navajo word for this shelter is *ca-oh*, but *ramada* is also widely used by the Navajo and other southwestern residents.

35 Stephen C. Jett, "Navajo Seasonal Migration Patterns," *Kiva* 44, no. 1 (1978): 70, 67.

36 Edwin N. Wilmsen, "The House of the Navaho," *Landscape* 10, no. 1 (1960): 15.

37 Stephen C. Jett, "Comments on the Navajo Hogan," *Places* 3, no. 2 (1976): 49.

38 Gordon Page, "Navajo House Types," *Museum Notes* (Museum of Northern Arizona), 9, no. 9 (1937): 47.

39 R. W. Shufeldt, "The Evolution of House Building among the Navajo Indians," *Proceedings of the National Museum* 15 (1892): 280.

40 Wesley R. Hurt, Jr., "Eighteenth Century Navaho Hogans from Canyon de Chelly National Monument," *American Antiquity* 8 (1942): 89–90; Jett and Spencer, *Navajo Architecture*, p. 56.

41 Detailed drawings of forked-stick hogans can be found in Page, "Navajo House Types," and excellent photographs appear in Clyde Kluckhohn, W. W. Hill, and Lucy W. Kluckhohn, *Navaho Material Culture* (Cambridge: Harvard University Press, 1971): 144–45.

42 Cosmos Mindeleff, "Navajo Houses," p. 498.

43 Corbett, "Navajo House Types," p. 107; Wilmsen, "The House of the Navajo," p. 16; Virginia Spencer and Stephen C. Jett, "Navajo Dwellings of Rural Black Creek Valley, Arizona–New Mexico," *Plateau* 43, no. 4 (1971): 171.

44 Spencer and Jett, "Navajo Dwellings," p. 166.

45 Jett and Spencer, *Navajo Architecture*, pp. 107–54.

46 Stephen C. Jett, "Pueblo Indian Migrations: An Evolution of the Possible Physical and Cultural Determinants," *American Antiquity* 29, no. 3 (1964): 281–300.

47 Trent E. Sanford, *The Architecture of the Southwest* (Westport, Conn.: Greenwood Press Publishers, 1950), p. 20.

48 J. B. Jackson, "Pueblo Architecture and Our Own," *Landscape* 3 (Winter 1953–54): 24.

49 A. F. Bandelier, *Report on the Ruins of the Pueblo of Pecos* (Boston: A. Williams and Company, 1881), pp. 43, 54, 67, 80.

50 Victor Mindeleff, "A Study of Pueblo Architecture," *Eighth Annual Report of the Bureau of Ethnology, 1886–1887* (Washington: Government Printing Office, 1891), p. 109.

51 Bainbridge Bunting, *Early Architecture in New Mexico* (Albuquerque: University of New Mexico Press, 1976), p. 9.

52 Elliot G. McIntire, "Changing Patterns of Hopi Indian Settlement," *Annals of the Association of American Geographers* 61, no. 3 (1971): 512.

53 Victor Mindeleff, "Study of Pueblo Architecture," pp. 102, 139, 152, 155, 179, 180.

54 Bunting, *Early Architecture in New Mexico*, pp. 30–31.

55 McIntire, "Changing Patterns," p. 517.

56 Much of the following discussion is based upon Bunting, *Early Architecture in New Mexico*, pp. 7–14.

57 J. W. Hoover, "House and Village Types of the Southwest As Conditioned by Aridity," *Scientific Monthly* 40 (March 1935): 244, mentions other typical materials used in this layer as arrowweed, ocatillo stems, and cactus ribs.

58 Victor Mindeleff, "Study of Pueblo Architecture," pp. 149–51.

59 Hugh Morrison, *Early American Architecture* (New York: Oxford University Press, 1952), p. 185.

60 T. A. H. Miller, *Adobe or Sun-Dried Brick for Farm Building*, Farmers Bulletin, no. 1720 (Washington: U.S. Dept. of Agriculture, 1949), p. 6.

61 Donald W. Meinig, *Southwest: Three Peoples in Geographical Change, 1600–1970* (New York: Oxford University Press, 1971), p. 11.

62 Richard L. Nostrand, "Mexican Americans Circa 1850," *Annals of the Association of American Geographers* 65, no. 3 (1975): 379; Edwin J. Foscue, "Historical Geography of the Lower Rio Grande Valley of Texas," *Texas Geographic Magazine* 3, no. 1 (1939): 8–9.

63 John J. Winberry, "The Log House in Mexico," *Annals of the Association of American Geographers* 64, no. 1 (1974): 62.

64 J. B. Jackson, "A Catalog of New Mexico Farm-Building Terms," *Landscape* 1, no. 3 (1952): 32.

65 Bunting, *Early Architecture in New Mexico*, pp. 13–14.

66 Janet A. Stewart, *Arizona Ranch Houses* (Tucson: Arizona Historical Society, 1974), p. 26.

67 Willard B. Robinson, *Gone from Texas: Our Lost Architectural Heritage* (College Station: Texas A & M University Press, 1981), p. 18.

68 A. W. Conway, "Southwestern Colonial Farms," *Landscape* 1, no. 1 (1951): 6.

69 A. W. Conway, "A Northern New Mexico House Type," *Landscape* 1, no. 2 (1951): 20–21.

70 Charles F. Gritzner, "Log Housing in New Mexico," *Pioneer America* 3, no. 2 (1971): 54–62.

71 Sanford, *Architecture of the Southwest*, p. 239.

9 French Houses in the Warm, Humid Mississippi Valley

1 Philippe Oszuscik, "French Creole Housing on the Gulf Coast: The Early Years," *PAST: Pioneer America Society Transactions* 6 (1983): 49.

2 Henry E. Chambers, *Mississippi Valley Beginnings* (New York: G. P. Putnam's Sons, 1922), p. 120.

3 Ibid., p. 67.

4 Harnett T. Kane, *The Bayous of Louisiana* (New York: William Morrow and Co., 1944), p. 178.

5 Fred B. Kniffen, "Louisiana House Types," *Annals of the Association of American Geographers* 26 (1936): 163; Oszuscik, "French Creole Housing."

6 Jay Edwards, "Cultural Syncretism in the Louisiana Creole Cottage," *Louisiana Folklore Miscellany* 4 (1976–1980): 21.

7 I first proposed the term *grenier* in "Rural Ethnic Islands," in *Ethnic Minorities in the United States*, ed. Jesse McKee (Dubuque, Iowa: Kendall Hunt Publishing Co., in press).

8 Kane, *Bayous of Louisiana*, pp. 179–80.

9 Harnett T. Kane, *Deep Delta Country* (New York: Duell, Sloan and Pearce, 1944), p. 21.

10 Fred Kniffen, "The Physiognomy of Rural Louisiana," *Louisiana History* 4, no. 4 (1963): 298.

11 Edwards, "Cultural Syncretism," p. 14.

12 Kane, *Bayous of Louisiana*, p. 181.

13 William B. Knipmeyer, *Settlement Succession in Eastern French Louisiana* (Ann Arbor: University Microfilms International, 1956), pp. 120–23.

14 William F. Rushton, *The Cajuns: From Acadia to Louisiana* (New York: Farrar, Straus, Giroux, 1979), pp. 183–84.

15 Knipmeyer, *Settlement Succession*, p. 88.

16 Milton B. Newton, Jr., *Atlas of Louisiana* (Baton Rouge: School of Geoscience, Louisiana State University, 1972).

17 Ibid.

18 Charles van Ravenswaay, *The Arts and Architecture of German Settlements in Missouri* (Columbia: University of Missouri Press, 1977), pp. 149, 170.

19 Edwards, "Cultural Syncretism," pp. 9–40.

20 Charles E. Peterson, "Early Ste. Genevieve and Its Architecture," *Missouri Historical Review* 35, no. 2 (1941): 216.

21 Ward A. Dorrance, "The Survival of French in the Old District of Sainte Genevieve," *University of Missouri Studies* 10, no. 2 (1935): 15.

22 C. Johnson, "Missouri-French Houses: Some Relict Features of Early Settlement," *Pioneer America* 6, no. 2 (1974): 10, n. 4.

23 Charles E. Peterson, *Colonial St. Louis: Building a Creole Capital* (St. Louis: Missouri Historical Society, 1949), p. 20n.

24 Charles E. Peterson, "The Houses of French St. Louis," in *The French in the Mississippi Valley*, ed. John Francis McDermott (Urbana: University of Illinois Press, 1965), p. 27.

25 Dorrance, "The Survival of the French," p. 16.

26 Peterson, "The Houses of French St. Louis," p. 25.

27 Peterson, *Colonial St. Louis*, p. 19, n. 5.

28 Peterson, "Early Ste. Genevieve and Its Architecture," p. 219.

29 Roulhac Toledano et al., *The Creole Faubourgs*, vol. 4 of *New Orleans Architecture* (Gretna: Pelican Publishing Co. and Friends of the Cabildo, 1974), p. 37.

30 Ibid., p. 40.

31 Milton B. Newton, Jr., "Louisiana House Types," *Melanges*, no. 2 (September 1971): 14.

32 John M. Vlach, "The Shotgun House: An African Architectural Legacy (Part I)," *Pioneer America* 8, no. 1 (1976): 51.

33 John M. Vlach, "Shotgun Houses," *Natural History* 86 (February 1977): 56.

34 John M. Vlach, "The Shotgun House: An African Architectural Legacy (Part II)," *Pioneer America* 8, no. 2 (1976): 57–61.

35 William A. Dakan, "Social Geography of Louisville," in *An Introduction to the Louisville Region: Selected Essays*, ed. Don E. Bierman (Louisville: University of Louisville, 1980), p. 63.

36 Toledano, *The Creole Faubourgs*, pp. 71, 72.

37 Ned Pratt, Wendy Nicholas, and Don Weber, *The Shotgun House* (Louisville: Preservation Alliance of Louisville and Jefferson County, Inc., 1980), p. 5.

38 Sylvia Ann Grider, "The Shotgun House in Oil Boomtowns of the Texas Panhandle," *Pioneer America* 7, no. 2 (1975): 47–55.

39 Dakan, "Social Geography of Louisville"; Pratt et al., *The Shotgun House*.

40 Newton, "Louisiana House Types," p. 16.

41 Vlach, "The Shotgun House, Part I," p. 49.

42 Samuel Wilson, Jr., *The Lower Garden District*, vol. 1 of *New Orleans Architecture* (Gretna: Pelican Publishing Co. and Friends of the Cabildo, 1971), p. 37.

43 Henry Glassie, *Pattern in the Material Folk Culture of the Eastern United States* (Philadelphia: University of Pennsylvania Press, 1968), p. 111.

10 The Diffusion and Modification of Eastern Houses

1 One important exception to the absence of bank barns in England is found in the Lake District, where they were fairly common. However, few early English settlers come from this area. See R. W. Brunskill, *Vernacular Architecture of the Lake Counties* (London: Faber and Faber, 1974), p. 84, for Lake District banked barns.

2 John Fraser Hart, *The Look of the Land* (Englewood Cliffs, N.J.: Prentice Hall, 1975), p. 128.

3 Fred Kniffen, "Folk Housing: Key to Diffusion," *Annals of the Association of American Geographers* 55, no. 4 (1965): 558.

4 Ibid., p. 559.

5 R. W. Brunskill, *Illustrated Handbook of Vernacular Architecture* (New York: Universe Books, 1970), p. 104.

6 These windows are sometimes erroneously called *eye-brow windows*, but this term should be reserved for small round-topped windows let into a roof slope.

7 This house is also referred to as a *Regency cottage*. See Marion Macrae and Anthony Adamson, *The Ancestral Roof: Domestic Architecture of Upper Canada* (Toronto: Clarke, Irwin, 1963), pp. 77–107.

8 Ibid., pp. 240–41.

9 Ibid., p. 94.

10 G. E. Mills and D. W. Holdsworth, "The B. C. Mills Prefabricated System: The Emergence of Ready-Made Buildings in Western Canada," *Canadian Historic Sites*, no. 14 (1975): 127–69.

11 R. W. Brunskill, *Illustrated Handbook*, p. 26.

12 Ibid., p. 25.

13 The problem of differentiating between *folk* and *popular* is discussed by Henry Glassie, *Pattern in the Material Folk Culture of the Eastern United States* (Philadelphia: University of Pennsylvania Press, 1968), pp. 5–19.

14 Richard Pillsbury and Andrew Kardos, *A Field Guide to the Folk Architecture of Northeastern United States* (Hanover, N.H.: Department of Geography, Dartmouth College, [1970]), p. 29.

15 Figure 10–20 is based upon Terry G. Jordan, *Texas Log Buildings: A Folk Architecture* (Austin: University of Texas Press, 1978); Fred Kniffen and Henry Glassie, "Building in Wood in the Eastern United States," *Geographical Review* 56, no. 1 (1966): 40–66; Eugene M. Wilson, "The Single Pen Log House in the South," *Pioneer America* 2, no. 1 (1970): 21–28; and Wilbur Zelinsky, "The Log House in Georgia," *Geographical Review* 43, no. 2 (1953): 173–93.

16 Martin Wright, "The Antecedents of the Double Pen House Type," *Annals of the Association of American Geographers* 48, no. 2 (1958): 117.

17 Stanley Willis, "Log Houses in Southwest Virginia: Tools Used in Their Construction," *Virginia Cavalcade* 21, no. 4 (1972): 38.

18 Eugene M. Wilson, *Alabama Folk Houses* (Montgomery: Alabama Historical Commission, 1975), p. 9.

19 Wilson, "The Single Pen Log House in the Old South," p. 24.

20 Warren Roberts, "Folk Architecture in Context: The Folk Museum," *Proceedings of the Pioneer America Society* 1 (1972): 38.

21 William C. Wonders, "Log Dwellings in Canadian Folk Architecture," *Annals of the Association of American Geographers* 69, no. 2 (1979): 200.

22 Jordan, *Texas Log Buildings*, p. 35.

23 Kniffen and Glassie, "Building in Wood," pp. 61–64; Zelinsky, "The Log House in Georgia," p. 174.

24 Fred Kniffen, "On Corner-Timbering," *Pioneer America* 1, no. 1 (January 1969): 3.

25 Kniffen and Glassie, "Building in Wood," pp. 59–61.

26 Charles van Ravenswaay, *The Arts and Architecture of German Settlement in Missouri* (Columbia: University of Missouri Press, 1977), p. 118.

27 An excellent description of the method of cutting a half-dovetail notch is given in *The Foxfire Book* (Garden City, N.Y.: Anchor Press, 1972), pp. 65–69.

28 Kniffen, "On Corner-Timbering," p. 3.

29 For Alabama, see Wilson, "The Single Pen Log House in the Old South," p. 25; for Ohio, see Donald A. Hutslar, *The Log Architecture of Ohio* (Columbus: Ohio Historical Society, 1977), p. 71; for Texas, see Jordan, *Texas Log Buildings*; and for the Ozarks, see Charles McRaven, *Building the Hewn Log House* (New York: Thomas Y. Crowell, 1978), p. 25.

30 Milton Newton and Linda Pulliam-DiNapoli, "Log Houses as Public Occasions: A Historical Theory," *Annals of the Association of American Geographers* 67, no. 3 (1977): 378.

31 Kniffen and Glassie, "Building in Wood," p. 65.

32 Ibid., p. 61.

33 Kniffen, "Folk Housing"; Glassie, *Pattern in the Material Folk Culture*; Kniffen and Glassie, "Building in Wood"; Wilbur Zelinsky, "Where the South Begins: The Northern Limit of the Cis-Appalachian South in Terms of Settlement Landscape," *Social Forces* 30, no. 2 (1951): 172–78.

34 The identifying traits were initially given by Zelinsky, "Where the South Begins," and later

L

were expanded and modified by Milton Newton, "Cultural Preadaptation and the Upland South," *Geoscience and Man* 5 (1974): 152 (special issue, *Man and Cultural Heritage*).

35 Charles A. Weslager, *The Log Cabin in America* (New Brunswick, N.J.: Rutgers University Press, 1969), p. 226.

36 See Kniffen, "Folk Housing," pp. 561–63; Henry Glassie, "The Appalachian Log Cabin," *Mountain Life and Work* 39 (1963): 14; and Francis B. Johnston and Thomas T. Waterman, *The Early Architecture of North Carolina* (Chapel Hill: University of North Carolina Press, 1941), p. 7.

37 Newton and Pulliam-DiNapoli, "Log Houses as Public Occasions," p. 377.

38 Wilson, *Alabama Folk Houses*; Henry Glassie, "Types of the Southern Mountain Cabin," in *The Study of American Folklore*, ed. J. H. Brunvand (New York: W. W. Norton, 1968), pp. 338–70.

39 Glassie, "Types of the Southern Mountain Cabin," pp. 355, 343.

40 E. Estyn Evans, "Cultural Relics of the Ulster Scots in the Old West of North America," *Ulster Folklife* 11 (1965): 34.

41 Glassie, "Types of the Southern Mountain Cabin," pp. 353, 355.

42 Jordan, *Texas Log Buildings*, p. 65.

43 Wilson, "The Single Pen Log House in the Old South," p. 24.

44 Glassie, "Types of the Southern Mountain Cabin," p. 341.

45 Ibid., p. 349.

46 Wilson, *Alabama Folk Houses*, p. 45.

47 Newton and Pulliam-DiNapoli, "Log Houses as Public Occasions," pp. 373–74.

48 Wilson, *Alabama Folk Houses*, p. 25.

49 James R. O'Malley and John B. Rehder, "The Two-Story Log House in the Upland South," *Journal of Popular Culture* 11, no. 4 (1978): 904–15.

50 This structure earlier was sometimes referred to as a *double-pen* cabin. See Edna Scofield, "The Evolution and Development of Tennessee Houses," *Journal of the Tennessee Academy of Science* 11, no. 4 (1936): 229–40, or Zelinsky, "The Log House in Georgia," pp. 173–93.

51 Zelinsky, "The Log House in Georgia," p. 180.

52 Eugene M. Wilson, "Form Changes in Folk Houses," *Geoscience and Man* 5 (1974): 70 (special issue, *Man and Cultural Heritage*).

53 Wright, "The Antecedents of the Double Pen House Type," p. 109.

54 Milton Newton, *Louisiana House Types: A Field Guide* (Baton Rouge: Museum of Geoscience, 1971), p. 9.

55 Peter O. Wacker and Roger T. Trindell, "The Log House in New Jersey," *Keystone Folklore Quarterly* 13 (Winter 1969): 265.

56 Terry G. Jordan, "German Houses in Texas," *Landscape* 14, no. 1 (1964): 26.

57 van Ravenswaay, *Arts and Architecture of German Settlement*, p. 113.

58 Hubert G. H. Wilhelm and Michael Miller, "Half-Timber Construction—A Relic Building Method in Ohio," *Pioneer America* 6, no. 2 (1974): 44.

59 van Ravenswaay, *Arts and Architecture of German Settlement*, p. 147.

60 Lawrence Kocher, "The Early Architecture of Pennsylvania," *Architectural Record* 49 (January 1921): 39.

61 van Ravenswaay, *Arts and Architecture of German Settlement*, pp. 169, 221.

62 Jordan, "German Houses in Texas," p. 24.

63 Hubert G. H. Wilhelm, "German Settlement and Folk Building Practices in the Hill Country of Texas," *Pioneer America* 3, no. 2 (1971): 21.

64 Dorothy Kendall Bracken and Maurine Whorton Redway, *Early Texas Homes* (Dallas: Southern Methodist University Press, 1956), p. 44.

65 Jordan, "German Houses in Texas," p. 24.

66 Richard W. E. Perrin, *The Architecture of Wisconsin* (Madison: State Historical Society of Wisconsin, 1967), p. 12.

67 M. S. Osborne, "The Architectural Heritage of Manitoba," in *Manitoba Essays*, ed. R. C. Lodge (Toronto: Macmillan Company of Canada, 1937), p. 65.

68 Peter N. Moogk, *Building a House in New France* (Toronto: McClelland and Stewart, 1977), pp. 28–30.

69 Wonders, "Log Dwellings in Canadian Folk Architecture," pp. 196–98.

70 Matti Kaups, "Log Architecture in America: European Antecedents in a Finnish Context," *Journal of Cultural Geography* 2, no. 1 (1981):138. (Fig. 10–49 reprinted by permission of Alvar W. Carlson, editor.)

71 Richard W. E. Perrin, *The Architecture of Wisconsin*, p. 22.

72 George Jorre, *The Soviet Union: The Land and Its People* (New York: John Wiley, 1967), p. 80.

73 Perrin, *The Architecture of Wisconsin*, p. 22.

74 Matti Kaups, "Finnish Log Houses in the Upper Middle West: 1890–1920," *Journal of Cultural Geography* 3, no. 2 (1983): 17.

75 Alvar W. Carlson, "German-Russian Houses in Western North Dakota," *Pioneer America* 13, no. 2 (1981): 49–60.

76 E. K. Francis, "The Mennonite Farmhouse in Manitoba," *Mennonite Quarterly Review* 28 (January 1954): 56–59.

77 Karl Stumpp, *The German-Russians: Two Centuries of Pioneering* (Bonn: Edition Atlantic Forum, 1967), p. 29.

78 Francis, "The Mennonite Farmhouse," p. 56; Albert J. Petersen, "German-Russian Catholic Colonization in Western Kansas: A Settlement Geography," Ph.D. diss., Louisiana State University, 1970, p. 146.

79 Jorre, *The Soviet Union*, p. 82.

80 William C. Sherman, "Prairie Architecture of the Russian-German Settlers," in Richard Sallet, *Russian-German Settlements in the United States* (Fargo: North Dakota Institute for Regional Studies, 1974), p. 186.

81 Petersen, "German-Russian Catholic Colonization," p. 139.

82 *Minnesota Farmscape: Looking at Change* (St. Paul: Minnesota Historical Society, 1980), p. 3.

83 Thomas W. Hanchett, "The Four Square

House Type in the United States," in *Perspectives in Vernacular Architecture*, ed. Camille Wells (Annapolis: Vernacular Architecture Forum, 1982), pp. 51–53.

84 Brian P. Birch, *Farmhousing in the United States Corn Belt in 1970* (Southampton: Department of Geography, University of Southampton, 1974), p. 32.

85 Ibid.

86 Robert Finley and E. M. Scott, "A Great Lakes-to-Gulf Profile of Dispersed Dwelling Types," *Geographical Review* 30, no. 3 (1940): 415.

87 Hanchett, "The Four Square House Type," p. 51.

88 Kay Halpin, "Sears, Roebuck's Best-kept Secret," *Historic Preservation* 33, no. 5 (1981): 24–29.

11 Style and Fashion: The Sequence of Nineteenth-Century Houses

1 For an introduction to the complexities of the concept of style see Marcus Whiffen, *American Architecture Since 1780: A Guide to the Styles* (Cambridge: M.I.T. Press, 1969), pp. vii–x.

2 Peirce F. Lewis, "Common Houses, Cultural Spoor," *Landscape* 19, no. 2 (1975): 2.

3 Whiffen, *American Architecture*; John J. G. Blumenson, *Identifying American Architecture* (Nashville: American Association for State and Local History, 1977); John Poppeliers, S. Allen Chambers, and Nancy Schwartz, *What Style is It?* (Washington: Preservation Press, 1977); Carol Rifkind, *A Field Guide to American Architecture* (New York: New American Library, 1980); Leland M. Roth, *A Concise History of American Architecture* (New York: Harper and Row, 1979).

4 Whiffen, *American Architecture*, p. 25.

5 Rifkind, *Field Guide to American Architecture*, p. 30.

6 Whiffen, *American Architecture*, p. 35.

7 Alan Gowans, *Building Canada: An Architectural History of Canadian Life* (Toronto: Oxford University Press, 1966), p. 69.

8 Todd R. Mozingo, "A Survey of Styles," in *The Iowa Catalog: Historic American Buildings Survey*, ed. Wesley I. Shank (Iowa City: University of Iowa Press, 1979), p. 128.

9 Wilbur Zelinsky, "The Greek Revival House in Georgia," *Journal of the Society of Architectural Historians* 13, no. 2 (1954): 9.

10 Talbot Hamlin, *Greek Revival Architecture in America* (1944; reprint, New York: Dover Publications, 1962), p. 266.

11 Henry-Russell Hitchcock, *Rhode Island Architecture* (New York: Da Capo Press, 1968), p. 51.

12 Whiffen, *American Architecture*, p. 56.

13 Andrew Jackson Downing, *The Architecture of Country Houses* (1850; reprint, New York: Dover Publications, 1962).

14 Carl W. Condit, *American Building Art* (New York: Oxford University Press, 1960), p. 16.

15 Raymond P. Jones and John E. Ball, *Framing, Sheathing and Insulation* (New York: Van Nostrand, Reinhold, 1973), p. 7.

16 Ibid., p. 10.

17 Ibid., p. 13.

18 Ibid., p. 14.

19 Blumenson, *Identifying American Architecture*, p. 35.

20 This section is based upon Allen G. Noble and Margaret Geib, "The Octagon House," *Places* 3, no. 3 (1976): 47.

21 Richard W. E. Perrin, "Circle and Polygon in Wisconsin Architecture," *Wisconsin Magazine of History* 47 (Autumn 1963): 50.

22 Clay Lancaster, "Some Octagonal Forms in Southern Architecture," *Art Bulletin* 28 (June 1946): 105.

23 Orson S. Fowler, *The Octagon House: A Home for All* (1853; reprint, New York: Dover Publications, 1973).

24 Carl F. Schmidt, *The Octagon Fad* (Scottsville, N.Y.: privately printed, 1960).

25 Walter Creese, "Fowler and the Domestic Octagon," *Art Bulletin* 28 (June 1946): 89–102.

26 Harley McKee, *Introduction to Early American Masonry* (Washington: National Trust for Historic Preservation, 1973), p. 68.

27 William A. Titus, "The Concrete Building in the United States," *Wisconsin Magazine of History* 24 (December 1940): 185, 187.

28 McKee, *Introduction to Early American Masonry*, p. 69.

29 Maurice M. Sloan, *The Concrete House and Its Construction* (Philadelphia: Association of American Portland Cement Manufacturers, 1912), p. 75.

30 Whiffen, *American Architecture*, p. 123.

31 J. Summerson, "The London Suburban Villa, *Architectural Review* 104 (August 1948): 63–72.

32 The roof style is written with a final *d*, whereas the architect's name ends in *t*.

33 Blumenson, *Identifying American Architecture*, pp. 52–53.

34 Ibid., p. 59.

35 Whiffen, *American Architecture*, p. 123.

36 Allan S. Everest, *Our North Country Heritage* (Plattsburg, N.Y.: Tundra Books, 1972), p. 78.

37 Whiffen, *American Architecture*, p. 118.

38 Sadayoshi Omoto, "The Queen Anne Style and Architectural Criticism," *Journal of the Society of Architectural Historians* 23, no. 1 (1964): 34.

39 Robert W. Bastian, "The Prairie Style House: Spatial Diffusion of a Minor Design," *Journal of Cultural Geography* 1, no. 1 (1980): 51.

40 Ibid.

41 Clay Lancaster, "The American Bungalow," *Art Bulletin* 40 (September 1958): 239.

42 Henry H. Saylor, *Bungalows* (Philadelphia: John C. Winston, 1911), pp. 5–6.

43 Richard Mattson, "The Bungalow Spirit," *Journal of Cultural Geography* 1, no. 2 (1981): 90.

44 Lancaster, "The American Bungalow," pp. 243–46, 248.

45 Use of a second floor prevented this house from being considered a bungalow by many early authorities. However, the continuous sweep of the roof, concealing much of the upper story, eventually made the structure acceptable within the classification, at least in popular usage.

Index